To:

From:

Your Time To Bake

A FIRST COOKBOOK FOR
THE NOVICE BAKER

Robert L. Blakeslee

SQUAREONE
PUBLISHERS

COVER DESIGNERS: Robert L. Blakeslee and Jeannie Tudor
COVER PHOTO: Getty Images, Inc.
INTERIOR PHOTOS AND GRAPHICS: Robert L. Blakeslee
EDITOR: Marie Caratozzolo
TYPESETTERS: Robert L. Blakeslee and Jeannie Tudor

Square One Publishers
115 Herricks Road
Garden City Park, NY 11040
(516) 535-2010 • (877) 900-BOOK
www.SquareOnePublishers.com

Library of Congress Cataloging-in-Publication Data

Blakeslee, Robert L.
  Your time to bake : a first cookbook for the novice baker / by Robert L. Blakeslee.
      p. cm.
  Includes index.
  ISBN 978-0-7570-0355-4 (hardback)
  1. Baking. 2. Cookbooks. I. Title. II. Title: Novice's guide to baking cakes, cookies, pies, and more.
  TX765.B58 2012
  641.8'15—dc22
                            2011014622

Printed in India by Nutech Print Services

10 9 8 7 6 5 4 3 2 1

Contents

Acknowledgments, xi

Words from the Author, xii

Introduction, 1

The What's & How To's of Baking

1. Essential Ingredients, 5

2. T 'n T (Tools 'n Terms), 31

3. This Is How to Do It, 49

Cookies, Cakes, Pies & More

4. Frostings, Fillings & Toppings, 73

5. Cookie Mania!, 103

6. Brownies, Squares 'n Bars, 135

7. Easy as Pie, 159

8. Cheesecake Shots, 205

9. Quick Breads, Biscuits & Muffins, 225

10. Coffeecake Break, 257

11. Big 'n Little Cakes, 279

12. Puff the Magic Pastry, 309

13. Sweet Holidays, 329

14. Decorating with Taste, 357

Metric Conversion Chart, 376

Index, 377

Contents
Expanded

1. Essential Ingredients

Easy Does It. 6
  Cool Dough, 6
  Mixing It Up, 8
  Easy as Pie, 9
You Need Some Stuff. 10
  Some Flours for You, 11
  Making Light of It, 11
  You Sure Are Sweet, Sugar, 12
  In the Thick of It, 13
  Spicy Is Nicey, 14
  Tantalizing Flavors, 15
  Thank Moo!, 16
  Egg-Centric, 17
  Cheeses!, 17
  That's Phat, 18
  OMG! I ♥ Chocolate, 19
  These Are Totally Nuts!, 20
  Bits and Pieces, 21
  Berry Tasty, 22
  Fresh Fruit Salad, 23
  Roots and Squash?, 24
  Canned, Frozen, and
    Dried Fruit, 25
Wrapping It Up. 26
What Else?. 28
How Much?. 29

2. T 'n T (Tools and Terms)

Basic Gadgets. 32
Electric Gizmos. 36
Potz and Panz. 37
Oven Vessels. 38
Home, Home on Your Range. . . 40
Baking Terms from A to Z 42

3. This Is How to Do It

Let's Get Started. 50
Fruit Processor. 52
All Mixed Up. 54
Sticky Situations. 58
Get Into Shape. 60
Roll with It, Baby!. 62
Now We're Cookin' 64
Are We Done Yet? 66
Taking Measure. 68
Baking a Mile High. 70

4. Frostings, Fillings & Toppings

Frost and Ice. 74
  Chocolate Buttercream, 76
  Vanilla Buttercream, 76
  Choc-Choc Frosting, 77
  Banana-Nut Frosting, 78
  Pineapple Frosting, 78
  Coconut Frosting, 79
  German Chocolate Frosting, 80
  Whipped Cream Frosting, 80
  Cream Cheese Frosting, 81
  Vanilla Ice, 82
  Chocolate Ice, 82
  Lemon Ice, 83
Very Saucy!. 84
  Fudge Sauce, 85
  Caramel Sauce, 86
  Raspberry Sauce, 86
  Butter Sauce, 87
How Filling!. 88
  Apple Filling, 89
  Blueberry Filling, 90
  Nut Filling, 90
  Lemon Custard, 91
  Chocolate Ganache, 92
  Pastry Cream, 93
  Cannoli Cream, 94
  Mascarpone Cream, 94
  White Chocolate Mousse, 95
  Mousse au Chocolat, 96
You're the Tops!. 98
  Whippy Cream, 99
  Streusel Toppings I and II, 100
  Pecan Topping, 101
  Fruit Glaze, 101

5. Cookie Mania!

Cookie Drops 104
  Chocolate Chip Cookies, 106
  Peanut Butter Cookies, 108
  Oat-Rageous Oatmeal
    Cookies, 110
  Oat-Butterscotch Cookies, 111
  Coconut Macaroons I, 112
  Coconut Macaroons II, 113
Nutty Cookies 114
  Flourless Chocolate Nut
    Cookies, 115
  Persian Walnut Cookies, 116
  Mexican Wedding Cakes, 117
  Walnut Puffs, 118

Biscotti Party. 120
  Chocolate Almond Biscotti, 122
  White Chocolate Macadamia
    Biscotti, 124
Cool Cookies 126
  Sugar Cookies, 128
  Ginger Snappies, 130
  Almond Crispies, 131
  Mama's Shortbread, 132

6. Brownies, Squares 'n Bars

Brownies Are Square, Man!. . . 136
  Bitchin' Brownies, 138
  Chocoroon Brownies, 140
  Soufflé Brownies, 142
  Beautiful Blondies, 144
Belly Up to the Bar 146
  E-Zay Lemon Squares, 148
  Chocolate Pecan Bars, 150
  Pumpkin Cheesecake
    Bars, 152
  5-Layer Choconut Bars, 154
  Chocoberry Oaties, 156

7. Easy as Pie

Humble Pies and Sweet Tarts . . 160
In Crust We Trust. 162
  Forming Methods
    For Cookie Crusts, 162
    For Pastry Crusts, 164
    For Lattice Tops, 168
    For Tart Crusts, 170
  Crust Recipes
    Standard Cookie Crust, 172
    Flaky Pastry Pie Crust, 173
    Sweet Tart Crust, 174

No-Bake and Low-Bake Pies . . 176
  Peanut Butter Pie, 177
  Chocolate Cream Pie, 178
  Key Lime Pie, 179
  Choco-Banana Cream Pie, 180
Beautiful Baked Pies 182
  Nuts 4 Pecan Pie, 183
  Mom's Apple Pie, 184
  Lemon Meringue Pie, 186
  Triple Berry Pie, 187
  Georgia Peach Pie, 188

Cobblers, Crisps & Crumbles. . . 190
  Peachy Blue Cobbler, 191
  Apple Crispy, 192
  Cherry-Apple Crumbly, 194
Sweet Tarts 196
  Strawberry Chocolate Tart, 197
  Fabulous Fruit Tart, 198
  Triple Nutty Tartlets, 200
  Canadian Butter Tartlets, 202

Contents Expanded

8. Cheescake Shots

No-Bake Cheesecake 206
  White Chocolate Cheesecake
    with Fruit Topping, 208
  Vanilla Cheesecake with
    Caramel Sauce, 210
  Lemon Chiffon Cheesecake, 212
Cheesecake Bake. 214
  Italian Cheesecake, 216

  Pumpkin Chiffon
    Cheesecake, 217
  New York Strawberry
    Cheesecake, 218
  Chocolate Swirl
    Cheesecake, 220
  White Chocolate-Raspberry
    Swirl Cheesecake, 222

9. Quick Breads, Biscuits & Muffins

Biscuits 'n Scones. 226
  Cranberry Butter Biscuits, 228
  Blueberry Corn Biscuits, 230
  Mom's Buttermilk Biscuits, 232
  Blueberry Scones, 234
Muffins, Man! 236
  Choc-Choc Muffins, 238
  Almond Poppyseed
    Muffins, 239
  Raisin Bran Muffins, 240
  Blueberry Buttermilk
    Muffins, 242
  Lemon Poppyseed
    Muffins, 244
  Cornberry Muffins, 246
Drop Dead Bread 248

  Pumpkin Bread, 249
  Banana Berry Bread, 250
  Date-Nut Bread, 252
  Zucchini Bread, 254

10. Coffeecake Break

Buttery-Nuttery Coffeecakes. . 258
  Chocolate Chunk
    Coffeecake, 260
  Butter Pecan Coffeecake, 262
  Cinnamon-Nut
    Coffeecake, 264
  Butter-Butter Coffeecake, 266
  Choco-Walnut Coffeecake, 268
  Apple-Pecan Coffeecake, 270
  Fresh Strawberry
    Coffeecake, 272
  Almond-Berry Coffeecake, 274
  Blueberry Buckle, 276

11. Big 'n Little Cakes

Easy as Cake (and Cupcakes). . 280
  Buttery Yellow Cupcakes, 282
  Chocolate Cupcakes, 283
  Coconut Cupcakes, 284
  Pumpkin Cupcakes, 286
  Chocolate Bomb
    Cupcakes, 287
Gimme Some Cake!. 288
  Buttermilk Pound Cake, 290
  Coconut-Coconut Cake, 291

Rich 'n Delicious Chocolate
  Cake, 292
Debbie's White Cake, 294
Greek Honeycake, 296
Pineapple-Carrot Cake, 298
German Chocolate Cake, 300
Devil's Food Cake, 302
Chocolate Heart Attack
  Cake, 304
Chocolate-Almond Torte, 306

12. Puff the Magic Pastry

Flaky Pastry Sheets. 310
  Apple Strudel, 312
  Apple Turnovers, 314
  Almond Triangle Puffs, 316
  Frangipane Puff Pie, 318
  Golden Palmiers, 320
Puffy Pastry Shells. 322
  Mascarpone Puffs, 323
  Cannoli Puffs, 324
  Blueberry Puffs, 325
  Chocolate Cream Puffs, 326
  White Chocolate
    Cream Puffs, 327

13. Sweet Holidays

Holiday Cookies. 330
  Holiday Rum Balls, 330
  Hanukkah Rugelach, 332
  Spanish Polvornes, 334
  Holiday Butter Crisps, 335
  Gingerbread Dudes
    'n Pals, 336
Holiday Pies. 338
  Pumpkin Pie, 338
  Sweet Po-Tater Pie, 339
  Fiadone Easter Pie, 340

Holiday Breads. 342
  Cranberry Bread, 342
  Fruity Christmas Loaf, 343
  Irish Soda Bread, 344
Holiday Puddings 346
  Yuletide Pudding, 346
  Bread Pudding, 347
  Mocha-Banana English
    Trifle, 348
Holiday Cakes. 350
  Southern Red Velvet
    Cake, 350
  Sponge Cake with
    Goodies, 352
  Holiday Honey Cake, 354

14. Decorating with Taste

Sweet Touches. 358
Ice Me Down!. 360
It's Raining Chocolate!. 362
Fruity Designs. 363
Dazzling Cupcakes. 364
Frost Me Up!. 366
That's Some Fancy
  Dec'ratin'. 368
Fond of Fondant. 372

Baking Trivia

Fantastic Fun-Filled Food Facts, 30
Some Like It Hot, 48
Shake and Bake, 72
Is It Icing or Frosting?, 102
Kooky for Cookies, 134
Cake and Pie to Go, 158
An Eye for Pye, 204
Wonderful World of Cheesecake, 224
Muffin Madness, 256
Coffee + Coffeecake = Good, 278
Classic Cake, 308
A Thousand Leaves, 328
Happy Holidaze, 356

This book is dedicated
in loving memory
of my Grandmother
Peg Becker.
I miss you –
and your cookies!

Acknowledgments

I would like to thank all my friends at Square One—
with special thanks to
publisher Rudy "Honey Cake" Shur,
my editor Marie "Easter Pie" Caratozzolo,
art director Jeannie "Angel Food" Tudor,
and reviewer Lesley "Coffecake" Steinberg
for their contributions to this book.

I'd also like to give a shout out
to some special people who have encouraged me
throughout the years—
my brother, Stephen "Cream Puff" Blakeslee,
Bruce "Pumpkin Pie" Howes,
Connie "Plum Pudding" Howes,
and last but not least,
"APat" and "UDave"—
Patricia and David Blakeslee.

Words from the Author

When I wrote my first cookbook *Your Time to Cook*, I wanted to create a new type of beginner's cookbook – one that took a strong visual approach to teach novices how to cook – because I know that's the easiest way to learn. A few months after the book was released, my publisher asked me to come up with some concepts for a second book.

After thinking about it, I remembered something I learned at an early age – that being good cook was not a guarantee for success in baking and vise-versa. My Grandma Becker (who this book is dedicated to) was just a so-so cook, but a fantastic dessert maker and cookie baker extraordinaire. My mother, on the other hand, was an absolutely amazing cook, but she couldn't bake her way out of a paper bag. I remember once she made a chocolate cake for my thirteenth birthday, and after a few bites, my older brother and I refused to eat it. Now *that's* bad.

Since cooking and baking are two different culinary disciplines, I decided to create a comprehensive baking book for novice and intermediate bakers. And I would use the same detailed visual approach as my first book. So *Your Time to Bake* was born.

This book has many similarities to my first. Not only are the style and look of the books similar, but all the photographs were taken without the use of a food stylist and without retouching. So what you see is what you get (assuming you follow the recipe instructions). Both books also have step-by-step photo instructions, with a finished shot of every recipe. And, of course, the recipes call for easy-to-find ingredients. If I couldn't find it in a standard grocery store or supermarket, then I didn't put it in this book.

I've been baking since I was a kid, so you can bet I've made a lot of mistakes along the way. I remember my first attempt at making chocolate chip cookies on my own. I was ten years old. When I read the recipe, which called for one teaspoon of salt, I thought it was one tablespoon (thanks to those dang abbreviations they use in some other cookbooks!). Trust me, you wouldn't have liked my very salty chocolate chip cookies. Of course, I ate them anyway – no sense in wasting perfectly good chocolate!

You will probably make some mistakes along the way, too; but don't worry. Even the most experienced baker faces less-than-perfect results at one time or another, especially when trying something new. Unlike cooking, which allows you to add an extra handful of spice to the soup or use more carrots and fewer potatoes in the stew, when it comes to baking, measurements must be precise and variables like oven temperatures and baking times exact. Baking is more about chemistry. That is why I have included a section in the Introduction called "Before You Bake, Read This." It is designed to give you a heads up regarding the important baking variables and how to control them for successful results.

I hope you have as much fun learning about baking and making the recipes in this book as I had putting it all together. What a life I have! I got to make my favorite desserts every day, take their pictures, and write some fun copy about them. I must have done something right in a past life.

I wish you all great success in the kitchen.

Enjoy and bon appétit!

Robert L. Blakeslee

How exciting that you've decided to try your hand at baking! With just a few ingredients, some basic techniques, and little practice, you'll be amazed at what you can create with a bowl, a wooden spoon, a baking pan, and an oven.

Your Time to Bake is the perfect starting place for the novice baker. With its comprehensive, reader-friendly, eye-catching approach, anyone can develop the skills to become a successful creator of all sorts of delectable baked goods. What makes this book especially helpful lies in how it guides you visually through full-color photos and illustrations (there are more than 1,500!), which are designed to make all of the information clear and accessible, whether it is showing you how to separate an egg, frost a cake, or add a top crust to a pie.

Kicking off the book are three "primer" chapters that provide helpful information on baking essentials—ingredients, equipment, and common baking terms and techniques. What follows next is a fantastic array of easy-to-prepare recipes, including a delectable assortment of cookies, brownies, pies and tarts, cakes and cupcakes, muffins, cheesecakes, quick breads, and puff pastry creations, as well as luscious frostings, fillings, sauces, and toppings. Each recipe includes clear, step-by-step instructions— and each step is accompanied by a full-color photo to ensure that even inexperienced bakers will enjoy success every time. Rounding out the book is a chapter devoted entirely to decorating your delicious baked goods. Simple instructions will guide you in putting the frosting on the cake—as well beautiful borders, edible fondant flowers, and much, much more.

With *Your Time to Bake* in hand, you will quickly discover how easy it is to become the baker you want to be—and have fun in the process. So grab your whisks and mixing bowls, ladies and gentlemen, and let's get started . . .

Before You Bake, Read This

When learning any new craft, whether it's baking a pie or riding a bike, most people learn through experience . . . and by making mistakes. To help keep your baking experiences enjoyable and to minimize those inevitable errors, keep the following advice in mind:

You must follow orders!

When it comes to cooking, you can usually let yourself get creative and make changes to a recipe and still wind up with a great dish. Baking, however, doesn't allow such freedom. Think of recipes for baked goods as formulas that must be followed exactly. They rely on the chemical interactions of ingredients for successful results.

For this reason, it is important to prepare the recipes *exactly as written*. This means using the specified ingredient amounts and carefully following the given instructions. It also means using the recommended baking pans, and paying attention to factors like oven temperature, timing, testing, and ingredient preparations as described in the recipe.

Read before you start

Before you start preparing a recipe, read through it first. Start by taking out all the ingredients you need. (You don't want to realize you're out of something while in the middle of the preparation.) And familiarize yourself with the instructions—make sure you are aware of any advanced prepping that may be required.

Hot, warm, and cold

Ingredient temperature is an important factor when preparing baked goods. Butter, for example will bind to flour differently when it's cold, softened, or melted. Unless otherwise specified, ingredients like eggs, dairy products, and most liquids should be at room temperature. Eggs at room temperature blend better with other ingredients.

A few words about eggs

▶ When raw eggs are used in a recipe, choose pasteurized varieties. Whipped raw egg whites, for instance, are used in a number of recipes, including no-bake pie fillings. Like milk, eggs that are pasteurized have been heated to reduce the risk of causing a food-borne illness.

▶ Egg size also matters. Always use large eggs unless the recipe calls for a specific size.

▶ *Never* crack an egg directly into a batter or other mixture. Crack it into a clear bowl or glass, and then carefully inspect for broken shells.

▶ If you drop a raw egg on the floor or counter, sprinkle it liberally with salt, which will make it clump and become easier to clean up.

Use the parchment

When a recipe recommends lining the pan or baking sheet with parchment paper, be sure to do it. This moisture- and grease-resistant paper, which is able to withstand high oven temperatures, prevents food from sticking to it, so it is especially helpful to use when baking certain cakes and sticky cookies. And it makes cleanup a snap!

Testing, testing . . .

Temperatures can vary from one oven to another by a few degrees. This means baking times can vary as well. To avoid overbaking or underbaking those cakes, cookies, and other baked goods, always begin checking on them for doneness a few minutes before the time indicated in the recipe. And be sure to check for the visual signs of doneness (page 66), which vary from recipe to recipe.

Altitude is everything

Unlike cooking, successful baking relies on air pressure, which has a dramatic effect on the way baked goods rise (and fall!). Air pressure varies depending on where you live— the higher the elevation, the lower the air pressure. For basic formulas and helpful tips on high-altitude baking, see page 70.

Keep ahead of "boilovers"

Because pie fillings (especially fruit pies) sometimes boil over during baking, it's a good idea to place the pan on a cookie sheet to catch any drippings before they land on the oven floor and create a burnt-on mess. I also recommend covering the cookie sheet with foil, which both protects it (the boiling hot sugar and fruit juice can cause it to discolor) and makes cleanup easier. This is also a good idea for cheesecakes, fruit cobblers, and other baked goods that may rise too high and spill over the sides of the pan.

Have no fear

Remember to have fun with your baking experiences. Enjoy your successes and learn from (and laugh at) your mistakes.

How to Read the Recipes

The recipes in this book all contain common elements that are arranged for easy reading. The "Stuff You'll Need" box shows the utensils and cooking vessels you'll need to create the recipe. An ingredient list, yield information, and clear step-by-step instructions with photos are also included. Then all you have to do is follow the instructions. If you do it right, the finished product should look like the finished recipe photo. Many of the recipes also have helpful Important Tips—these pointers will help you make better baked goods or save you from making mistakes that could ruin them.

Step-by-step photo instructions

Step-by-step written instructions

Recipe title

Recipe introduction

Ingredient list

Important tip

Stuff You'll Need (tools and utensils)

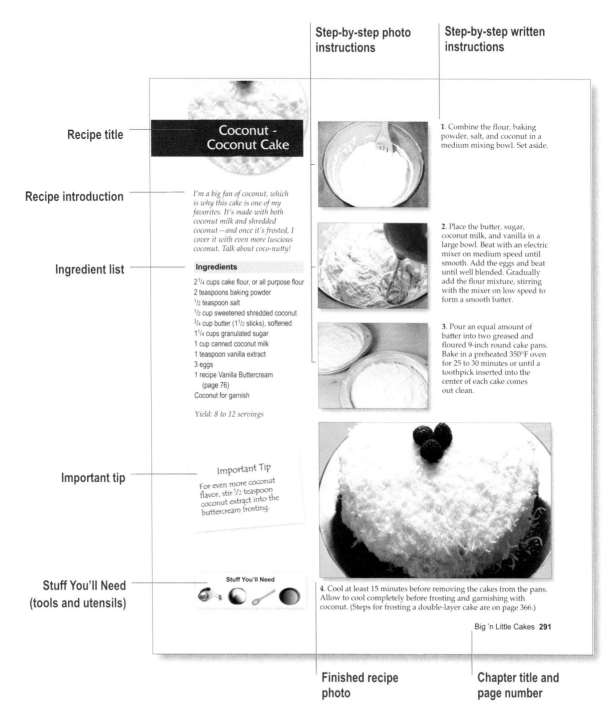

Coconut - Coconut Cake

I'm a big fan of coconut, which is why this cake is one of my favorites. It's made with both coconut milk and shredded coconut—and once it's frosted, I cover it with even more luscious coconut. Talk about coco-nutty!

Ingredients

2¹/₄ cups cake flour, or all purpose flour
2 teaspoons baking powder
¹/₂ teaspoon salt
¹/₂ cup sweetened shredded coconut
³/₄ cup butter (1¹/₂ sticks), softened
1¹/₄ cups granulated sugar
1 cup canned coconut milk
1 teaspoon vanilla extract
3 eggs
1 recipe Vanilla Buttercream (page 76)
Coconut for garnish

Yield: 8 to 12 servings

Important Tip

For even more coconut flavor, stir ¹/₂ teaspoon coconut extract into the buttercream frosting.

Stuff You'll Need

1. Combine the flour, baking powder, salt, and coconut in a medium mixing bowl. Set aside.

2. Place the butter, sugar, coconut milk, and vanilla in a large bowl. Beat with an electric mixer on medium speed until smooth. Add the eggs and beat until well blended. Gradually add the flour mixture, stirring with the mixer on low speed to form a smooth batter.

3. Pour an equal amount of batter into two greased and floured 9-inch round cake pans. Bake in a preheated 350°F oven for 25 to 30 minutes or until a toothpick inserted into the center of each cake comes out clean.

4. Cool at least 15 minutes before removing the cakes from the pans. Allow to cool completely before frosting and garnishing with coconut. (Steps for frosting a double-layer cake are on page 366.)

Big 'n Little Cakes **291**

Finished recipe photo

Chapter title and page number

Easy Does It. 6
  Cool Dough, 6
  Mixing It Up, 8
  Easy as Pie, 9

You Need Some Stuff. 10
  Some Flours for You, 11
  Making Light of It, 11
  You Sure Are Sweet, Sugar, 12
  In the Thick of It, 13
  Spicy Is Nicey, 14
  Tantalizing Flavors, 15
  Thank Moo!, 16
  Egg-Centric, 17
  Cheeses!, 17
  That's Phat, 18
  OMG! I ♥ Chocolate, 19
  These Are Totally Nuts!, 20
  Bits and Pieces, 21
  Berry Tasty, 22
  Fresh Fruit Salad, 23
  Roots and Squash?, 24
  Canned, Frozen, and
    Dried Fruit, 25

Wrapping It Up. 26

What Else?. 28
How Much?. 29

How sweet it is!

I enjoyed shopping for all the ingredients called for in this book – I even discovered a few new products. And it was always fun to see the reaction of the cashiers when they rang up my orders, which often consisted entirely of dessert items. One day, a cashier at my regular grocery store said, "You just buy all the good stuff," and I had to agree.

Amazingly, I lost weight during the six-month period that I tested the recipes in this book. Although they are irresistible, I didn't make an "oink oink" out of myself. I believe that desserts are for sharing, and I was fortunate to have at least forty friends and acquaintances who selflessly volunteered to help me test out the treats. (*Did I mention how popular I was at the time?*)

This chapter is about the "good stuff" that goes into making all types of delicious baked goods, as well as frostings, fillings, toppings, and the many tasty ingredients that are used to decorate them. Starting out is a section on easy-to-make-and-bake items, such as cake mixes and premade products like cookie and pie dough. These can be excellent choices to help the novice baker get comfortable using the oven, working with utensils, and trying simple baking techniques.

Next comes a look at the standard ingredients that go into making homemade baked desserts from scratch, including dry, fresh, bottled, canned, dehydrated, and frozen goodies. There are also tips on how to select and store these items, as well as helpful tables on ingredient substitutions, product yields, and much more.

Easy Does It

Before presenting the ingredients used to make homemade baked goodies from scratch, I want to talk about some of the premade items and boxed mixes that are readily available in most grocery stores. If you are new to baking, starting out with some of these products can be a good way to gain both experience and confidence as a baker. They are also good choices when time is a factor. In some cases, these items are better than what most people can make on their own.

I have found great success with many of the prepared items found on the following pages.

Cool Dough

Rather than making dough from scratch – whether for pastries, sweet rolls, or cookies – be aware that you can buy it already made. Boxed mixes that simply require the addition of a few ingredients are also available. Ready-made doughs are often found in the refrigerated section, although certain varieties like phyllo and puff pasty dough come frozen. Making these two doughs from scratch is very difficult – even experienced bakers have difficulty making them. For this reason, I recommend buying premade varieties. Aside from resulting in perfect pastries every time, they take just minutes to bake!

Cookie Dough

Boxed mixes that contain all the necessary dry ingredients for cookies, as well as premade refrigerated cookie dough are found on most grocery store shelves. The refrigerated dough needs only to be broken apart or sliced, placed on a cookie sheet, and baked according to package directions.

Vacuum-Packed Dough

You'll find canned dough for making sweet rolls, biscuits, turnovers, and a number of other pastries in your store's refrigerated section. Simply pop open the can to release the dough. For the dough to rise properly, be sure to preheat the oven first. And although the directions may suggest placing the dough on an ungreased pan or baking sheet, I've found that it often sticks – even to nonstick surfaces. So I recommend adding at least a light spray of cooking oil to the pan.

Puff Pastry Dough

When baked, puff pastry's compressed layers of butter and dough puff up to a light and flaky multi-layered crust that is buttery rich. Used to make such classic favorites as turnovers, strudels, napoleons, and fruit tarts, puff pastry is sold in sheets and preformed shells. I love this versatile dough so much, I have dedicated an entire chapter to it. (See "Puff the Magic Pastry," beginning on page 309.)

Puff pastry sheets

Most commercial puff pastry sheets are about 9-x-9-inches in size and come two to four in a box. (Pepperidge Farm brand is recommended.) You can use the sheets as they are or cut them into various shapes according to the recipe.

Puff pastry shells

These preformed frozen shells have a scored circle in the middle, as seen in the photo above. When baked, the shells puff up about three-inches. The round top can be easily removed, and the inside hollowed out. Then you can load the shell with your favorite filling. Ice cream, fruit, and pudding are popular choices. These shells are also perfect for cream puffs! Mini shells are also available for making "one-bite" dessert puffs.

Phyllo Dough

Tissue-thin sheets of phyllo dough are used in layered and strudel-type desserts. Phyllo is very fragile, dries out quickly, and breaks easily, making it difficult to work with. It is because of this that there are no recipes in this beginner's book that call for phyllo. Be aware, however, you can buy premade frozen phyllo cups that you can heat up and serve with the filling of your choice. These crispy cups come in standard and mini-tart sizes.

Mixing It Up

Boxed mixes are available for all types of baked goods, from cakes and muffins to brownies and quick breads. When you're strapped for time, or if you've never baked anything before and you just want to see how the dang oven works, check 'em out. You will find that my recipes are just about as easy – and they taste even better. One reason they taste better is because they are made with pure, fresh ingredients. Keep in mind that the majority of commercial mixes for baked goods contain artificial colors and flavors, as well as chemicals and preservatives.

Cake Mixes and Frostings

If you've never baked a cake before, it may seem a little intimidating. Enter the cake mix – an almost foolproof way to make a cake by following a few simple directions. Typically, these mixes contain all of the necessary dry ingredients. To create batter, they require only a few added items – usually water, eggs, and oil. Other than that, all you'll need are a measuring cup, a mixing bowl, a hand-held electric mixer, and a cake pan . . . and you're off to the races!

And talk about variety! In addition to standard yellow, white, and chocolate cakes, there are mixes for just about every type imaginable, from carrot and angel food cakes to pound cakes, Bundt cakes, and sponge cakes. There are super-moist varieties that come with their own pudding packets, and others that include fillings and/or toppings. You can even find sugar-free and reduced-sugar mixes.

Boxed frosting mixes are also available, as are canned ready-made frostings. These are pretty convenient, although making your own frosting is actually pretty easy (you'll find lots of recipes in Chapter 4.) When buying ready-made frostings, be sure to check the ingredients. Many contain hydrogenated oils, which have a negative impact on good health and should be avoided.

Brownie Mixes

One of my first baking experiences was making brownies from a mix. It was really easy and they came out pretty good. Since those days, I have made brownies dozens of times, both from mixes and from scratch. Because I find it pretty hard to tell the difference between the two, I often opt for the mix to save time. When I do, I usually add ingredients like nuts, chocolate morsels, or peanut butter chips to give the brownies more of a homemade taste.

Easy as Pie

From the crust to the filling to the topping, everything you need to make a pie comes premade and is available in your grocery store. You can have a pie ready to pop into the oven in just a few minutes.

Fillings

Regular and instant pudding mixes come in a wide variety of flavors. By reducing the amount of milk, you can also use the pudding as a pie filling. Canned fillings are available for most types of fruit pies – cherry, apple, blueberry, pumpkin, and peach are standard varieties.

Although they may not be as fresh as a real fruit filling, they do taste pretty good and are very convenient.

Boxed pudding mixes, which come in many flavors and in regular and instant varieties, also make popular pie fillings. In order for the filling to be thick enough to use in a pie, you'll have to use less liquid than what is used to make the pudding. Directions are available on the package.

Crusts

Graham cracker and cookie crusts are great for cream pies and cheesecakes. You'll find them in the baking aisle. Standard pastry crusts, which are best for fruit pies, come frozen in regular and deep-dish pie tins. Refrigerated premade pie dough is also available – just unfold the dough and press it into a pie plate. I have tried a few of these refrigerated doughs, but haven't found any that hold up as well as the frozen varieties.

Whipped Cream vs Whipped Topping

Making whipped cream is easy, but not as easy as buying it ready-made in a tub or getting one of those fun dispensers that let you shoot the topping into your mouth. Be sure to look at the ingredient label before buying. Just because it looks like and tastes like whipped cream, does not mean that it is whipped cream. Many prepared whipped toppings contain unhealthy trans fats, as well as preservatives, chemicals, and other additives – and not a drop of cream. To make your own whipped cream, see page 99.

You Need Some Stuff

It's amazing how many different types of baking products are readily available. Here are some grocery lists of the items you'll need to make most of the recipes in this book. These items are discussed in detail on the following pages.

Try to have all of the dry goods on hand. If you have the space, I also recommend having the canned and bottled items, too. Unless you are a strict vegan, most of the dairy products – butter, eggs, milk, and possibly cream – may already be staple ingredients in your fridge. It is also a good idea to stock up on some fresh fruit. Although it isn't always needed in a recipe, fruit can often make a perfect garnish or accompaniment to a dessert. And you can always enjoy it as a healthy snack. For the freshest fruit at the best price, buy it in season and from local growers if possible.

Dry Goods

All-purpose flour
Baking powder
Baking soda
Brown sugar– light or dark
Chocolate–baking, chips, morsels
Cocoa powder, unsweetened
Coconut, sweetened– shredded or flaked
Coffee, instant
Confectioner's (powdered) sugar
Cornstarch
Cream of tartar
Gelatin, unflavored
Granulated sugar
Nuts–blanched almonds, pecans, walnuts
Raisins
Spices–allspice, cinnamon, ground cloves, ginger, nutmeg, salt

Canned and Bottled Goods

Cooking spray
Corn syrup
Extracts–almond, coconut, maple, imitation rum, vanilla
Honey
Jams
Milk–condensed, evaporated
Molasses
Pineapple–crushed or chopped
Pumpkin purée

Dairy Products

Butter
Buttermilk
Cream, whipping
Cream cheese
Eggs
Milk, whole
Ricotta cheese
Sour cream

Fruit – fresh or frozen

Apples–Granny Smith or McIntosh (best for baking)
Bananas
Berries–blackberries, blueberries, raspberries, strawberries

Some Flours for You

Just about any grain, as well as certain seeds, nuts, and legumes, can be ground into flour; wheat, however, is the most popular. One of the reasons for wheat flour's popularity is due to its gluten-forming capability. (Gluten is necessary for baked items to rise properly.) Here are some of the most popular flour varieties.

All-purpose flour

As its name implies, this flour, which comes in bleached and unbleached varieties, works in just about any recipe for bread and other baked goods. It is also used a thickener for sauces and pie fillings. Bleached flour is whiter than unbleached and has a longer shelf life; however, the chemicals used in the bleaching process can affect the strength of the gluten. For this reason, some bakers prefer unbleached flour, especially for making bread.

Bread flour

Milled specifically for the purpose of making bread, this flour, sometimes sold as "bread machine flour," has a very high gluten content, which causes bread to rise into larger, lighter-textured loaves than it would with other flours.

Cake flour

This flour's low gluten content results in baked goods that are very light and tender.

Cornmeal

This coarse yellow flour is milled from corn and used to make tortillas and cornbread.

Self-rising flour

Already sifted, this light all-purpose flour contains a leavening (rising) agent in the form of baking powder or soda.

Whole wheat flour

All parts of the wheat berry are contained in this nutritionally superior flour that is brownish in color. Because it results in heavy, dense baked goods, whole wheat flour is usually combined with other white refined flours. It offers nutrition (especially protein and fiber), texture, and body to the finished product.

Whole wheat pastry flour is more finely milled than whole wheat flour. It is rich, light, and used in many baked goods.

Making Light of It

There are three primary rising agents – also called leavening or activating ingredients – that cause cakes, cookies, and breads to rise and become light and fluffy.

Baking soda

Also called bicarbonate of soda, baking soda has no leavening power when it is used alone. However, when it is added to a batter or dough that contains an acidic ingredient (such as lemon, molasses, honey, or buttermilk), it causes baked goods to rise.

Baking powder

Baking powder is a mixture of baking soda and other ingredients, of which the most important is an acidic compound (such as cream of tartar). When this product is mixed in a batter or dough, leavening occurs. Unlike baking soda, no acidic ingredients are needed as the acid is already in the powder.

Yeast

Yeast is actually a microscopic organism that comes to life when moistened with warm (not hot) water and fed some form of carbohydrate (sugar, flour). When activated, yeast produces carbon dioxide, which cases batters and doughs to bubble and rise. It has a distinct flavor and aroma and is used primarily in breads.

You Sure Are Sweet, Sugar

Once called "white gold" because it was so scarce and expensive, sugar was a luxury only the wealthy could afford. Today, this ingredient staple is used to sweeten both foods and beverages. It adds tenderness to dough and gives baked goods a warm golden hue. There are many sugar varieties and popular sweeteners that are used in baking. The most common ones are listed here.

Important Tips

▶ Store crystallized sugar varieties in airtight containers and keep in a cool, dry place. Exposure to the air will cause this type of sugar to clump, especially brown sugar, which forms into rock hard lumps.

▶ To soften hardened brown sugar, place it in a plastic storage bag with an apple wedge and seal tightly for a day or two. For a quick fix, place the open bag in the microwave next to a cup of water, and heat on high for about two minutes.

Crystallized Sugar

Granulated white sugar

This most commonly used sugar dissolves easily and sweetens everything from beverages and sauces to baked goods and other dessert treats.

Brown sugar

This is white sugar combined with molasses, which gives it a soft texture. Light varieties have less molasses and a more delicate flavor than dark.

Raw sugar

This is the crystallized juice that has been extracted from sugar cane. It has a coarse texture and a flavor similar to brown sugar.

Confectioner's sugar

The superfine crystals of this "powdered" granulated sugar have a little added cornstarch to prevent clumping. Because it dissolves so easily, this sugar is often used for icings. It's also used to decoratively "dust" the top of some desserts.

Liquid Sweeteners

Corn syrup

This thick sweet syrup, made from the starch in corn, doesn't crystallize, so it is often used in frostings, candies, and pie fillings. It adds chewiness to cookies, and because it holds moisture, it allows baked goods to stay fresher longer. Corn syrup comes in both dark and light varieties.

Molasses

Molasses – light, dark, and blackstrap varieties – is created from the boiled-down juice of the sugar cane. Dark molasses is the most popular type with bakers and is used to flavor cookies, gingerbread, puddings, and pie fillings.

Honey

Honey is the sweetest of the liquid sweeteners. It is 20 to 30 percent sweeter than granulated sugar. Store honey at room temperature in the pantry.

Artificial Sweeteners

Most artificial sweeteners do not provide the same flavor, browning, and texture to baked goods as sugar does. Those containing aspartame (Equal, NutraSweet) lose their sweetness when exposed to high heat. Sucralose (sold as the brand Splenda) is one substitute that can be used successfully. Recipes made with this sweetener do, however, tend to bake a little faster and come out a little drier.

In the Thick of It

There are a number of ingredients used to thicken soups and stews, sauces and gravies. Many of these products also add body and thickness to dessert items like puddings and custards, as well as fruit sauces, toppings, and pie fillings. On this page, you'll find some of these more commonly used thickeners.

Helpful Tips

▶ When thickening a sauce or filling on the stovetop, be sure to stir or whisk it briskly and constantly to prevent lumps from forming.

▶ Before adding a starchy thickener like cornstarch or flour into a hot liquid, first mix it with an equal amount of cold water until it forms a paste. Otherwise, the powder will be difficult to blend and is likely to form lumps.

▶ Add thickeners near the end of cooking time.

Important Tip

If lumps form while thickening a custard or other liquid ingredient, remove them with a strainer.

Powdered Thickeners

Cornstarch

This "flour" that comes from the corn kernel is often used to thicken puddings, sauces, and pie fillings. It is the best choice to use in dairy-based sauces and fillings. Avoid using it to thicken acidic liquids as it will lose its potency.

Arrowroot

Arrowroot is another popular thickening agent for puddings and sauces. Unlike cornstarch, it is a good choice for thickening acidic liquids, but it becomes slimy when combined with dairy products. Arrowroot is tasteless and becomes clear when cooked.

Flour

Along with thickening sauces and gravies, flour is a good choice for thickening the liquid filling of fruit pies and tarts. You can either sprinkle the flour over the fruit once it is in the pie shell, or toss the fruit in the flour before adding it to the shell.

Gelatin

Odorless, tasteless, and colorless, gelatin is used as a thickener for jams, jellies, and "jelled" desserts. It is also called for in some cheesecake recipes.

Tapioca flour

This popular thickener, which comes from the cassava plant, has a slightly sweet flavor and gives a glossy sheen to sauces, glazes, and fruit pie fillings.

Concentrated Milks

Condensed milk

This thick sweet mixture of whole milk and sugar is heated until about 60 percent of the liquid evaporates. It is used to add thickness and creamy richness to custards, puddings, and pie fillings.

Evaporated milk

The same as condensed milk only without the sugar, evaporated milk comes in lowfat and skim varieties.

Spicy Is Nicey

Sometimes a little bit of spice can add just the right touch to an already delicious dessert. Apples for example, may be the featured ingredient in a luscious apple pie, but adding a sprinkle of cinnamon or a pinch of nutmeg can enhance their flavor even further.

The spices on this page are popular choices in a wide range of dessert favorites, including delicious baked goods. All have interesting origins. Cinnamon comes from the inner bark of a laurel tree, allspice is from the dried berries of a myrtle tree, ginger is a root, nutmeg is from the nut of the nutmeg tree (makes sense), and cloves are the dried flower buds of a tropical evergreen.

Cream of Tartar

Although it is found near the spice section of your grocery store, cream of tartar (*potassium bitartrate*) is actually not a spice at all. It comes from the sediment that is produced while fermenting wine in barrels and is used mainly to help stabilize and add volume to beaten egg whites. It also prevents sugar from crystallizing, making it a good choice to use in sugary frostings and meringues.

Allspice

The name "allspice" was coined by the British due to its flavor, which has been described as a combination of cinnamon, nutmeg, and cloves. It is often used to flavor pies, spice cakes, and cookies.

Cinnamon

This sweet aromatic spice comes in many forms, from powder to chips to rolled sticks. Ground cinnamon is commonly used to flavor fruit (especially apples), pies, and cookies, as well as sweet rolls, breads, and muffins.

Cloves

Sweet and pungent, cloves are available as dried buds or in ground powdered form. Ground cloves lend flavorful depth to a number of baked goods, including gingerbread, spice cakes and cookies, and fruit pies like peach and pear.

Ginger

Often sold as a fresh root, ginger is also available in pickled, dried, crystallized, and ground forms. Ground ginger is what gives ginger snaps their classic flavor. It is also used in cookies, muffins, and other baked goods.

Nutmeg

The strong nutty taste of this spice is used in many desserts and sauces. It is an essential ingredient in eggnog (especially if you leave out the rum!).

Tantalizing Flavors

Extracts are highly concentrated flavorings that come from various foods or plants. A small amount adds powerful flavor to foods without adding a lot of liquid. Although there are over sixty extract flavors, most grocery stores carry only a dozen or so. Pure extracts are more expensive than artificial, but they are superior in taste. Use them whenever possible.

Vanilla extract, which comes from the beans of a certain orchid variety, is a baking staple because it is used in so many recipes. Here is a list of the most commonly used extracts in baked goods and other dessert treats.

▶ Almond
▶ Anise
▶ Butterscotch
▶ Caramel
▶ Cinnamon
▶ Clove
▶ Coconut
▶ Coffee
▶ Ginger
▶ Lemon

▶ Maple
▶ Orange
▶ Pear
▶ Pecan
▶ Peppermint
▶ Pistachio
▶ Rum
▶ Spearmint
▶ Vanilla
▶ Walnut

Homemade Extracts

Making your own baking extracts is pretty easy. Here are recipes for some of the more popular ones. Although they call for vodka, you can use brandy or rum with equally good results. As a general rule, the longer you allow these extracts to steep, the deeper-flavored they will be.

Vanilla Extract

4–5 whole vanilla beans
Fifth bottle of vodka
(about 3 cups)

1. Split the vanilla beans and add to the bottle.
2. Store in a cool dark spot and steep at least two months before using.
3. Gently shake the mixture often as it steeps.
4. When the extract is ready, transfer some to a smaller bottle for regular use.
5. Add more vodka to the large bottle to keep it topped off.
6. After a year, replace the beans with fresh ones.

Lemon or Orange Extract

1 large lemon or navel orange
1/2 cup vodka
1/4 cup water

1. Remove the rind (but not the white part) from the fruit and coarsely chop.
2. Add the rind to a clean glass jar along with the vodka and water. Cover tightly and let steep in a cool dark spot at least five days before using.
3. Gently shake the mixture often as it steeps.
4. Use up to a year.

Thank Moo!

Back when I was a child, there were still milkmen that delivered milk, cream, and cheese from local dairies right to your door. The milk came in glass quart bottles with foil caps. My brother bears a striking resemblance to our old milkman, but I've never said a word to him about it.

Unless otherwise specified, when milk is called for in a recipe, it usually means whole milk. Using a different variety may (or may not) result in differences in the richness, texture, and color of the baked goods.

Remember the Following:

▶ Milk has a short shelf life, so be sure to inspect the "good to" date on the container.

▶ Keep milk refrigerated. Never leave it out for more than a minute or two.

▶ Milk absorbs flavors, so keep the container closed when storing in the refrigerator.

▶ Keep in mind that the higher the milk's fat content, the quicker it sours. Skim milk lasts longest, cream the shortest.

▶ If milk is past its expiration date, just throw it out.

Whole milk

Rich and creamy, whole milk contains at least 3.25-percent fat.

Reduced-fat milk

This milk contains 2-percent fat. Most contain added vitamins A and D, which are removed during the fat-reducing process. This is a good lowfat alternative to whole milk.

Lowfat milk

Containing only 1-percent fat, lowfat milk is generally fortified with added nutrients.

Skim milk

Considered "nonfat," skim milk has as much fat removed as possible (it must contain less than 0.5 percent). It has half the calories of whole milk. It is also thin, watery, and not a good choice for most dessert recipes.

Cream

This rich layer of milk fat is skimmed from the top of milk before it is homogenized. It is light or heavy, depending on the amount of fat it contains. Light cream is often added to coffee, while heavy cream is used for whipping and as an ingredient in cream-style toppings, sauces, and desserts.

Half-and-half

Equal parts whole milk and cream, half-and-half is a lower-fat version of cream (although it still contains 10- to 12-percent milk fat). Neither half-and-half nor light cream can be whipped.

Buttermilk

Buttermilk is the slightly thick, tangy flavored liquid that remains after butter is churned. Today it is made commercially. Buttermilk is excellent to use in biscuits, cakes, and many other baked goods.

Rice milk

Cholesterol- and lactose-free, rice milk is a good choice for those who are allergic to dairy or soy.

Soymilk

This milky-flavored, lowfat nondairy liquid is cholesterol-free and a great alternative for those who are lactose intolerant or allergic to dairy.

Lactose-free milk

People who cannot digest lactose (a sugar found naturally in milk) are able to tolerate lactose-free milk. This milk variety can be substituted for regular milk in any recipe.

Egg-Centric

Eggs are extremely versatile and used in most baked goods and other dessert items. Along with color and flavor, they add lightness and texture to cakes and cookies. They also act as binders and thickeners for custards and many pie and pastry fillings.

Remember the Following:

▶ Before buying eggs, inspect them for cracks and leaks; then give them a twist to make sure they aren't stuck to the carton.

▶ Keep your eggs refrigerated, where they can stay fresh for several weeks.

▶ Check the expiration dates on cartons.

▶ Once an egg is cracked, if it smells funny or is discolored, throw it away.

▶ Use pasteurized eggs for recipes that call for uncooked eggs, like some mousses and whipped fillings.

▶ For best results, eggs should be at room temperature before using them in recipes for baked goods.

▶ As far as color, there is no difference between brown and white eggs other than the breeds that lay them.

Size matters

Egg are sold in small, medium, large, extra large, and jumbo sizes. Unless a recipe instructs otherwise, use large eggs. Egg size makes a difference in the consistency of batters and dough, and ultimately affects the outcome of the final product.

Cage free

Most hens are raised in "battery cages," which confine them to small areas. Eggs sold in cartons marked "cage free" were laid by hens that were able to walk around, spread their wings, and lay their eggs in nests – but did not necessarily have access to the outdoors.

Organic

Organic eggs come from hens that are free to roam outdoors and are fed organic feed. They are free of antibiotics, pesticides, and synthetic hormones; and high in beneficial omega-3 fatty acids.

Pasteurized

Like milk, eggs can be pasteurized to reduce the risk of food-borne illness. The process involves heating the eggs for several minutes at a temperature in excess of 150°F.

Cheeses!

A number of soft cheese varieties add wonderful creamy richness to cakes, pies, and pastry fillings.

Cream cheese

The thick, creamy richness of this fresh cow's milk cheese makes it a cheesecake staple, as well as an excellent base for some frostings.

Neufchâtel

Similar to cream cheese in flavor, texture, and appearance, Neufchâtel (named for the French town in which it originated) is made with milk instead of cream, so it contains about one-third less fat.

Mascarpone

An excellent choice for creamy desserts and pastry fillings, mascarpone is a rich, triple-cream Italian cheese that may be best known as the main ingredient in tiramisu.

Ricotta

The very fine curd of this Italian cheese makes it similar to cottage cheese. It is the main ingredient in Italian cheesecake (recipe on page 216), as well as the classic filling for cannolis.

Remember the Following:

▶ Keep cheese refrigerated until ready to use.

▶ Soft cheese absorb flavors easily, so wrap it well before refrigerating.

▶ If the cheese smells funny or is covered with mold, throw it out.

▶ For best results, bring soft cheeses to room temperature before using in a recipe.

That's Phat

Butter, margarine, and shortening are the fats used most often in baking. Solid at room temperature, they are responsible for adding flavor and crispness to cookies, as well as richness and tenderness to cakes and many other baked treats. Oil, which is a liquid fat, is also used in certain cookie and quick bread recipes.

Remember the Following:

▶ With the exception of butter, which should be refrigerated, fats can be stored at room temperature.

▶ Butter tends to absorb flavors easily, so wrap it well before refrigerating.

▶ When using oil for baked goods, avoid strong-flavored varieties like olive, sesame, and peanut. Mild-tasting canola and vegetable oils are best for baked desserts.

Butter

Butter comes in two varieties – salted and unsalted. Salted butter can contain anywhere from one-half to three-quarter teaspoon of salt per four-ounce stick. Unsalted butter (also known as sweet butter) is the preferred type for baking. It allows bakers to control the amount of salt in the recipe. Unless otherwise specified, use unsalted butter for baked goods and sweet desserts.

Margarine

Margarine is a butter substitute that can be used interchangeably with butter in any recipe.

Light Varieties

Butter and margarine that are labeled "light," "lower fat," "reduced fat," "reduced-calorie/diet," or "fat-free" should not be used for baking. These products have a lower fat content than traditional stick butter/margarine and will not produce proper results.

Oils

The best oils to use for baking are vegetable and canola because their mild flavors will not be detectable in the final product. Although corn oil has a slightly stronger flavor, it is also acceptable. Do not use strong-flavored oils like olive oil, unless you enjoy olive-flavored cookies and cupcakes!

Cooking/Baking Spray

Cooking spray is a good choice for greasing baking sheets and pans. It's fast and easy. Like oils, cooking sprays come in a variety of flavors, including butter. For baking, use those with mild flavors.

Shortening

The word shortening can refer to butter, lard, and margarine; however, when you see it listed as a recipe ingredient, it refers to solid vegetable oil. Virtually flavorless, vegetable shortening has a slightly higher fat content than butter and is used to make baked items like pie crusts and biscuits light and flaky.

OMG!
I ♥ Chocolate

Chocolate is made from cocoa beans. The beans are roasted and ground into cocoa "solids," which are combined with cocoa butter to make chocolate. Sugar and milk may also be added.

The highest percentage of cocoa is found in unsweetened chocolate varieties (also called bitter or baking chocolate). Next in line is bittersweet chocolate, followed by semi-sweet, and then sweet-dark chocolate. Milk chocolate, which gets its name from the fact that it contains milk, has the least amount of cocoa (and the most sugar).

Important Tip

When you are making a dessert with chocolate as the main flavoring, try to use the best-quality chocolate you can find.

Baking chocolate

Bars of baking chocolate come in individually wrapped one-ounce squares (usually eight to a pack). Each square is scored down the middle, so it can be easily broken in half. It comes in unsweetened, bittersweet, semi-sweet, and German sweet chocolate varieties.

Chocolate morsels

Although they can be used in most recipes that call for chocolate, chocolate chips or morsels are best known as an ingredient in chocolate chip cookies. They come in many varieties, including milk, semi-sweet, and white chocolate.

Cocoa powder

Cocoa powder comes in unsweetened and sweetened varieties. It easily dissolves in liquids, making it a good choice for hot cocoa and other chocolate beverages. Unsweetened cocoa adds chocolate richness to many baked goods and other desserts.

Chocolate candy

For most recipes, you don't have to use chocolate made specifically for baking. Try candy-coated chocolate like M&M's in your next batch of chocolate chip cookies. If a recipe calls for baking chocolate, try using a good-quality chocolate candy bar instead.

White chocolate

White chocolate is used in baked goods and desserts, but it is not actually chocolate since it does not contain cocoa solids. It's made of sugar, cocoa butter, milk solids, and vanilla. Inferior brands contain vegetable fat instead of cocoa butter.

These Are Totally Nuts!

Feeling a little nutty? I do all the time. Nuts are a welcome addition to cookies, cakes, and breads, and great for topping off a bowl of ice cream or frozen yogurt. Many nuts, like Brazil nuts, are actually seeds; others, like peanuts, are legumes. Most nuts are available raw or roasted, with or without salt, and plain or flavored. They also come whole, halved, sliced, slivered, and chopped.

Keep 'em Fresh

Freshness is an extremely important consideration when cooking or baking with nuts. The flavor of a stale nut will ruin any type of dish – guaranteed! Because of their high fat content, nuts get stale quickly. To keep them fresher longer, place them in an airtight container and store in the refrigerator or freezer. In the refrigerator, they will last three to four months; in the freezer, they will stay fresh up to eight months. Before adding nuts to a recipe, *always* taste them to be sure they're fresh.

Toasting nuts enhances their flavor; it also makes them easier to chop. You can easily toast nuts yourself. Simply spread them out on a baking sheet in a single layer, then pop them into a 350°F oven for five to twenty minutes (depending on the size of the nut). Keep an eye on them because they can burn very quickly. Cool them completely before storing.

Nutty Paste

Almond Paste
Made primarily of ground almonds and sugar, this paste is typically used as a pastry filling (ever had an almond croissant, strudel, or bear claw?). It is also used in some cookies like macaroons.

Marzipan
Made mostly of almond paste and sugar, marzipan is a pliable mixture that can be colored and rolled out or molded into edible decorative shapes (like ribbons or bows).

Almonds

Pecans

Cashews

Peanuts

Macadamias

Walnuts

Bits and Pieces

One trip down the baking aisle and you'll be amazed at the wide range of luscious little bits and pieces you can add to cookies, cakes, and quick breads; mix with your favorite ice cream, pudding, or frozen yogurt; or use to decorate all sorts of delicious treats. You can even make your own by chopping up your favorite candy bars.

Tasty Treats

Of the wide variety of tasty morsels found in the baking aisle, pictured here are some of the more popular choices. Chips of various flavors, which are typically added whole to cookies and ice cream, also melt well and can be used in just about any recipe that calls for melted chocolate. This also makes a great dip for fresh fruits like strawberries and bananas.

Coconut comes sweetened or unsweetened and shredded or flaked. Colored candy sprinkles are perfect to decorate cookies doughnuts, and cupcakes, while rich, buttery toffee pieces add flavor and texture to cookies and frostings. And let's not forget raisins, also known as "nature's candy." They are great in everything from puddings and cookies to quick breads and muffins.

Light and fluffy marshmallows come in regular and miniature sizes. They are the perfect glue for holding together S'mores and Rice Krispies Treats.

Chips

Coconut

Sprinkles

Toffee pieces

Raisins

Marshmallows

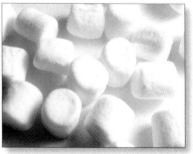

Berry Tasty

Americans sure love their berries. Did you know that the United States is the world's leading producer of blueberries and strawberries? Not only are fresh ripe berries wonderful in pies, cakes, and muffins, they are often the perfect choice for decorating the finished products. Be sure to check out some of the ways they add visual beauty (as well as delicious taste) to pies and cakes in Chapter 14 "Decorating with Taste," beginning on page 357.

Berries are berry, berry delicious, but they are also berry, berry fragile. Keep the helpful tips at right in mind when purchasing, storing, and using fresh berries.

Berry Good Tips

▶ All berries are delicate, especially raspberries and blackberries, and they are easily crushed and bruised. Handle them carefully.

▶ When buying berries, use color as an indication of their ripeness. They should be richly colored and plump. (Once picked, they won't ripen further, but they *will* begin to spoil.)

▶ Be sure to check packaged berries carefully for mold, which is a sign that they are spoiled.

▶ Avoid unripe berries, which are very sour. For some berries – strawberries, blueberries, and blackberries – a greenish color is an indication.

▶ Because berries spoil quickly when damp, don't rinse them until just before using.

▶ Berries are highly perishable and have a very short shelf life – most varieties don't last longer than five days. Use them shortly after buying.

▶ Store berries uncovered in the refrigerator.

▶ Berries are popular with pests and, unless they are organically grown, have most likely been sprayed with pesticides. Rinse them thoroughly before using.

▶ Fresh blackberries, blueberries, and raspberries tend to fall apart and "bleed" when they are stirred into a batter. Freezing them for about an hour before adding them will help them stay firm.

▶ When using fresh or frozen blueberries, be sure to inspect them for stems.

Blackberries

Cranberries

Raspberries

Blueberries

Gooseberries

Strawberries

Fresh Fruit Salad

The fresh, naturally sweet taste of fruit makes it the perfect choice to include in a wide variety of baked goods and dessert treats. From apple pies and pear tarts to peach cobblers and banana bread, fruit has always played a starring role. Along with berries, the fruits on this page are among the most popular ones used in baking – but they are certainly not the only ones.

As a general rule, inspect all fresh fruit before purchasing. As detailed in the tips at right, use your eyes, nose, and sense of touch to make good selections. And when fresh is not available, canned or frozen varieties will often work just as well (see page 25).

Fresh Fruit Tips

▶ Avoid bruises, holes, dents, or mold when choosing any fruit.

▶ Apples, pears, and peaches should feel firm when you give them a gentle squeeze.

▶ Citrus fruits should be firm, heavy, and bright in color. Those with thin skins are often the juiciest.

▶ For many fruits, a faint clean smell of the fruit itself is a sign of freshness. Overripe fruit will smell too sweet because its natural sugars become stronger with age.

▶ Bananas ripen quickly. Unless you plan to use them immediately, buy them when they're still a little green. Store in a cool, dry place – not the refrigerator.

▶ The juice and zest from lemons, limes, and oranges are used in many dessert recipes. Opt for fresh when possible, but if buying a commercial brand, choose one that is pure juice with no added chemicals.

▶ A ripe pineapple will have a faint pineapple smell and brownish skin. It will be slightly firm, but not rock hard. And if you can easily pluck out one of its leaves, it's ripe.

▶ The tart, crisp Granny Smith and the sweet, slightly tart McIntosh are the most popular apples for baking. Both have firm juicy flesh that holds up well to heat.

▶ Because of their firm texture, Bosc and Asian pears are the preferred varieties for baking.

Apples

Lemons

Pears

Bananas

Peaches

Pineapples

Roots and Squash?

How about using some sweet veggies the next time you decide to bake a cake, a pie, a quick bread, or some muffins? Don't laugh. Carrots, sweet potatoes, pumpkins, and even zucchini are called for in many delicious dessert recipes. I guess it makes sense, considering they all have a mild sweet flavor when cooked.

Important Tip

If you are grating fresh carrots or zucchini for a recipe, it isn't necessary to peel them. They should, however, be thoroughly washed.

Sweet potatoes

The mashed flesh of sweet potatoes is used to make the filling for sweet potato pie – the favorite alternative to the classic pumpkin pie. To remove the skin from sweet potatoes, boil them first, then drop them into cold water. The skin will slip right off.

Carrots

When naturally sweet carrots are cooked, their sweet flavor becomes deliciously mild, making them a popular ingredient choice for cupcakes, muffins and, of course, everyone's favorite – the carrot cake.

Zucchini

When zucchini is cooked, it lends a mildly sweet and buttery flavor to quick breads, cakes, and muffins. Although zucchini has seeds, they are tiny and soft, and not detectable in baked goods.

Making Pumpkin Purée?

Pumpkin purée is the star ingredient in pumpkin pie. Although it isn't very difficult to make your own, it does take a lot of time and work . . . plus it makes a big mess. First, you have to remove the stem, seeds, and inner strings from the pumpkin. Then you have to cut it up, boil it until tender, and then purée it in a food processor.

What's more important is that canned pumpkin purée works beautifully, so there is no need to knock yourself out and make it from scratch. Just be sure to choose brands that are 100-percent pumpkin.

Canned, Frozen, and Dried Fruit

Although fresh fruits are superior in appearance and nutritional value (especially when freshly picked), they may not always be available. For some recipes, canned, frozen, or sometimes dried varieties can be good substitutions. They are also convenient and may even be preferred. Personally, when a recipe calls for a cup or so of pineapple, I'll use canned because I don't need to buy a whole fresh one. I have also found frozen fruit to work well in a number of baked goods – once the fruit bakes, there's really not much difference between fresh and frozen. Dried fruits are naturally better in certain baked items. Take raisins, for instance. Cinnamon-raisin bread works . . . Cinnamon-grape bread? Not so much.

Canned fruit

Canned fruits go through an extensive heating process that compromises their nutrient content, as well as texture and appearance. Be aware that many canned fruits also contain added sweeteners, artificial colors, and preservatives. When using canned fruit, choose varieties that are packed in their own juice. Unless otherwise instructed, drain the fruit before adding it to batters, dough, or pie fillings.

Frozen fruit

Frozen fruits that are packaged shortly after they are picked are closer to fresh in taste, nutrients, and appearance than canned. Unless the recipe calls for the fruit to be defrosted first, it can be added directly to most batters. Be aware that frozen blueberries, raspberries, and blackberries tend to "bleed" when added to batter, so add them at the last minute and stir gently.

Dried or dehydrated fruit

Dried fruit is wonderfully concentrated and flavorful. Adding a handful of dried cranberries, raisins, apricots, apples, or dates to cookies, quick breads, scones, or muffins gives them a delicious spark of flavor. Special "baking raisins" are also available in most grocery stores. Extra moist and plump (thanks to a special handling process), these raisins tend to maintain their moistness during baking. Most dried fruit has a long shelf life. Tightly wrapped, it will keep about six months in the pantry and about a year in the refrigerator.

Wrapping It Up

When you are ready to put on your baker's cap, you'll want have all of the ingredients ready to go. You will also want to make sure that everything – the nuts, the chocolate chips, the flour – is fresh.

To keep ingredients fresh, it is important to store them properly. Luckily there are wraps and bags and containers to help maintain product freshness. These items are also perfect for storing leftovers – those extra chocolate chip cookies you just made, that leftover banana bread, or that last delicious piece of homemade apple pie.

Depending on what you are storing, the food will have different requirements for air, temperature, and the size and shape of the containers. Here are some basic food-storage items, methods, and materials.

Wax paper

Although it is not very good for storing food, wax paper has a nonstick, moisture-proof surface that makes it perfect for preventing layers of stored items like cookies and brownies from sticking together.

Plastic wrap

Along with wrapping up certain foods, plastic wrap is also used to "seal" the tops of bowls and plates that contain food. Use it for short-term storage only.

Plastic containers

These handy containers, which come in a variety of shapes and sizes and have resealable lids, are great for storing everything from dry ingredients like nuts and sugars to leftover cookies and cakes to whipped cream and frostings.

Storage canisters

Glass jars and canisters with airtight lids (like Mason jars) are great for storing dry goods like flour, sugar, coffee, and nuts. If your kitchen cabinets are cramped for space, you can even leave the filled containers right on the countertop.

Foil

This short-term storage wrap also acts as a barrier, preventing light and outside odors from reaching the food inside. Foil is also good for covering the tops of bowls and pans, and it makes a good liner for cookie sheets.

Parchment Paper

This heavy-duty paper may not be good for wrapping up leftovers or covering bowls, but it is a great product for anyone who bakes. Also called "baking paper" or "baking parchment," this paper is moisture and grease resistant. It is used primarily to line cookie sheets and baking pans, eliminating the need to grease them. This means there is virtually no cleanup. And food doesn't stick to parchment, which makes it especially handy when baking sticky cookie dough. Once baked, the cookies practically slide right off. You can even lift the parchment and transfer an entire batch of cookies to a cooling rack in one step! As an added bonus, you can use parchment like wax paper to prevent layers of stored foods like cookies or brownies from sticking together.

Parchment is suitable for use in microwaves and conventional ovens up to 450°F. Do not, however, use it in a toaster oven, under a broiler, or over an open flame.

Zippered storage bags

Great for day-to-day storage, these bags come in various sizes and thicknesses. If you are going to freeze the food, use bags that are designed specifically for the freezer. Before sealing the bag, try to remove as much air as possible, which will keep the food fresher longer. When freezing food, I recommend writing what you are freezing along with the date on the bag itself. Most items freeze well for about three months.

What Else?

If you are getting ready to prepare a recipe (or you're in the middle of preparing one) and you discover that you're missing an ingredient – don't worry. Here is a list of some common items you can use as ingredient substitutes if you ever find yourself in a pinch.

Ingredient Substitutions

Ingredient	Amount	Substitution
Baking powder	1 teaspoon	$1/3$ teaspoon baking soda plus $1/2$ teaspoon cream of tartar.
Bread crumbs, dry	1 cup	3 slices bread, dried or toasted.
Butter	1 cup	$7/8$ cup oil plus $1/4$ teaspoon salt.
Buttermilk	1 cup	1 cup milk plus 1 tablespoon lemon juice (let stand five minutes).
Corn syrup	1 cup	1 cup granulated or packed brown sugar plus $1/4$ cup water
Cornstarch	1 tablespoon	2 tablespoons all-purpose flour.
Eggs	1 whole	2 egg whites plus 2 teaspoons oil, or $1/4$ cup egg substitute.
Flour (for thickening)	2 tablespoons	1 tablespoon cornstarch or 4 tablespoons arrowroot.
Flour, cake	1 cup	1 cup less 2 tablespoons sifted all-purpose flour.
Honey	1 cup	$1 1/4$ cups granulated sugar plus $1/4$ cup water
Lemon juice	1 teaspoon	$1/2$ teaspoon vinegar.
Molasses	1 cup	1 cup honey or maple syrup, or 1 cup brown sugar and $1/4$ cup water.
Pumpkin pie spice	1 teaspoon	$1/4$ teaspoon allspice, $1/4$ teaspoon nutmeg, and $1/4$ teaspoon cinnamon.
Sour cream	1 cup	1 cup plain yogurt.
Sugar, brown	1 cup, packed	1 cup granulated sugar plus 2 tablespoons molasses.
Sugar, confectioner's	1 cup	$1/2$ cup plus 1 tablespoon granulated sugar.
Sugar, granulated	1 cup	1 cup firmly packed brown sugar, or $1 3/4$ cups confectioner's sugar
Vinegar	1 teaspoon	2 teaspoons lemon juice.
Yogurt, plain	1 cup	1 cup buttermilk or sour cream.

How Much?

How many apples will yield 1 cup of slices? How many lemons will produce 3 tablespoons of juice? How many cups of brown sugar are in a pound? Here is a chart of common baking ingredients and their approximate weight or volume equivalents.

 =

Ingredient Yields

Ingredient	The Recipe Needs . . .	You Will Need . . .
Apples	1 cup slices	1 medium apple
	1 pound	3 or 4 medium apples
Bananas	1 cup mashed	2 medium bananas
Bread (white)	1 cup soft crumbs	1$\frac{1}{2}$ slices
	1 cup dry crumbs	5 fully toasted slices
Butter	1 cup	2 sticks or 8 ounces
Carrots	1 cup grated	1 large or 1$\frac{1}{2}$ medium carrots
Cranberries	1 cup whole	4 ounces
Cream	2 to 2$\frac{1}{2}$ cups whipped	1 cup ($\frac{1}{8}$ pint) heavy cream
Cream cheese	1 cup	8 ounces
Eggs	1 cup	4 large eggs
Egg whites	1 cup	8 large eggs, separated
Flour	3$\frac{1}{2}$ cups	1 pound
Lemon	2 to 3 tablespoons juice	1 medium lemon
Lime	2 tablespoons juice	1 medium lime
Orange	$\frac{1}{4}$ to $\frac{1}{2}$ cup juice	1 medium orange
Peaches	1 cup sliced	8 ounces or 2 medium peaches
Pears	1 cup chopped	8 ounces or 2 medium pears
Ricotta cheese	1 cup	8 ounces
Shortening	2$\frac{1}{4}$ cups	1 pound
Strawberries	3 cups whole or 2 cups sliced	1 pound
Sugar, brown	2$\frac{1}{4}$ cups packed	1 pound
Sugar, confectioner's	4 cups	1 pound
Sugar, granulated	2 cups	1 pound

Fantastic Fun-Filled Food Facts

Most baked goods have a few common ingredients like flour, eggs, milk (or other dairy products), and flavorings – often vanilla extract. Where do these products come from? When were they first used? How much do we consume as a nation? Here is some interesting "stuff" about these foodstuffs.

Milking It

Check out these interesting facts about milk:

▶ There is evidence that the Britons were milking cows over 6,000 years ago.

▶ Just about every large mammal is milked, including camels, buffalos, horses, goats, donkeys, sheep, reindeer, and yaks. (The donkey's milk is one of the closest to human's.) Pigs, whose milk is very similar to human's, are never milked!

▶ The milk of a reindeer contains 22.5 percent milkfat, while cow's milk has only 5.5 percent.

▶ The average cow produces 7 gallons of milk a day – and it takes about 350 squirts to make 1 gallon.

▶ Currently, the record amount of milk produced by a cow in one year is 72,170 pounds. That's roughly 8,400 gallons at an average of 23 gallons per day.

▶ Do you know that it takes 21 pounds of whole milk to make 1 pound of butter?

▶ On average, chocolate manufacturers use about 3.5 million pounds of milk per day.

▶ Know why milk is white? It's due to a calcium-rich protein called *casein*. Also, the cream in milk contains fat, which is white. The more cream in the milk, the whiter it is. Because low-fat and fat-free milk contain less cream, they are more grayish in color.

Orchid Beans

The majority of the world's vanilla extract is produced in Madagascar. Vanilla beans, which come from a certain species of orchid, are soaked in alcohol to produce the extract.

God Bless Our Hens

▶ There are over 240 million laying hens in the United States that produce over 50 billion eggs. The average hen lays 300 to 325 eggs per year. That is about 1 laying hen and 1 egg per day for every person in the country.

▶ The largest egg on record weighed 1 pound. It had a double yolk and a double eggshell. That hen must have been the size of a goose!

Flours Are Pretty

The word "flour" is a variation of the French word *fleur*, which means "flower" or "blossom." Although most flour comes from different varieties of wheat, it is also made from cereal grains like rice, barley, corn, and oats. Flour can also come from potatoes, chickpeas, peanuts, soybeans, and other nuts and seeds.

Flour Bomb

Did you know that flour is flammable? When flour dust is suspended in the air, it can explode. On May 2, 1878, a spark ignited airborne flour dust within the Washburn 'A' Mill in Minneapolis, Minnesota – the largest flour mill in the United States at the time. The explosion, which instantly killed fourteen workers, set off a fire that caused the deaths of four more people, destroyed two other nearby mills, and completely decimated the surrounding area. Known as the Great Mill Disaster, this tragic event led to many reforms in the milling industry, including the installation of ventilation systems and other safety devices.

2. T'n T (Tools 'n Terms)

Basic Gadgets 32

Electric Gizmo 36

Potz and Panz 37

Oven Vessels 38

Home, Home on Your Range 40

Baking Terms from A to Z 42

Slap it, flip it, spin it around . . .

Thank goodness for kitchen gadgets and gizmos! If it wasn't for these handy little time savers, I probably wouldn't have taken the time to learn how to bake. Imagine if you had to whip cream with sticks or grind nuts with rocks. You might think that sounds funny, but that's how they did it in the not-too-distant past. Now if someone would invent one of those machines you see in science fiction movies that can make anything you want by just pushing a couple buttons, I'd probably make a birthday cake every day.

This chapter presents a list of basic supplies that are commonly used to prepare most baked goods and other dessert creations. It begins with a glossary of small gadgets and utensils, and then gives an overview of helpful electric appliances, cookware, and cutlery. Rounding out this section is a list of essential bakeware . . . the standard baking sheets and pans you'll need to bake up those delectable cookies, cakes, muffins, and pies. There's a good chance that you may already own many of these items. And for those who are true novice bakers, there is even a short tour of your oven – just so you can become familiar with it!

The final section is dedicated to "bake talk," or baking terminology. It is the place to turn when you come across an unfamiliar word or phrase while preparing a recipe. These are terms you "knead" to know, or you might find yourself in a real "bind" while you're baking. *(Punny, huh?)*

This photo is of a stand mixer I own that was manufactured by GS Blakeslee & Co. The company was started in 1870 by my great grandfather, who invented and manufactured the first commercial automatic dishwasher. The dishwasher, which was made out of wood, was considered a success because it washed more dishes than it broke. The company was sold after it had been in the family for 100 years and is still in operation today (but they don't make wooden dishwashers anymore).

Basic Gadgets

Although the gadgets and small utensils found on the following pages are among the most useful for baking, it isn't necessary to own them all. Select the ones that are right for your particular needs. For example, you don't have to buy a timer if your stove already has one built in (you can even use the alarm on your cell phone). You'll find that if you enjoy baking, over time, you'll probably want to own many of these items. But here's a word of advice . . . Don't be a cheapskate and shop for them at the 99-cent store. Really splurge and go to the dollar store! I'm just kidding, of course. Many of these items are actually not that much money (under twenty dollars), and I usually recommend buying the best ones that you can.

Purchasing Pointers

▶ Make sure that equipment like mixing bowls, spatulas, and measuring cups are dishwasher safe. Even if you generally wash them by hand, there may be times (like when you're baking for a big party or for the holidays) that you may prefer to use a dishwasher.

▶ I tend to purchase better-quality small kitchen utensils like vegetable peelers, spatulas, and can openers. They cost just a few dollars more than cheaper ones, but the difference in the way they perform and wear can be significant.

▶ If it's within your budget, buy good-quality knives. They are worth the investment – with proper care, they can last a lifetime.

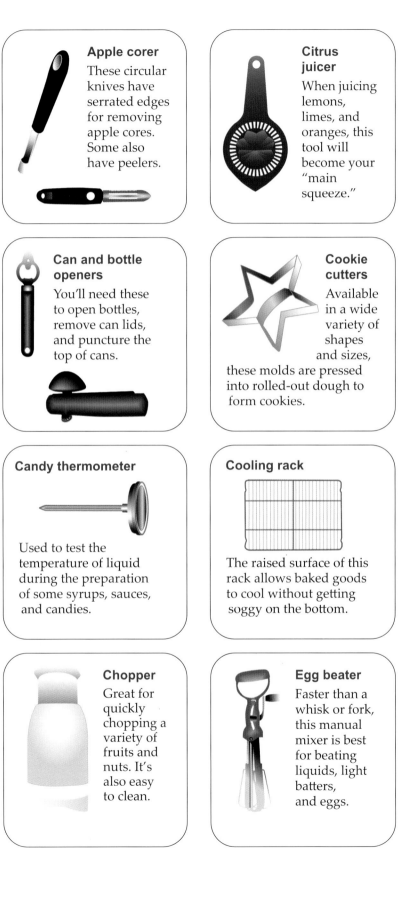

Apple corer
These circular knives have serrated edges for removing apple cores. Some also have peelers.

Citrus juicer
When juicing lemons, limes, and oranges, this tool will become your "main squeeze."

Can and bottle openers
You'll need these to open bottles, remove can lids, and puncture the top of cans.

Cookie cutters
Available in a wide variety of shapes and sizes, these molds are pressed into rolled-out dough to form cookies.

Candy thermometer
Used to test the temperature of liquid during the preparation of some syrups, sauces, and candies.

Cooling rack
The raised surface of this rack allows baked goods to cool without getting soggy on the bottom.

Chopper
Great for quickly chopping a variety of fruits and nuts. It's also easy to clean.

Egg beater
Faster than a whisk or fork, this manual mixer is best for beating liquids, light batters, and eggs.

Dough scraper

Use this flexible plastic or metal tool to divide dough and remove sticky remnants from work surfaces.

Nut cracker

This tool is specifically designed for cracking open nuts with shells.

Grater/shredder

This tool has large holes for shredding and small holes for grating.

Oil can

Use this handy container for drizzling oil, syrups, and dessert sauces.

Ladle

This long-handled spoon has a deep bowl that is good for transferring batter to baking pans.

Oven glove/mitt

You should have at least two oven mitts for taking hot baked goods from the oven. They come in cloth and synthetic material.

Mixing bowls

A large mixing bowl is all you really need, but it is helpful to have a variety of sizes.

Pastry bag

Used for cake decorating, pastry bags (made of cloth or disposable plastic) are filled with frosting that is piped out through special tips.

Knives

Chef's knife

Good for chopping, slicing, and mincing, the all-purpose chef's knife is the one you will find most useful. Chef's knives are available with blade lengths of 6, 8, 10, and 12 inches.

Paring knife

Resembling a smaller, thinner chef's knife, a paring knife has a 3- to 4-inch blade that tapers to a point. It offers more control than a chef's knife, making it especially good for peeling, slicing, and trimming small fruits.

Serrated bread knife

With its 8- or 9-inch blade and serrated edge, this knife is designed to easily cut bread and cakes without squashing or tearing them.

Utility knife

This multipurpose knife has a 4- to 7-inch plain or serrated blade. Good for jobs like cutting up fruit and slicing pies and cakes.

Basic Gadgets

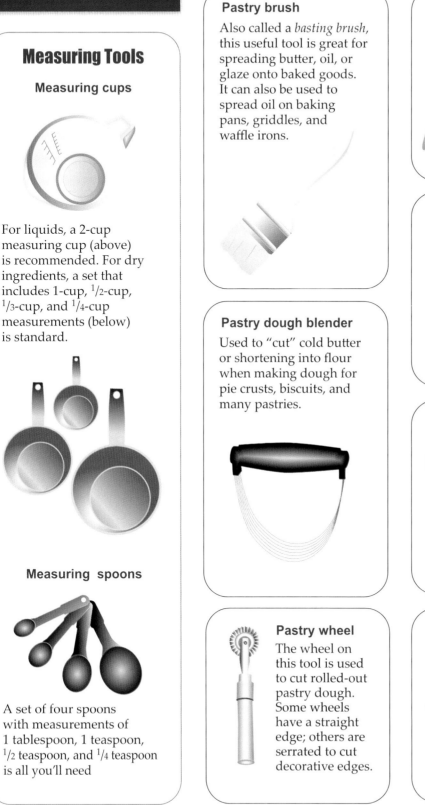

Measuring Tools

Measuring cups

For liquids, a 2-cup measuring cup (above) is recommended. For dry ingredients, a set that includes 1-cup, $^1/_2$-cup, $^1/_3$-cup, and $^1/_4$-cup measurements (below) is standard.

Measuring spoons

A set of four spoons with measurements of 1 tablespoon, 1 teaspoon, $^1/_2$ teaspoon, and $^1/_4$ teaspoon is all you'll need

Pastry brush

Also called a *basting brush*, this useful tool is great for spreading butter, oil, or glaze onto baked goods. It can also be used to spread oil on baking pans, griddles, and waffle irons.

Pastry dough blender

Used to "cut" cold butter or shortening into flour when making dough for pie crusts, biscuits, and many pastries.

Pastry wheel

The wheel on this tool is used to cut rolled-out pastry dough. Some wheels have a straight edge; others are serrated to cut decorative edges.

Pie/cake server

A combination knife/server that is specially shaped for cutting and serving a slice of cake or pie.

Pizza wheel

This large "pastry wheel" can be used to cut rolled-out dough.

Potato masher

Resembling a large garlic press, this tool is used to mash foods like ripe fruits and cooked potatoes.

Rolling pin

This cylindrical-shaped utensil, often made of wood, is used to flatten and shape dough.

Rubber spatula

Use this tool to scrape batter and soft mixtures from bowls and utensils. I sometimes use it to spread frosting on cake.

Strainer

Used to separate solids from liquids, strainers come in a variety of sizes.

Whisk

Excellent tool for whipping and beating light batters and ingredients like heavy cream, eggs, and egg whites. Whisks come in a variety of sizes.

Sifter

Gadget used for aerating flour, sugars, and other dry ingredients.

Sugar shaker

Container for sprinkling dry ingredients such as powdered sugar, cinnamon, and cocoa powder.

Wooden spoon

Used to stir batters, sauces, and just about everything else, wooden spoons are a must-have for bakers. Get a few!

Serving spoon

Use this oversized, long-handled spoon to scoop out servings of cobblers and crisps from baking pans.

Timer

This essential cooking gadget should have at least a one-hour capacity and an alarm.

Spatula

Useful tool for removing cookies from cookie sheets, as well as brownies and bar cookies from baking pans.

Trivets

Set hot pans or dishes on these little stands, which protect tables and counters from heat damage.

Zester

Used to scrape the outer layer (zest) of citrus fruits.

Preparing certain foods and ingredients with electric appliances can speed up preparation time and improve your results. A few essential items—a food processor, an electric mixer, and a blender—will help you prepare just about anything. From general preparation techniques like chopping and grating to mixing and blending batters, toppings, and fillings, these appliances can do it all.

Generally, I don't find it necessary to buy top-of-the-line small electric appliances like blenders and hand-held mixers. Those that are moderately priced usually work well enough. For all the extra money you'll spend on the higher-priced items, there is often little difference in the jobs they do. (A twenty-speed blender, for example, will cost you more, when three speeds are all you really need.)

Blender

The short blades of a blender can chop small amounts of food like nuts and chocolate, but this appliance is best for puréeing fruits and blending sauces, beverages, and other liquids. Its tall, narrow container does not allow much air to be incorporated into the liquid, so it is not a good choice for whipping ingredients like cream and egg whites.

Electric hand-held mixer

For creaming, mixing, and whipping ingredients, and for the best consistency in batters and frostings, you'll need a hand-held electric mixer. This portable appliance is lightweight with beaters that pop right off for easy cleaning. I recommend a model with five speeds.

Food processor

Speedy and efficient, the food processor can chop, dice, slice, grind, and purée most foods. Some even knead dough. A medium-size model with a five- to seven-cup capacity bowl is good for most baking needs. All come with a standard set of attachments, including chopping blades and disks for slicing and shredding.

Stand mixer

This stationary mixer, which sits on the countertop, is a heavy duty version of the portable hand-held type. It has a more powerful motor that can handle heavier mixing jobs. Most models come with at least two mixing bowls of different sizes. And along with a set of standard beaters, they are usually equipped with attachments like whisks and dough hooks.

Potz and Panz

Most cookware, including the basic pieces shown on this page, comes in stainless steel, aluminum, copper, or cast iron. Cookware with nonstick surfaces is also available and often a good choice for the new baker.

Aluminum

Lightweight and an excellent conductor of heat, aluminum cookware is very popular. Be sure to choose pieces that are at least $\frac{1}{8}$ inch thick (3.2 millimeters).

Cast Iron

The most durable cookware available, cast iron distributes and retains heat very well. It is also very heavy and needs to be seasoned.

Copper

Copper cookware is both beautiful and a good conductor of heat. It is also pretty heavy and expensive.

Stainless Steel

Very durable and reasonably priced, stainless steel cookware was once the popular choice of most home cooks. Its biggest drawback is that it does not conduct heat as well as copper or aluminum.

Small saucepans and pots

A one-quart saucepan and a two-quart pot are standard cookware for the stovetop preparation of sauces, fillings, and toppings for many baked goods. For easier cleaning, I prefer nonstick varieties. This is because many sauces and other dessert items have a high sugar content, making them sticky and hard to remove from cookware.

Dutch oven or four-quart pot

A four-quart pot or a similar size Dutch oven will come in handy for cooking or blanching large quantities of fruit and for boiling foods like sweet potatoes (for luscious sweet potato pie, like the one found on page 339).

Double boiler

A double boiler uses indirect heat to melt chocolate and to gently cook delicate sauces and custards. It consists of two stackable pots – the bottom pot holds boiling water, which heats up the ingredients in the upper pot.

Oven Vessels

Here's the essential bakeware you'll need to prepare most baked goods, including those in this book. Most are available in aluminum and tempered (heatproof) glass. Be aware that glass cooks food faster than aluminum in electric ovens, so you may have to adjust the baking time, depending on what you're using. Some aluminum varieties have a nonstick coating – a big plus when it comes to cleanup. Most also come in disposable aluminum.

Important Tip

For best results when baking items like cakes and quick breads, use the size pan that is indicated in the recipe. Using pans that are larger or smaller will alter baking time, as well as the size and texture of the finished products. A cake baked in a pan that is too large will be thin and dry. And if the pan is too small, the batter may rise too high and flow over the sides. Plus, the interior won't be thoroughly baked.

Cookie sheets

Perfect for baking cookies and anything that requires a large surface area, cookie sheets come in a variety of sizes. Some have shallow sides; others have none.

13-x-9-inch baking pans

Multipurpose 13-x-9-inch rectangular baking pans range from 2 to 3 inches deep. They are used to make brownies, bar cookies, and single-layer cakes.

Square pans

Like the rectangular pans, standard 8- and 9-inch square baking pans also range from 2 to 3 inches deep. They are used for single-layer cakes, brownies, and bar cookies. Deeper pans are also good for cobblers and coffee cakes.

Loaf pans

Great for baking yeast breads and quick breads, standard loaf pans come in a few sizes. The recipes in this book require a 9-x-5-inch loaf pan.

Cake pans

Standard cake pans come in 8- and 9-inch rounds and are about 1 1/2 inches deep. To make a double-layer cake, you'll need two of the same size. The cake recipes in this book call for 9-inch round pans.

Pie pans

Standard pie pans are 8, 9, and 10 inches in diameter and $1^1/4$ inches deep. They are also available in deep-dish varieties, which are $1^1/2$ to 2 inches deep.

Tart pans

Tart pans range from 4 to 11 inches in diameter and are about an inch deep. They also have fluted edges. Many varieties have removable bottoms, which make it easy to remove the tart from the pan. Mini 2- to 3-inch tartlet pans are also available.

Muffin pans

Most pans for making standard-size muffins have twelve cups. They are also used to make cupcakes. Pans for larger muffins typically have six cups (shown at left), while those for making mini muffins have twenty-four cups. Unless the pan has a nonstick surface, I recommend using paper muffin cups to keep the muffins from sticking.

Springform pan

There are two pieces to a springform pan – a round flat base and a removable side piece that is locked into place with a clamp (see page 215). When the cake is baked and cooled, the clamp is opened and the side piece is removed, leaving the cake intact on the pan's base. Springform pans are best for creamy cheesecakes, dense flourless cakes, and delicate tortes.

Tube Pans

Bundt pan

This round tube pan with fluted sides was originally designed for making a particular German ring-shaped coffee cake, but it can be used for just about any dessert cake. Because of the pan's fluted interior, when the cake is turned out of the pan, it has a beautiful curved shape. To prevent the cake from sticking to the pan, be sure to grease it well or use a nonstick pan.

Angel food pan

This tall round tube pan is designed specifically for baking angel food cakes. The pan's center tube promotes even baking and encourages the batter to rise higher. Some pans have removable bottoms.

When the baked cake is removed from the oven, the pan is inverted while the cake cools. This prevents the cake from falling in on itself. Although a Bundt pan can also be used for angel food, its fluted sides make it difficult to release the cake.

Most kitchen stoves/ranges are all-in-one units that have a stovetop or rangetop (for cooking food in pots and pans on top of the unit) and an oven (for baking or broiling food in an enclosed area). They are powered by gas or electricity. Standard stovetops have four burners, also called "elements." The temperature of both the burners and the oven is controlled by a panel of knobs on the stovetop.

A quick overview of the different types of stovetops and ovens is presented on the following pages. And in an effort to help you get to know your oven, we'll even take a peek inside!

Hot! Hot! Hot!

You'll need oven mitts or gloves to handle hot pans and to remove hot dishes from the oven. And don't forget that you will also need a safe place to rest the hot bakeware – placing it directly on countertops or kitchen tables can cause damage. For this reason, be sure to have a few trivets of various sizes on hand. What are trivets, you ask? They are little stands or supports, usually made of metal, wood, ceramic, or silicone, on which hot pans or dishes are placed. They are designed specifically to protect the surface of tables and counters from heat damage.

Stovetops

Basically, there are two types of stovetop burners—gas and electric.

Gas

Natural or propane gas is the preferred method of stovetop cooking by most people, including chefs from around the world. This is because it offers several advantages over electric burners. The flame on a gas burner ignites instantly and its heat level is very easy to control.

Electric

All electric stovetops have the same drawback—the burners take time to heat up and cool down. Today's electric stoves, however, heat up faster and the temperatures are much more precise than they were in the past. What follows are different types of electric stovetops.

Electric coil burners

These are the most common heating elements found on electric stoves. They are the least expensive, very durable, and easy to replace. One drawback of coil burners is that the drip pans below them can be hard to reach and difficult to clean.

Glass-ceramic cooktop

This flat, one-piece cooktop is heated from beneath by electric coils or infrared halogen lamps. The burner areas heat up and cool down quicker than coil burners, and because food cannot get underneath the elements, cleanup is a snap.

Induction cooktop

This type of cooktop creates an electromagnetic field that heats up special magnetic-based pans, not the cooktop itself. Because the cookware becomes the heat source and cooks the food, the cooktop stays cool to the touch.

Ovens

There are many types of ovens. Here is some basic information on the most common ones.

Conventional Oven

Conventional ovens are powered by gas or electricity. Gas ovens heat up faster than electric, but once the oven is preheated, there is little difference in how they cook food. The heat comes from elements located at the bottom of the oven.

Convection Oven

Also known as *fan ovens*, convection ovens work the same way as conventional units, only with the addition of a high-temperature fan. The fan causes air to circulate around the food, making it cook faster and at lower temperatures than in a conventional oven. The air circulation (convection) also tends to cook the food more evenly and eliminate any hot spots.

Toaster Oven

Because of their reduced size, standard toaster ovens preheat faster and use less energy than conventional ovens. They are great for baking small batches of cookies or reheating most baked goods.

Microwave Oven

Microwave ovens use microwave energy to heat or cook food in a fraction of the time it takes in a conventional oven. I don't recommend them for baking because they cook unevenly. They may, however, be useful for heating or melting ingredients like butter or chocolate to use in recipes.

Be aware that you cannot place any object containing metal in a microwave. This includes aluminum pans and foil, forks and other cutlery, and dishes that are decorated with metal paint. These items can create an electric arc, cause sparks, and possibly result in fire.

This type of oven cooks food with superheated steam. It's like a pressure cooker without the pressured environment. Steam ovens make breads crisper and brownies moister. Convection models are also available.

Meet Your Range

Although oven designs vary considerably, they have the same essential features. This illustration is of a typical electric oven. Gas models are slightly different since there are no electric elements, and broiling is often done on a shelf below the main oven body.

Control Panel

Typically, stoves have two sets of controls. One set is for regulating oven temperature, and the other is for controlling the stovetop burners. Depending on your oven, you may have one control, as with most gas ranges, or two if you have a separate broiler. Many ovens are equipped with lights that will tell you when the oven is at the right temperature, or if the electric elements on the stovetop are still hot.

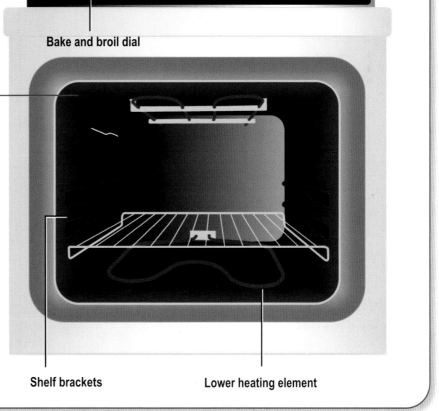

Stovetop burner controls

Oven temperature dial

Bake and broil dial

The Interior

Along with heating elements, oven interiors have two common features: racks and shelf brackets. The racks hold bakeware on a level surface and the shelf brackets let you place the racks at different heights. For most baked goods, it is best to place the pan on a rack in the middle of the oven. If it is placed too low, the bottom of the cake, pie, or whatever you are baking may cook too quickly. When placed too high, the top may burn.

Shelf brackets

Lower heating element

Baking Terms from A to Z

Don't worry if you come across an unfamiliar baking term when preparing a recipe. Simply turn to this glossary for an easy, concise definition. These terms are fairly basic. They're the ones you will find in most cookbooks, but by no means is this list complete – there are hundreds more out there.

Once you venture past basic baking and try your hand at more challenging recipes, chances are you are going to come across a term or technique that is unfamiliar. Don't let it stop you from trying the recipe. With the Internet at your fingertips, the information you need is just a mouse-click away. And the technique or procedure may be easier than it sounds. Who would imagine, for example, that to cook food "en crocite" simply means "wrapped in pastry dough"? Besides, even if the instruction is challenging, go for it!

Everything you make – each success and failure – adds to your experience, and with experience comes confidence. Have fun and enjoy the adventure.

A

Aerate

To incorporate air into an ingredient to make it lighter. Sifting a dry ingredient like flour is an example of this process, as is whipping cream or butter.

B

Bake

To cook food using dry heat, usually in an oven.

Batter

A pourable mixture of flour and liquid, often with the addition of eggs and shortening. Batters are used for muffins, cakes, and other baked goods.

Beat

To combine ingredients by mixing them briskly with a spoon, whisk, or an electric mixer until well combined and smooth.

Bind

To thicken a sauce, custard, or other hot liquid by stirring in an ingredient such as egg, flour, or cornstarch.

Blanch

To briefly cook food, usually a fruit or vegetable, in boiling water before plunging it into ice water to stop the cooking process and to maintain the food's color and crispness. Blanching is also a way to loosen the skin of fruits and vegetables, such as plums, peaches, and tomatoes, for easy removal.

Blend

To mix together ingredients, often liquids, with a spoon or blender until well combined and smooth.

Bloom

Whitish streaks or dots that appear on the surface of chocolate, bloom occurs when the chocolate gets warm and the cocoa butter separates and forms crystals. This does not affect the taste of the chocolate – it just looks funny.

Boil

To heat liquid to the point that it bubbles.

Broil

To cook directly under a high heat source.

Brush

To coat food with a liquid, such as melted butter, sauce, or glaze, with a pastry brush.

C

Caramelize

The process of cooking sugar over medium heat until it melts and begins to brown. Grilling or slow cooking certain vegetables with a high-sugar content, like onions and carrots, as well as many fruits, like peaches, pears, and pineapples, will cause them to caramelize. This intensifies their sweetness.

Chiffon

This is generally a puréed filling or topping that is made light and fluffy by adding beaten egg whites, whipped cream, or gelatin.

Chop

To cut food into small, often irregular pieces.

Coat

To completely cover food with an ingredient such as flour, oil, sugar, or spices.

Coddle

To simmer slowly and gently in liquid that is just below the boiling point. Eggs, for example, are typically coddled.

Cool

To bring hot food to room temperature (68°F–77°F), or until it is no longer hot to the touch.

Combine

To mix two or more ingredients together.

Core

To remove the inedible center of certain fruits such as apples, pears, and pineapples.

Cream

To beat together a fat (usually butter, margarine, or shortening) with sugar until smooth and creamy.

Crimp

To pinch or seal the edges of a double-crust pie with your fingertips or the tines of a fork.

Crumble

To break apart food, such as bread or cookies, into small pieces with your fingers.

Crush

To smash food or ice into smaller pieces.

Cube

To cut food into pieces with six equal sides – usually ranging from $1/4$ to 1 inch in size.

Curdle

To coagulate or thicken a liquid – typically milk, cream, a cream-based sauce, or egg whites – either through overheating or by adding an acidic ingredient.

Cut-in

To work a semi-solid ingredient like shortening or cold butter into a dry ingredient like flour.

D

Dash

Measurement of $1/8$ teaspoon.

Dice

To cut food into small cube-shaped pieces.

Dissolve

To thoroughly combine a dry ingredient like sugar or salt with a liquid until no solids remain.

Dilute

To thin a liquid by adding water or another liquid.

Dot

To add small pieces of an ingredient, usually butter, over a food or mixture to ensure even distribution during cooking or baking. (Dots of butter, for example, may be scattered over the filling of an apple pie before baking.)

Dough

A pliable mixture of flour, liquid, and often other ingredients that is baked into breads, cookies, pie crusts, and pastries. Unlike batter, which is thin and pourable, dough is firm and workable with the hands.

Dredge

To lightly coat food with flour, cornmeal, or another dry ingredient, often before it is baked or fried.

Drizzle

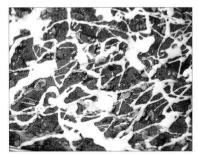

To slowly pour a liquid – such as icing, a glaze, or melted butter – over food in a very thin stream.

Dust

To sprinkle a food, usually baked goods, with a dry ingredient such as confectioner's sugar or cinnamon.

E

Egg wash

A glaze made of beaten egg (yolk, white, or both) and a little water or milk. Breads and other baked goods are sometimes brushed with egg wash before baking. This gives them a glossy shine and color when baked.

Elastic

Term describing the flexible ability of yeasted dough to return to its original shape after being stretched.

Emulsion

A well-blended mixture of two liquids, such as oil and water, that normally do not combine well.

F

Fallen

Term used to describe a cake or soufflé that rises while baking, but then collapses in the center.

Filter

To remove impurities or solids from a liquid by running it through a strainer or filter.

Flour

To sprinkle food, utensils, baking pans, or work surfaces with a light coating of flour. Flouring countertops, rolling pins, and even your hands helps prevent dough from sticking and makes it easier to work with. Flouring greased pans prevents cakes and other baked goods from sticking and allows for their easy removal.

Flambé

Cooking technique in which a dish, usually a dessert, is sprinkled with liquor and set aflame just before serving.

Flute

To press a decorative pattern into the raised edge of a pie or pastry crust, usually with your fingers.

Fold

To gently combine a whipped, airy mixture with a dense batter to make the batter lighter.

Fondant

Soft pliable "dough" made of cooked sugar and water that is used to create edible flowers and other decorations for cakes and pastries.

Frost

To decorate a cookie, cake, or pastry by covering it with frosting.

G

Ganache

This rich blend of semi-sweet chocolate and whipping cream is used as a pastry filling, as well as an icing that is poured while lukewarm over cakes and tortes.

Garnish

To decorate baked goods with an edible item, such as grated chocolate, shredded coconut, or colorful fresh berries, for added visual appeal.

Glaze

To give food a shiny coating by brushing it with a thin layer of icing or sauce either before or after it is baked.

Grate

To finely shred food.

Grease

To spread a thin layer of oil, butter, margarine, or shortening on a cookware surface to prevent food from sticking to it.

Grind

To cut food into fine pieces with a food processor, blender, or grinder.

Ice

To spread or drizzle icing or glaze on baked goods.

Infuse

To extract the flavor of certain ingredients – coffee, herbs, tea – by steeping them in heated liquid. The resulting liquid is called an infusion.

Jell

To cause a liquid to become firm or solidify, usually by adding gelatin.

Knead

To work dough with the heel of your hands in a folding motion until it becomes smooth and elastic.

Leavening

An ingredient, such as baking powder, baking soda, or yeast, that causes breads and other baked goods to rise.

Line

To place wax paper, parchment paper, or foil on the bottom of a baking sheet or pan to prevent food from sticking to it.

Lukewarm

Temperature that is neither hot nor cold. Usually used to describe a liquid.

Marbling

The gentle swirling or folding of two different colored mixtures (often cake and cheesecake batters) into one another to create the look of marble.

Mash

To press or mix food, such as bananas or boiled potatoes, until the mixture is smooth and free of lumps.

Meringue

A mixture of stiffly beaten egg whites and sugar that is typically used as a topping for puddings and pies, such as the classic lemon meringue.

Mince

To chop a food (often a spice) very finely so that it disperses evenly throughout the dish.

Mix

To stir ingredients together, usually with a spoon or fork, until they are evenly distributed.

Moisten

To add enough liquid to a dry ingredient to just dampen it.

P

Pack
To press an ingredient (typically brown sugar) firmly into a measuring cup to compact it.

Pare
To remove the thin outer skin of a fruit or vegetable with a knife or vegetable peeler.

Peaks

Mounds that form on a whipped ingredient or mixture when it has become thick and stiff.

Peel
To remove the rind or skin from a fruit or vegetable with a knife or vegetable peeler. The skin of some foods, like oranges and bananas, can be peeled with your fingers.

Pinch
Measurement of $1/16$ teaspoon.

Pipe
To squeeze frosting or a semi-soft food through the tip of a pastry bag.

Pit
To remove the seed or stone from fruit.

Press
To pat or flatten dough on the bottom of a pie plate or baking pan.

Prick

To make small holes in pastry dough with a fork before baking. This technique, which is used for prebaked pie and tart crusts, prevents bubbles or blisters from forming as the dough bakes.

Proofing
A technique for testing yeast to see if it is alive.

Purée
To grind or mash food in a blender or food processor until it is completely smooth.

R

Reconstitute
To bring a dehydrated item (such as powdered milk or instant coffee) back to its original consistency by adding water or another liquid.

Reduce
To cook a liquid, such as a sauce, until it is reduced in volume due to evaporation. This makes it thicker and more flavorful.

S

Sauté
To briefly cook food in oil or butter in a skillet or sauté pan over medium to medium-high heat.

Set
To allow food to become firm, such as a gelatin, pudding, or pie filling.

Scald

To briefly heat a liquid, usually milk, just below the boiling point until tiny bubbles form around the edge of the pan and a thin skin forms on top.

Score
To make shallow cuts or slashes in food, such as the top crust of a pie, so steam can escape during baking. Scoring some foods, such as bread, before baking, adds a decorative touch.

Shred

To cut food into long, thin, uniform strips, either by hand or by running it over the larger holes of a grater.

Sift

To pass a dry ingredient, such as flour or confectioner's sugar, through a fine mesh screen or a sifter for the purpose of making it lighter and airier. This is also done to remove any large pieces.

Simmer

To cook food gently in liquid that is heated just below the boiling point.

Skim

To remove the top layer from a liquid, such as cream from milk or foam from a sauce.

Slice

To cut through food.

Thin

To reduce the thickness of a mixture by adding liquid.

Thicken

To increase the thickness of a mixture by adding a dry ingredient like flour or cornstarch, or a liquid ingredient like condensed or evaporated milk.

Toss

To gently mix ingredients together with two spoons or forks, using a lifting motion.

Unleavened

To term that describes breads or other baked goods that do not contain a leavening (rising) agent – yeast, baking powder, or baking soda.

Vent

To cut holes or slits into the top crust of a pie, turnover, or other sealed crust with a filling. This allows steam to escape during baking.

Whip

To briskly beat an ingredient, typically cream or egg whites, until it is light and fluffy.

Whisk

To whip soft or liquid ingredients together, usually with a wire whisk.

Zest

To remove the outermost colored rind of a citrus fruit, usually an orange or lemon, with a fine grater, zester, or knife.

Some Like It Hot

In one form or another, cooking utensils and appliances have been around since the discovery of fire. The first kitchen tools were made from crude materials like sticks and stones and animal bones. Ovens were actually invented before the wheel, but, unfortunately, before the invention of oven mitts!

Oven Evolution

▶ Ancient Greeks were the first to use ovens for baking bread. Most early ovens were made of brick or stone. Monstrous-looking masks were sometimes hung on the outside to keep the children away from the hot ovens as a safety measure.

▶ The first cast iron ovens were manufactured in Germany in 1728.

▶ In 1826, British inventor James Sharp patented the first gas oven.

▶ The development of the electric oven took place during the early 1880s. The general public got its first glimpse of the new invention in 1883, when it was on display at the Chicago World's Fair. The first patent for the electric oven was given to American inventor William Hadaway in 1896. The appliance, however, did not become popular until the 1930s, when electricity became more available to the masses.

You're Waring on Me

Polish-American inventor Stephen Poplawski is credited with inventing the blender in 1922. The machine, which was sold almost exclusively to soda fountains, was designed specifically for making milk shakes and malts. Inventor Fred Osius improved upon Poplawski's design and created the first home model, which he named the Waring Blender (after Fred Waring, the project's financial backer). Hamilton Beach began manufacturing the blenders in 1937.

I Feel Strange

Percy Spenser was an engineer who worked for Raytheon Company – a major American defense contractor. The company had a giant microwave-generating magnetron that was used to improve radar capabilities for the military. One day in 1945, as Spencer was standing in front of the magnetron, he felt a strange sensation and noticed the chocolate bar in his pocket had melted. Then he decided to place some popcorn kernels by the giant machine . . . and they popped! For the next several years, Spencer worked on developing the first microwave oven, which weighed 750 pounds and was over 5 feet tall. Modern microwaves took decades longer to develop.

How Things Got All Mixed Up

In 1908, engineer Herbert Johnson, who worked at Hobart Corporation – a manufacturer of kitchen equipment – attempted to mechanically recreate the motion that bakers used when stirring dough. The result of his efforts was the first electric mixer. Initially, it had a giant 80-quart bowl and was used only commercially. In 1915, Hobart began manufacturing the first home models. Sunbeam introduced the first hand-held electric mixer in 1952.

Mom Doesn't Make Much Bread Anymore

Before the 1920s, about 70 percent of bread in the United States was made in the home. By the late 1920s, over 80 percent was made in factories. In the 1990s, the first automatic home bread makers became available.

Let's Get Started 50

Fruit Processor 52

All Mixed Up 54

Sticky Situations 58

Get Into Shape 60

Roll with It, Baby! 62

Now We're Cookin'. 64

Are We Done Yet? 66

Taking Measure 68

Baking a Mile High 70

3. This Is How to Do It

It's all in the techniques, baby!

I remember when I first started baking, I was about halfway through a recipe when I came across an instruction telling me to "fold" two mixtures. Immediately my mind went into a state of panic. I thought, "How can you fold something that isn't solid?" I knew that I could fold a piece a paper and fold my laundry, but how the heck was I supposed to fold two liquidy mixtures? What the heck did "fold" mean?!

That experience is why I spent so much of my valuable time writing and photographing this chapter – to help you avoid any baking-related mind-twisting panic attacks like I had. If you're new to baking, this is an especially important chapter – probably the most important one in the book. That's why I'm not making any silly comments or stupid wisecracks right now. If you take the time to learn the basic techniques on the following pages, you will be able to follow all the recipes in this book (and just about any others you come across) – with perfect results.

You'll learn how to mix, roll, and shape batters and doughs, as well as measure ingredients properly and test different types of baked goods for doneness. You'll also learn how to prepare pans and baking sheets to prevent cakes and cookies from sticking to them. And if you live in the mountains, you'll even discover the tricks for successful high-altitude baking.

Always be prepared.

Before you pull out the mixing bowl and wooden spoon, you may need to prepare some ingredients first. It's kinda difficult to make a graham cracker crust with whole crackers, or the perfect cookie without softened butter. Preparation also includes preheating your oven. If you want your cakes to rise high and your cookies to hold their shape, a preheated oven is essential for the best results.

Get Ready

Ingredient Temperature

▶ Proper ingredient temperature is an important key to successful baking. Unless otherwise instructed, ingredients like eggs, milk, and other dairy products should be at room temperature to produce the most consistent results. This makes it easier to mix the items evenly. Mixing a cold ingredient into a batter, for example, can create lumps and cause overmixing.

▶ To quickly take the chill out of cold eggs, dip them in a bowl of warm – not hot – water about ten minutes.

▶ If your mixing bowls are cold, run them under hot water to warm them up.

Preheated Ovens

▶ Unless otherwise instructed, always preheat the oven. Baking times are based on it. Products won't bake properly if started in a cold oven. And ovens heat up at different speeds, another cause of inconsistent results.

▶ Even a properly preheated oven can still have "hotspots," which cause uneven baking. If your oven has hotspots, rotate the dish midway through the baking process.

▶ Most ovens have a light or other signal that indicates when the desired temperature is reached. If yours does not, consider buying an inexpensive oven thermometer, which hangs on or clips to oven racks.

Sifted Flour

▶ Many recipes call for flour that has been sifted, a process that incorporates air and makes the flour lighter. Most flour in stores has been presifted, so this step is often not necessary.

▶ To sift your own flour, simply shake it through a strainer or run it through a sifter.

Basic Techniques for Preparing Ingredients

Softening
Ingredients like butter and cream cheese often need to be softened before using. Simply leave the item out at room temperature (68°F to 77°F) for three to four hours. To test, lightly press into it with your fingertip. If you can make an impression, it's ready. To speed up the softening process, cut the cold butter or cream cheese into chunks. It will soften within thirty minutes or so.

Grinding
Before nuts are added to a recipe, they often need to be ground. You can either buy them this way or do it yourself with the help of a blender, food processor, or coffee grinder. Depending on what is called for in the recipe, you can grind the nuts coarsely into small irregular pieces, or finely into almost a powder.

Crushing
Crunchy cookies and graham crackers need to be crushed before they are turned into pie crusts. Although a food processor or blender can do the job, it's easier to use a large, sturdy zip-lock bag and a rolling pin (and cleanup is easier). Partially fill the bag with the ingredient, squeeze out the air before sealing, then roll over the bag with a rolling pin.

Cracking eggs
There's more than one way to crack an egg, but I feel the best way is to use the edge of a bowl. Hold the egg firmly in the palm of your hand with part of the shell exposed. Using a swift downward motion, crack the egg against the side of the bowl. Use your fingers to separate the shell into two pieces.

Separating Eggs

Step 1
Crack the egg as described at left. (Try to make the halves about the same size.) Do this directly over the bowl. The two half shells will form "cups" that are large enough to hold the yolk.

Step 2
Pass the yolk back and forth from one "cup" to the other, letting the white fall into the bowl. Place the yolk in a separate bowl. Try not to break the yolk, but if you do, don't let it spill over the side of the shell. If you make a complete mess, make yourself a scrambled egg . . . then start over.

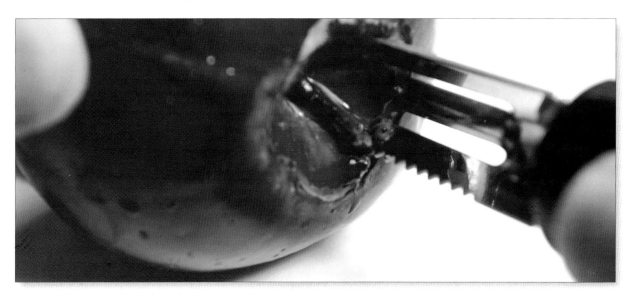

Getting to the core of it.

Did you know the easiest way to peel a banana is to pinch it at the bottom, then peel it from the bottom? That's how a monkey does it, and it's very efficient. Fruits, veggies, and tubers are often used in baked desserts. It's important to know how to prepare these ingredients, whether they need to be peeled or shredded or juiced or zested or . . .

Basic Techniques for Preparing Fruits 'n Veggies

Chopping

To chop items like apples or peaches, cut them into small pieces that are not necessarily uniform in shape. A "coarsely" chopped item is cut into bite-sized pieces, while a "finely" chopped ingredient is cut much smaller.

Slicing

To slice an ingredient, cut through it with a knife into smaller pieces that are fairly similar in width. This is a way to cut fruits like strawberries and bananas, as well as rolled cookie dough.

Mashing

Mashing ingredients like soft bananas and fresh strawberries or cooked sweet potatoes and pumpkin makes them smooth and easy to incorporate into batters and pie fillings. You can mash the ingredients against the side of a bowl with a wooden spoon or use a potato masher.

Basic Techniques for Preparing Fruits 'n Veggies

Peeling

Although you can use a sharp knife for this job, I always use a vegetable peeler. Be sure to hold the food firmly and always peel away from yourself. Don't let the blade of the peeler get close to your hands; it is, after all, a knife and very sharp. I usually do my peeling over a lined garbage bag, but you can use the kitchen sink as well.

Coring

Many utensils are designed for coring apples. My favorite is an apple corer that has a peeler attached. Simply insert the corer into the top of the apple (about ¼ to ½ inch from the stem) and push it through to the bottom. Next, use the serrated side of the corer to cut a circle around the stem, and then push out the core.

Stemming

Tree fruits and berries, like cherries, pears, grapes, and blueberries, usually have stems attached. Stems are actually designed by nature to fall off, so all you have to do is pinch them at their base to remove them. The stem and leafy hull from strawberries can also be easily plucked. Don't cut them off with a knife, as this will waste some of the fruit itself.

Juicing

Fruit juices are used in many dessert recipes. There are several types of mechanical juicers on the market, but all you will likely need is a simple manual citrus press. My favorite type is the one pictured above. It has a container that catches the juice for easy pouring. To juice a fruit, simply twist it over the ribbed top and apply pressure. Look out for any small seeds that may fall through. Use a teaspoon to fish them out.

Zesting

Zest is the very flavorful outer rind of citrus fruits. Lemon, orange, and lime zest add a spark of flavor to many recipes. To remove zest, I recommend using the tool that is designed specifically for the job – a zester! Simply run its steel edge along the top of the rind, but be careful not to include any of the bitter white part of the fruit that's just below the surface. You can also remove zest with a sharp knife or a fine grater.

Shredding

Shredding is a method for cutting foods like carrots, zucchini, and coconut into long, thin uniform strips. To shred an ingredient, either cut it by hand or simply slide it over the large holes of a grater. If you are using a grater, be careful not to continue shredding the food if it gets too small (less than an inch long) or you will risk shredding your fingers!

I was whipped and mixed up, so I folded and beat it.

There are a number of different ways to combine ingredients. Folding is the gentlest technique, requiring just a few easy strokes. Whipping (as the word suggests) is the most vigorous and is usually done with a high-speed electric mixer. Between these two extremes are a number of other basic techniques you'll need for combining ingredients and mixing 'em up.

Basic Techniques for Combining Ingredients

Mixing
Mixing involves combining ingredients – usually with a spoon or fork – until they are evenly distributed. Often the ingredients need to be only loosely combined and the mixture does not necessarily have to be completely smooth.

Stirring
Although you stir when you mix, when a recipe instructs that you "stir" ingredients, it is implying that you combine them completely, but not as vigorously as when beating. This technique also implies using a circular motion to combine the ingredients.

Blending
Blending involves mixing liquid ingredients together until they are well combined and usually smooth. A blender is the perfect appliance and specifically designed for this job (and a few others, like grinding and puréeing).

Basic Techniques for Combining Ingredients

Whipping

Whipping involves vigorously beating an ingredient – typically cream or egg whites – to incorporate air until it is light and fluffy and has increased in volume. Usually done with an electric mixer, whipping can also be done by hand with a whisk, but only by someone with good endurance. More information on the different whipping stages is found on page 56.

Creaming

Creaming is the first step when making many cakes, cookies, and other baked goods. Essentially, it involves beating sugar with a fat, like butter, margarine, or shortening, until it is light, fluffy, and fairly smooth. This should be done slowly with an electric mixer on low speed. For successful creaming, the butter (or other fat) should be softened.

Beating

Beating involves vigorously mixing a single ingredient (like eggs) or a combination of ingredients (like those in a cake batter) until smooth and well combined. This can be done with an electric mixer or by hand with a whisk or wooden spoon. Beating also incorporates some air into the mixture. Generally, 100 strokes by hand is equal to one minute with an electric mixer.

Whisking

Whisking is the vigorous whipping of ingredients (like creams, eggs, sauces) by hand with a wire whisk. This is done with a rapid circular motion that incorporates air into the mixture, giving it lightness and volume. Some master chefs whisk just about everything.

Cutting

Cutting cold butter (or other fat) into a flour mixture is often the first step in making flaky pastry dough. It involves pressing small pieces of butter into the flour mixture with a pastry blender until it resembles a crumbly meal that sticks together when pressed with your hands. Instead of a pastry blender, you can also use two knives in a criss-cross motion, or a wooden spoon with a stabbing motion.

Folding

Folding is a method used to lighten a dense batter or heavy mixture by gently combining it with a whipped airy mixture. The method, which is described in detail on page 57, involves first placing all or part of the lighter mixture on top of the heavier one. Then, using a rubber spatula and starting from the bottom of the bowl, one ingredient is brought up and gently mixed (folded into) the other.

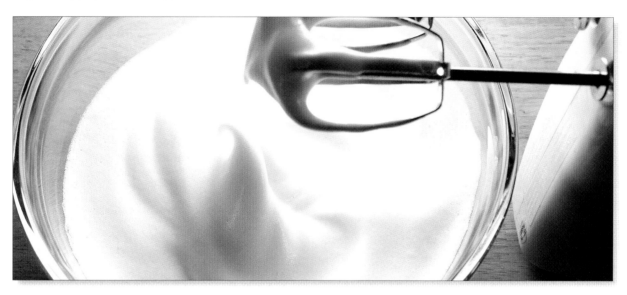

Totally whipped!

Whipping typically involves vigorously beating ingredients, such as cream or egg whites, until they have increased in volume and are light and airy. For the best results, there are a couple of tricks you should know. To get the lightest whipped cream, for example, chill the bowl first. Also chill the electric mixer blades or whisk before beating. For stiffer egg whites, add a little sugar, cream of tartar, or pinch of salt.

The Three Levels of Whipping

Thickened

This is the first (and longest) stage of whipping in which the volume of the cream has increased and the mixture is thick enough to coat the blades of an electric mixer (or whisk). It won't, however, be able to hold any shape. Thickened cream makes a delicious topping for fresh berries.

Foamy

In this next visible whipping stage, the blades of the mixer can hold some of the whipped ingredient and the mixture can form very small soft peaks that curl over and droop. Eggs or egg yolks that are whipped into foam are used in a number of baked goods, such as biscotti, brownies, and some cakes.

Peaked

A mixture that is fully whipped (usually cream) has more than doubled in volume. It is also thick, airy, and able to form stiff peaks that stand straight up. Recipes often instruct "beating the ingredient until stiff peaks form." If, however, it instructs "beating until stiff but not dry," this suggests soft peaks.

Come into the fold.

As described on page 55, folding is the method used to lighten a heavy mixture, such as a dense batter, by gently combining it with a whipped, airy ingredient. The outcome is a well-blended mixture that maintains the light airiness of the whipped ingredient.

The Three Stages of Folding

1. Lighten the base mixture
Place less then half of the lighter whipped mixture on top of the heavier one. Using a spatula and a circular motion, bring up some of the heavy mixture from the bottom of the bowl and place it on top of the lighter mixture. Do this a few times to partially combine the mixtures. This will make it easier to mix with the rest of the whipped ingredient.

2. Add the remaining ingredient
Once the base mixture has been lightened a bit, add the rest of the whipped ingredient. Continue folding the ingredients, using smooth circular strokes and carefully running the spatula around the base and edges of the bowl. Be very gentle and patient – it is important to preserve the airiness.

3. Combine completely
Continue folding, making sure all of the heavy mixture has been brought up from the bottom of the bowl. As soon as the ingredients are completely blended – uniform in color and without any streaks – stop folding immediately. Continuing will compromise the airiness of the mixture.

Greased and floured and ready to go.

After spending your valuable time and money making homemade quick breads, brownies, cakes, or muffins, the last thing you want is to have them stick to the pan. Although they'll probably still taste good, the presentation will be ruined! To prevent this from happening, many recipes will instruct you to first grease (or grease and flour) the bakeware.

Greasing Pans

If a recipe instructs you to "grease" the pan, either spray it with cooking spray or spread it uniformly with a dab of butter or margarine. If using cooking spray, use one that is plain, not flavored. The flavor of sprays like olive oil will transfer to the final product.

How to Flour a Pan

Step 1
In addition to greasing a pan, if a recipe instructs you to also "flour" it, first grease the pan (as instructed at left). Then place a small handful of flour (a tablespoon or two) in the middle.

Step 2
Rotate the pan to shift the flour around until it coats the entire surface – the sides as well as the bottom. If the pan is not completely coated, add a little more flour. If there is excess flour, toss it out.

I'm not lining to you.

Some desserts (like the coconut macaroons pictured above) are so sticky even flouring and greasing a pan won't do. That's when parchment paper comes in handy. This paper is not only nonstick, it is also designed to withstand oven temperatures up to 425°F. When lining a baking pan, rather than fold the parchment, which can be bulky and uneven, I cut it to fit perfectly. As you can see below, it's an easy task. (For more information on using parchment paper, see page 27.)

How to Line a Pan with Parchment

1. Trace
For the parchment to fit properly, first trace the bottom of the pan on the paper before cutting. Hold the pan firmly while tracing, and make certain that the angle of the pen is consistent as you outline.

2. Cut
Since the traced exterior of the pan will be slightly wider than the interior, you'll have to cut the paper a fraction of an inch inside the traced line. Use sharp scissors and be sure to follow the contours as best you can. The better job you do, the better the lining will fit.

3. Line
Place the paper in the bottom of the pan. If it is too large, trim it to fit. If it's too small, place a scrap of parchment paper under the larger piece to make up the difference. You can secure the paper to the bottom of a pan with a dab of grease.

Wish I had more dough to play with . . .

Dough can be rolled, cut, sculpted, and molded into many forms – from simple shapes like circles and squares to structures as complex as gingerbread houses. Dough is very elastic, which makes it very workable, no matter how it's shaped. And once it's ready for the oven, it will be baked into sweet treats that look as good as they taste.

Basic Techniques for Shaping Dough

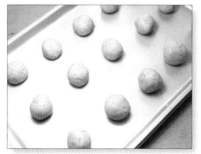

Dropping

This is the probably easiest way to form many cookies. Just scoop some dough into a spoon and drop it onto a cookie sheet. If the dough sticks to the spoon, either push it off with your finger or with another spoon.

Rolling

Some cookies are rolled into balls before they're baked. To form a ball, pinch off a small amount of dough and roll it between your palms. Try to use the same amount of dough for each ball, so the cookies are consistent in size and take the same time to bake.

Flattening

After they are rolled into balls, some cookies need to be flattened. You can use anything with a clean flat surface to do this. In the photo above, I used the bottom of a drinking glass.

Basic Techniques for Shaping Dough

Pan shaping

Another easy way to shape cookie dough is to simply press it on the bottom of a baking pan. I always use a round pan. Score the dough with a sharp knife or pastry wheel so the cookies are easy to cut once baked. Also poke holes in the dough with a fork (as shown above) to vent the dough and keep it from bubbling up as it bakes.

Slicing

When slicing cookie dough from a refrigerated roll, use a sharp knife and cut the dough in uniform slices ($1/4$ inch is standard). To form your own cookie dough rolls, shape the dough into an oblong piece and roll it on a nonstick surface until it is about 2 inches in diameter. Cover with plastic wrap and refrigerate until firm.

Free-form shaping

Dough can be shaped by hand into just about any form you can imagine. Most beginners are comfortable with simple shapes like rings and half circles. I thought about putting these pretzel-shaped cookies in the book, but felt they might be a little too advanced for beginners. Whatever shape you make, try to keep them consistent in size.

Molding

When making mini tarts that require a bottom crust, you can mold the dough into the baking cups with your fingers. You need to work fast, because the dough will become sticky from the warmth of your hands. Special tampers are also available for molding the dough. If prebaking the crusts before filling, vent the dough with a fork to prevent blistering.

Spreading

Many sour cream based cake and coffeecake recipes, which are baked in a pan, have doughy batters that are too thick to pour but not stiff enough to press into the pan by hand. Drop large even spoonfuls of the dough on the bottom of the pan. Using a rubber spatula, spread it into an even layer.

Rolling out

Many doughs are flattened with a rolling pin. The rolled-out dough is usually cut into shapes with a cookie cutter or formed into a crust for pies or pastries. If you want to get creative, try cutting out your own freeform cookie shapes. You'll find steps for rolling out dough and some of the ways it is used beginning on page 62.

Now you're rolling in dough!

Rolled-out dough is used in many baked goods, including cookies, pastries, and pie crusts. This section shows the basic technique for rolling out dough, as well as the different ways to use it, trim it, cut it, and more. Once you get the hang of it, you'll be rolling you way into the hearts of everyone you know.

Basic Steps for Rolling Out Dough

Step 1

Sprinkle a clean work surface with flour to keep the dough from sticking. Also sprinkle a little flour over the dough and rub some on the rolling pin. (You can also place the dough between two pieces of wax paper that have been sprinkled with flour.)

Step 2

With the palm of your hand, flatten out the dough a little. Starting at the center and using firm, even pressure, begin to flatten the dough in one direction with the rolling pin. Place the rolling pin back at the center and roll out the dough in the opposite direction. Then change the angle and roll back and forth again.

Step 3

Continue rolling out the dough from side to side, back and forth, and diagonally until it reaches the desired thickness (for most cookies and crusts, this is usually $1/8$ or $1/4$ inch). As you roll, continue to sprinkle the rolling pin, dough, and counter with flour as needed to prevent sticking.

Cutting, Venting, Crimping . . .

Cookie cutting

In addition to using cookie cutters – which come in hundreds of different shapes and sizes – you can also cut out cookies using something as simple as the rim of a glass. To cut the shape, place the cutter on top of the dough and press it through to the bottom. Without twisting or turning, lift the cutter straight out. Peel away the excess dough, and roll it out again to cut more cookies!

Freehand cutting

Along with using cookie cutters with rolled-out dough, you can create freehand shaped cookies with a knife. I usually find that geometric shapes like triangles, diamonds, and rectangular strips are easiest. Sometimes I give the strips a twist for fun. When cutting dough, be sure to use a sharp knife.

Wrapping

Dough that is rolled into sheets makes the perfect wrapper for a wide variety of baked goods including strudels, turnovers, and jam-filled cookies. When wrapping dough around a filling, be careful not to add too much filling or place it too close to the edge of the dough – it is likely to spill out during baking.

Trimming

When rolling out a crust to put in a pie plate or baking pan, it is impossible to get it the exact shape you need. For this reason, make the dough a little larger than the pan itself, and then trim away the excess. Using a sharp knife at a 45-degree angle and the edge of the pan as a guide, trim the dough with a gentle sawing motion.

Crimping

When making a double-crust pie, one with a bottom and top crust, you'll need to seal the edges of the dough together – a method called *crimping*. The most common way to crimp is by pinching the edges together with your thumb and forefinger. Sealing the edges with the tines of a fork (as shown above) is another.

Venting

Cutting small slits in the top crust of a pie, turnover, or other sealed crust with a filling is called *venting*. Vents allow steam to escape during baking. Without them, the steam created by the filling will build, causing the crimped edges to open and the filling to boil over and seep out.

Hot off the stove.

Most sauces and fillings for baked goods are cooked in a saucepan or double boiler on the stovetop. Chocolate is another ingredient that is usually melted in a pot. When preparing these types of items, it is important for any good baker to know the difference between a simmer, a medium boil, and a rolling boil. Heating or cooking ingredients over heat that is the wrong intensity can cause them to burn, boil over, or never reach the proper consistency. The point here is simple, always follow the recipe's heating instructions carefully.

Heat Me Up

When you're cooking dessert ingredients on the stovetop, remember that you are dealing mostly with fats, sugars, and starches, which are all fairly volatile when you cook them, and even more so when they're combined. Sugar and butter have a tendency to burn, melted chocolate can suddenly seize or harden, and creams tend to boil over or curdle.

Sauces and fillings – especially those containing butter, chocolate, or cream – often appear thinner and more "liquidy" in their heated state than when they have cooled.

Keep this in mind if you feel the mixture isn't thick enough as you cook it. It may thicken as it cools. If, however, the mixture hasn't thickened sufficiently, you can usually heat it up some more to reach the desired thickness.

Helpful Tips

▶ Don't leave your pots and pans unattended on the stove. In the blink of an eye, the ingredients can boil over. Not only is this likely to ruin the contents of the pot, it will also make a mess.

▶ Use a wooden spoon to stir sauces, and be sure to scrape the bottoms and sides of the pot to prevent burning.

▶ If you are adding a starchy powdered thickener like cornstarch to a hot sauce, first mix it with a little cold water until it forms a paste. Otherwise, the powder will be difficult to blend and will likely form lumps.

▶ Add thickeners near the end of cooking time.

▶ When thickening a sauce or filling on the stovetop, be sure to stir or whisk it briskly and constantly to prevent lumps from forming.

▶ Use oven mitts to remove hot pans that don't have insulated handles.

The Three Boils

Simmer
A liquid simmers when it is heated just enough to cause tiny bubbles—a few at a time—to rise to the surface. Simmering is typically used for cooking delicate sauces, custards, and fillings that need to be cooked slowly over low heat.

Gentle or medium boil
For a gentle or medium boil, the liquid is set over medium to medium-low heat until a steady stream of pea-sized bubbles rise to the surface. This boil is a controlled one with very little splashing and a modest amount of steam.

Rolling or hard boil
This rollicking frolicking boil splashes and bubbles furiously. To prevent the boiling contents of the pot from splashing onto your stovetop, don't fill the pot more than three-quarters full. To reach and maintain a rolling boil, the heat should be set on medium-high to high.

Basic Techniques for Stovetop Preparations

Melting
Some ingredients, like chocolate and delicate sauces, need to be heated very slowly. Although this can be done carefully in a saucepan, the best pot to use is a double boiler (see page 37), which cooks or melts ingredients using indirect heat. It consists of two stackable pots – the bottom pot holds boiling water, which heats up the ingredients in the upper pot.

Thickening
Thickening sauces, fillings, or toppings in a pot on the stove is usually done over low or medium-low heat. The mixture, which may or may not include a starch or other thickening agent, should be stirred often to prevent it from clumping.

Toasting
Although you can toast nuts in the oven (see page 20), you can also toast them in a pot or skillet on the stove. It is best to place the nuts in a single layer and toast them over medium-low heat. And don't veer too far from the stove as the nuts need to be stirred often for even toasting. They also tend to burn easily, so be careful.

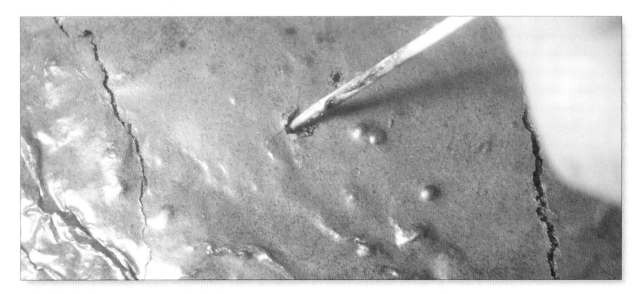

I didn't know there was going to be a test!

Because of all the variables that can occur during baking – oven variations, differences in bakeware material, even the altitude where you live – the "bake" times given in recipes are approximate. For this reason, it is important to be aware of the other signs that indicate when a product has finished baking.

Basic Techniques for Testing Baked Goods

You would think that if you preheated the oven properly, used the recommended bakeware, and followed the baking time indicated on the recipe, the dish would come out perfect. Unfortunately, that's not always the case. There are a number of factors that determine how long a product takes to bake. For example, if you use a glass baking pan and an electric oven, which uses radiant heat, the recipe will cook faster than it would with a metal baking pan.

The oven shelf you use also makes a difference. Top and bottom shelves tend to cook the tops and bottoms of food faster or slower, depending on where the heat source is located. Many ovens also have "hotspots" — areas that are hotter than others. My oven is characteristically hotter in the back than in the front. (I learned this the first time I baked a batch of chocolate chip cookies – the ones near the back of the oven got darker faster than the others.) Once I discovered this, I began rotating my cookie sheets and baking pans halfway through the baking process to ensure even heating.

Although the time given in a recipe is a good indicator, keep in mind that it is also "approximate" – a starting point. As you will see, there are other methods for verifying doneness – and they differ depending on the type of product you are baking.

The Pick

To determine when most batter-based goods – cakes, cupcakes, quick breads – are done baking, simply insert a wooden toothpick into the center. If it comes out clean, the cake is done; but if it comes out with batter (as shown in the photo above), more baking time is needed.

The Jiggle

Some cakes, particularly cheesecakes, as well as certain pies and baked custards, need to become firm or "set" before they are ready to be removed from the oven. To test these types of baked goods for doneness, place your hands (make sure you're wearing oven mitts) on both sides of the pan and shake very gently. If the center jiggles, it needs more time. Just remember to shake gently (you can make just about anything jiggle if you shake it hard enough!).

How Now, Brown Cow

Color is one indicator of doneness for dough-based items like cookies, yeast breads, and puff pastry. Most recipes indicate readiness by stating how brown they should be – light brown, golden brown, or (simply) brown, as shown in the photo below. They also state whether they are browned on top, on the edges, and/or on the bottom. You can usually determine crispness by the level of brownness – the darker it is, the drier and crispier the product.

Many of these baked goods, cookies in particular, can change dramatically in the matter of a minute. One minute, they look like they are nearly done, and the next, they're burned and ready for the garbage. Not only is it important to check the product around the time specified in the recipe (I start checking a few minutes before), but also to keep an eye on how brown they are to prevent them from burning.

Tap, Tap, Tap . . .

When it comes to checking yeast breads for doneness, color is one indicator – their tops are often supposed to be golden brown. In addition, you can remove the pan from the oven and turn it over to release the bread. Tap the bottom of the loaf with your knuckles. If the bread sounds hollow, it is done. If it doesn't, return it to the oven for a few minutes. If you're not sure, carefully cut a slice from the loaf and examine it. If it's still doughy, place the bread and the slice back in the pan and return it to the oven for another few minutes. With experience, you'll be able to tell when bread is done just by the way it smells.

Important Tip

If you are using Splenda (sucralose) to sweeten baked goods, don't expect them to brown. The chemical composition of this artificial sweetener doesn't allow it. (Sugar, honey, and other natural sweeteners are responsible for the browning of baked goods.) When using Splenda, you can, however, spray the products before or during baking with nonstick cooking spray to achieve a browning effect.

Light Brown

Brown

Golden Brown

Taking Measure

Measuring ingredients accurately with the right type of equipment is key to achieving successful recipe results—especially when it comes to baked goods like breads and cakes.

Glass Measuring Cup

Common sizes:

1 cup
2 cup (most common)
4 cup

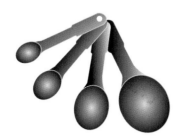

Proper usage:

Place the cup on a flat surface. Pour the ingredient to the desired mark, and then check it at eye level. If there is too much, pour it out. If you need just a little more, add it with a spoon.

Dry Measuring Cups

Common sizes:

¼ cup
⅓ cup
½ cup
1 cup

Proper usage:

Use the proper cup for the proper measurement. If, for example, you need ¼ cup of a particular ingredient, use a ¼ measuring cup. For an exact measurement, slightly overfill the cup, then use the back of a knife to level the surface and scrape the excess back into the original container.

Measuring Spoons

Common sizes:

¼ teaspoon
½ teaspoon
1 teaspoon
1 tablespoon

Proper usage:

Most recipes require level spoon measurements. After filling the spoon, level it off with the back of a knife. For a heaping amount, overfill the spoon and let the ingredient round off the top in a small mound.

Metric Conversions

Unlike the United States, which uses a system for measuring ingredients based on cup and spoon amounts, most countries use the metric system. During your culinary adventures, if you happen to run across a recipe that uses metric amounts, don't automatically give up on it. Instead, turn to page 376. There, you'll find a convenient, easy-to-use metric conversion chart to help you translate those unfamiliar ingredient amounts into familiar ones.

Important Tip

If you have a semi-solid ingredient like shortening or a lumpy ingredient like brown sugar you'll have to "pack" it into the measuring cup. First, overfill the cup. Then press the ingredient into the cup with your hand or a rubber spatula.

Butter and Margarine

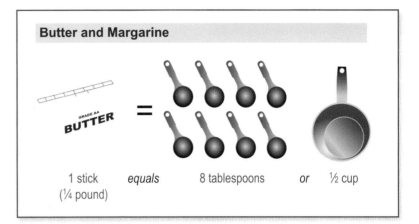

1 stick *equals* 8 tablespoons *or* ½ cup
(¼ pound)

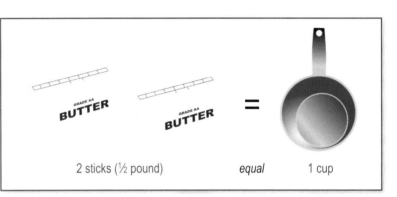

2 sticks (½ pound) *equal* 1 cup

Conversions

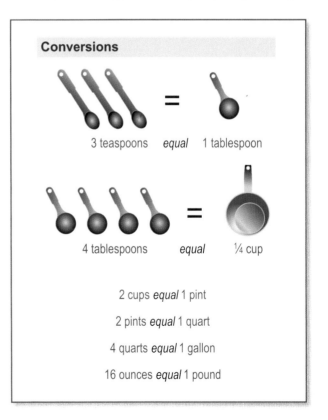

3 teaspoons *equal* 1 tablespoon

4 tablespoons *equal* ¼ cup

2 cups *equal* 1 pint

2 pints *equal* 1 quart

4 quarts *equal* 1 gallon

16 ounces *equal* 1 pound

Abbreviations Used in Some Cookbooks

t or tsp.	teaspoon
T or Tbsp.	tablespoon
c.	cup
oz.	ounce
pt.	pint
qt.	quart
gal.	gallon
lb or #.	pound

The rise and fall of high altitude baking.

This photo shows you what baking at a high altitude can do. I made this cake recipe at a 7,000-foot elevation. (I live in the mountains.) When I put it in the oven, the batter rose too high, spilled over the sides of the pan (thankfully, I had put a drip pan below it), and fell. The recipes in this book are written for people who live at an altitude of up to 3,000 feet, which, thankfully, includes most of this country's population. But for the "mountain people," there are a few simple adjustments you can make to find recipe success.

High Altitude Adjustments

Why do recipes for baked goods need to be prepared differently at high altitudes? The answer is air pressure. The higher the elevation, the thinner the air. The thinner the air, the more the air pressure is reduced. Reduced air pressure causes baked goods to rise faster. This is because leavening agents – yeast, baking powder, baking soda – activate quickly, creating large gas bubbles in batters and doughs that expand rapidly. As a result, cakes, muffins, and breads rise too quickly and then collapse. The good news is that a simple adjustment or two can remedy the problem.

Reducing the amount of leavening is the main solution. If that doesn't do the trick, adding a little more flour or other dense ingredient to the mixture may help. The tables on the next page give the proper adjustments for different altitudes.

When I bake something for the first time at a high altitude, I adjust the leavening and then test a small amount. If it's cake batter, I'll put a little into a single cupcake cup and bake it to see if it rises properly. If it bakes up and has a round top, I know the recipe will work. If, however, the top is flat or concave, I'll add an ingredient to make the batter

denser. If the mixture is mostly liquid, I'll add a little flour – about one tablespoon for every cup of flour used in the recipe. If another ingredient that has body, like crushed pineapple or grated carrots, is appropriate for the recipe, I may add a little of that instead of flour. Usually a tablespoon of a dense ingredient per cup of flour will do the trick. You can, however, add a little more if necessary.

"Rule of Thumb" Altitude Baking Guide

Altitude	Leavening Adjustment	Flour (or dense ingredient) Adjustment
0 to 3,000 feet	None	None
3,000 to 5,000 feet	Reduce leavening by $1/8$	Add 1 teaspoon per cup of flour
5,000 to 8,000 feet	Reduce leavening by $1/4$	Add 1 tablespoon per cup of flour
8,000 feet plus	Reduce leavening by $1/3$ to $1/2$	Add $1 1/2$ to 2 teaspoons per cup of flour

Approximate Leavening Conversions

3,000 to 5,000 feet		5,000 to 8,000 feet		8,000 feet plus	
If recipe calls for:	Reduce to:	If recipe calls for:	Reduce to:	If recipe calls for:	Reduce to:
1 teaspoon	$7/8$ teaspoon	1 teaspoon	$3/4$ teaspoon	1 teaspoon	$2/3$ teaspoon
$1 1/2$ teaspoons	$1 1/4$ teaspoons	$1 1/2$ teaspoons	$1 1/8$ teaspoons	$1 1/2$ teaspoons	1 teaspoon
2 teaspoons	$1 3/4$ teaspoons	2 teaspoons	$1 1/2$ teaspoons	2 teaspoons	$1 1/4$ teaspoons
1 tablespoon	$2 1/2$ teaspoons	1 tablespoon	$2 1/4$ teaspoons	1 tablespoon	2 teaspoons

This photo is of a buttermilk muffin recipe made at an elevation of 7,000 feet. I divided the batter into thirds before adding the leavening (baking powder). I made one batch without any ingredient adjustments (muffin #1). For the second batch, I reduced the baking powder and added flour, which resulted in the slightly rounded muffin (muffin #2). For the third batch, I reduced the baking powder, which produced the tallest muffin (muffin #3). Initially, muffin #1 rose higher than the other muffins, but fell before it finished baking.

Shake and Bake

The first recorded references to baking are found on Egyptian reliefs that were carved around 2600 BC. The ancient Greeks were believed to be the first ones to bake bread. Here are some other interesting bits of baking trivia.

Let's Get Organ-iz-ized

The Greeks were the first to bake extensively with ovens. The Romans, who loved to copy the Greeks, helped perfect the art of baking. By 500 BC, the pastry cook became a respected profession. The first pastry cook association or *pastillarium* was formed by the Romans in 400 AD.

A Doughnut "First"

The ancient Greeks are also credited with making the first doughnuts – small rings of honey-sweetened dough that were dipped in wine and eaten hot.

Whisk Me Away

Whipped egg whites are the basis for many light desserts. To incorporate air into the whites, which makes them light and fluffy, you can beat them with a whisk. The first whisks were made of thin branches that were tied together in bundles. Often the branches, such as those that came from peach trees, were aromatic and added flavor to the whipped ingredient. The French invented the modern whisk in the early 1900s.

"It's the Greatest invention Since Sliced Bread"

Originally bread was sold only in whole loaves. In 1912, Otto Frederick Rohwedder came up with the idea of an automatic bread-slicing machine. Bakers, however, weren't sure they liked the idea because sliced bread got stale quickly. So Rohwedder also looked for ways to keep the bread together after it was sliced. In 1917, his factory burned down along with his prototype and blueprints, but he continued to work on his invention. In 1928, he patented the first automatic slicing machine, which not only sliced bread but also wrapped it. At first, the bakeries were hesitant to use his machines, but when Wonder Bread came on the market with the first packaged sliced bread, they quickly followed suit. Toaster sales went through the roof!

Street Sweets

Before bakeries became popular, bakers would often peddle their wares on the street. During the Middle Ages, you could find pancake cooks selling their goods all throughout Europe. Gingerbread merchants were popular in London, and the "pie man" was a common sight on the streets of Germany.

Pinching Some Dough

In England, before people had ovens in their own homes, housewives would bring the dough they prepared to a baker, often their landlord, who would bake it for them. Some bakers had secret trap doors in the back of their ovens so an apprentice could pinch off some of that dough, which the baker would then use to make other baked goods to sell. This unethical practice and others like it led to the enactment of the "Assize of Bread and Ale" – the first law in England, written during the thirteenth century, to regulate practices in the sale of food and beverages.

Frost and Ice 74
   Chocolate Buttercream, 76
   Vanilla Buttercream, 76
   Choc-Choc Frosting, 77
   Banana-Nut Frosting, 78
   Pineapple Frosting, 78
   Coconut Frosting, 79
   German Chocolate Frosting, 80
   Whipped Cream Frosting, 80
   Cream Cheese Frosting, 81
   Vanilla Ice, 82
   Chocolate Ice, 82
   Lemon Ice, 83

Very Saucy! 84
   Fudge Sauce, 85
   Caramel Sauce, 86
   Raspberry Sauce, 86
   Butter Sauce, 87

How Filling! 88
   Apple Filling, 89
   Blueberry Filling, 90
   Nut Filling, 90
   Lemon Custard, 91
   Chocolate Ganache, 92
   Pastry Cream, 93
   Cannoli Cream, 94
   Mascarpone Cream, 94
   White Chocolate Mousse, 95
   Mousse au Chocolat, 96

You're the Tops! 98
   Whippy Cream, 99
   Streusel Toppings I and II, 100
   Pecan Topping, 101
   Fruit Glaze, 101

Stuff that goes with other stuff

I love sweet stuff so much that I often put it on top of, underneath, and inside of other sweet stuff. When I was a kid (and could eat anything without gaining a pound), my favorite dessert was Chocolate Heart Attack Cake topped with lots of sweet raspberry sauce, a handful of chopped nuts, and a heavy dollop of whipped cream. But now that my metabolism is no longer capable of handling such feats without expanding my waistline, I have just a small slice with nothing (*sigh*) on it. (*I'm just kidding. I still add a drizzle of raspberry sauce.*)

I start off this chapter with some of my favorite frostings and icings, followed by special sauces that go with just about everything. Luscious fillings for a wide assortment of cakes and pastries come next. And then there are toppings. Don't forget the toppings! You'll find lots of them, including four – *count 'em four* – whipped cream recipes!

The great thing about all the recipes in this chapter is that they are basic, easy to prepare, and can be used to fill or crown many different types of baked goods, whether homemade or store bought. As an added bonus, some recipes – like the creamy mousses and the heavenly pastry cream – can be enjoyed as is. Once you become more familiar with baking, you may want to do a little experimenting with different filling, frosting, topping, and sauce combinations. And the cool thing about this kind of 'sperimentin' is that all your results will be *saw-weet!*

Sweets for the sweet.

People often use the words "frosting" and "icing" interchangeably, but there is a difference. Frosting, which can be cooked or uncooked, is usually beaten or whipped, very thick, and normally used to fill or spread on cakes and cupcakes. Icing is typically thinner than frosting, and usually poured or drizzled over cookies, coffeecakes, and pastries. Icing also hardens, while frosting tends to remain soft. For decorating tips on how to frost or ice your baked goods, check out Chapter 14 beginning on page 357.

Basic Steps for Making Frosting   . . . and Icing

1. Soften

The base for many uncooked frostings is some sort of fat, like butter or cream cheese, which needs to be softened for best results. To do this, simply leave it out at a room temperature (68°F to 77°F) for three to four hours. Additional softening methods are found in the Helpful Tips at right.

2. Beat

Once the base is softened, it's time to beat in the remaining ingredients (which usually includes confectioner's sugar) until the mixture is light and fluffy. Although you can use a wooden spoon to beat the ingredients, an electric mixer is far more efficient and produces superior results in a fraction of the time.

1. Whisk or stir

Icing is made by stirring a liquid like milk, juice, or water with confectioner's sugar. This is easily done by hand with a spoon or whisk. Icing is much thinner than frosting, but not too thin. It should run in long, thick ribbons from the whisk or spoon.

Helpful Tips

▶ Getting homemade icing to achieve the right consistency can be a little tricky. Even a drop too much liquid can result in icing that is too thin – too little liquid and the icing will be too thick. It is best to add the liquid slowly, a few drops at a time, while stirring.

▶ Icing that is used for "drawing" should be thicker than icing used for drizzling.

▶ When preparing frosting that calls for confectioner's sugar, use a large bowl and add the sugar gradually, or you'll wind up with a dust storm! (There is a good reason, it's also called "powdered" sugar.) After each addition, be patient and allow it to blend fully before adding more.

▶ If a frosting recipe calls for softened butter (or other fat) and you don't have the time to let it sit out at room temperature, cut it into cubes, which will speed up the process. Just don't let it get too soft or the frosting will be too thin. If this happens, put it in the refrigerator for a few minutes to let it harden a bit.

▶ Make sure cakes and other baked goods are completely cool before adding frosting or icing. If they are warm, the frosting/icing will melt into the cake or become runny.

▶ You can also soften cream cheese in a microwave (don't forget to remove the wrapping!) by heating it about fifteen to twenty seconds.

▶ For frosting and icing decorating techniques, see Chapter 14 beginning on page 357.

Storing Frosting and Icing

▶ Try to use frosting or icing almost immediately after making it. Icing especially will harden quickly when it is exposed to the air.

▶ To store frosting, place it in an airtight container and refrigerate. Most buttercream frostings will keep up to two weeks. You can also freeze buttercream for several months. Before using, let it come to room temperature and then stir for easier spreading. Whipped cream frostings will keep in the refrigerator for a day or two.

▶ To keep your freshly frosted cake picture perfect, it is best to store it on a cake plate with a dome top. If you need to wrap the cake, refrigerate it first to harden the frosting, and then loosely cover it with plastic wrap or foil. You can also stick a few toothpicks in the top of the cake to keep the wrapping from touching the frosting. (See the inset on page 289.)

▶ Cakes with whipped cream frostings must be refrigerated.

Chocolate Buttercream

Buttercream is light and fluffy and easy to spread.

Ingredients

$^1/_2$ cup vegetable shortening
$^1/_2$ cup butter (1 stick), softened
$^3/_4$ cup unsweetened cocoa powder
1 teaspoon vanilla extract
3–4 tablespoons milk
4 cups confectioner's sugar

Yield: About 2$^1/_2$ cups

Stuff You'll Need

1. Place the shortening and butter in a medium bowl and beat with an electric mixer on low speed until light and fluffy.

2. Add the cocoa, vanilla, milk, and the confectioner's sugar one-third at a time. Continue beating until the mixture is smooth, thick, and uniform in color. Use immediately, or cover and refrigerate up to two weeks.

Vanilla Buttercream

Vanilla buttercream is a classic. For different flavors, try other extracts (like maple, coffee, rum, coconut) instead of vanilla.

Ingredients

$^1/_2$ cup shortening
$^1/_2$ cup butter (1 stick), softened
2 tablespoons milk
1 teaspoon vanilla extract
4 cups confectioner's sugar

Yield: About 2$^1/_2$ cups

Stuff You'll Need

1. Place the shortening and butter in a medium bowl and beat with an electric mixer on low speed until light and fluffy.

2. Add the milk, vanilla, and the confectioner's sugar one-third at a time. Continue beating until the mixture is smooth, thick, and uniform in color. Use immediately, or cover and refrigerate up to two weeks.

Choc-Choc Frosting

The chocolate used in this recipe makes it especially rich and delicious. When it comes to chocolate frostings, this one is my favorite.

Ingredients

$1/2$ cup (1 stick) butter
6 ounces semi-sweet baking chocolate
$1/4$ cup milk
2 teaspoons vanilla extract
$3 1/2$ cups confectioner's sugar

Yield: About $2 1/2$ cups

Stuff You'll Need

1. Melt the butter and chocolate in a medium saucepan over medium-low heat. Stir until smooth, then transfer to a medium bowl and let cool a few minutes.

2. Add the milk, vanilla, and half the confectioner's sugar to the cooled chocolate, and beat with an electric mixer on low speed until well blended.

3. Gradually add the rest of the sugar and beat until the mixture is smooth, thick, and uniform in color.

4. Use immediately, or cover and refrigerate. (Even at room temperature, this frosting will begin to harden quickly.)

Banana-Nut Frosting

If you love bananas, you'll love this frosting! It's kinda nutty, too.

Ingredients

$^1/_2$ cup butter (1 stick), softened
1 teaspoon vanilla extract
1 medium banana, cut up
4 cups confectioner's sugar
1 cup sweetened flaked coconut
1 cup chopped pecans

Yield: About 3 cups

Stuff You'll Need

1. Place the butter, vanilla, and banana in a medium bowl and beat with an electric mixer on low speed until light and fluffy. Add the confectioner's sugar one-third at a time, and continue beating until the mixture is smooth, thick, and uniform in color.

2. Add the coconut and pecans, and stir until thoroughly combined. Use immediately, or cover and refrigerate up to two weeks.

Pineapple Frosting

The refreshing pineapple flavor of this frosting adds the perfect touch to many cakes and other baked goods. Try it on yellow cupcakes, or any mildly flavored cake.

Ingredients

$^1/_2$ cup butter (1 stick), softened
$^1/_3$ cup crushed canned pineapple
4 cups confectioner's sugar

Yield: About 3 cups

Stuff You'll Need

1. Place the butter and pineapple in a medium bowl and beat with an electric mixer on low speed until well combined.

2. Add the confectioner's sugar one-third at a time, and continue beating until the mixture is thick and uniform in color, and the sugar is fully incorporated. It will be a little lumpy from the pineapple. Use immediately, or cover and refrigerate up to two weeks.

Coconut Frosting

This recipe makes enough frosting for a dozen standard cupcakes. Because this is a very sweet and solid frosting I suggest using it on smaller desserts like cupcakes. For a large cake I prefer buttercream frosting that is flavored with coconut extract.

Ingredients

1/4 cup butter (1/2 stick), softened
4-ounce package cream cheese, softened
1 tablespoon heavy cream
1/4 teaspoon coconut extract
1/2 teaspoon vanilla extract
2 cups confectioner's sugar
1/2 cup sweetened shredded or flaked coconut

Yield: About 2 cups

Stuff You'll Need

1. Place the butter and cream cheese in a medium bowl and beat with an electric mixer on low speed until light and fluffy.

2. Add the cream, coconut extract, vanilla extract, and the confectioner's sugar one-third at a time. Beat until the mixture is smooth and thick.

3. Add the coconut and stir until well combined. Use immediately, or cover and refrigerate up to three days.

German Chocolate Frosting

This classic German chocolate cake topper is buttery rich and laced with coconut and pecans.

Ingredients

1¹/₂ cups (12 ounces) evaporated milk
1¹/₂ cups granulated sugar
³/₄ cup butter (1¹/₂ sticks)
4 egg yolks*
1 teaspoon vanilla extract
1 cup sweetened flaked coconut
1¹/₂ cups chopped pecans
* For egg separating instructions, see page 51.

Yield: About 3 cups

Stuff You'll Need

1. Place the evaporated milk, sugar, butter, egg yolks, and vanilla in a medium pot over medium heat. Stir constantly until the mixture is lightly boiling.

2. Add the coconut and pecans, and reduce the heat to low. Stirring occasionally, simmer for 10 minutes or until the mixture is very thick. Refrigerate at least 8 hours before using.

Whipped Cream Frosting

This creamy frosting is light and fluffy with a touch of sweetness. For best results, use a cold bowl and beaters.

Ingredients

2 cups heavy cream, cold
1 cup confectioner's sugar
1 teaspoon vanilla extract

Yield: About 3¹/₂ cups

Stuff You'll Need

1. Place the cream, sugar, and vanilla in a medium bowl. Beat with an electric mixer on low speed for about 1 minute.

2. Increase the speed to high and continue to beat for several minutes until the mixture is thick, smooth, and spreadable. Use immediately or cover and refrigerate up to two days.

Cream Cheese Frosting

1. Place the cream cheese in a medium bowl and mash with a spoon.

Although this thick creamy frosting is traditionally paired with carrot cake, don't hesitate to try it on lots of other cake and quick bread varieties. Especially delicious on pumpkin muffins, spiced cakes, and even devil's food.

2. Add the vanilla, cream, and half the confectioner's sugar, and beat with an electric mixer on a low speed until blended. Gradually add the rest of the sugar and continue to beat until the mixture is smooth and thick.

Ingredients

8-ounce package cream cheese, softened

1 teaspoon vanilla extract

$1/4$ cup heavy cream

$3^{1}/_{2}$ cups confectioner's sugar

Yield: About $2^{1}/_{2}$ cups

3. Use immediately or cover and refrigerate up to two days.

Stuff You'll Need

Vanilla
Ice

You don't have to be a rapper to love this simple icing. It's great drizzled over cookies, coffeecakes, and muffins.

Ingredients

1 cup confectioner's sugar
1 tablespoon milk
$1/4$ teaspoon vanilla extract

Yield: About $1/2$ cup

Stuff You'll Need

1. Place all the ingredients in a medium bowl and stir until well combined.

2. Continue to stir until the mixture is smooth and thick enough to drip in long ribbons from the whisk or spoon. If it's too thin, add a few more tablespoons sugar; if it's too thick, add more milk – one drop at a time. Use immediately or store in an airtight container.

Chocolate
Ice

Chocolaty and sweet, this icing can be easily doubled or tripled.

Ingredients

1 cup confectioner's sugar
1 tablespoon unsweetened cocoa
  powder
2 teaspoons milk
$1/4$ teaspoon vanilla extract

Yield: About $1/2$ cup

Stuff You'll Need

1. Place all the ingredients in a medium bowl and stir until well combined.

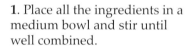

2. Continue to stir until the mixture is smooth and thick enough to drip in long ribbons from the whisk or spoon. If it's too thin, add a few more tablespoons sugar; if it's too thick, add more milk – one drop at a time. Use immediately or store in an airtight container.

Lemon Ice

I love to pucker, so I love lemons. This icing is sweet and tart and super-terrif to drizzle over muffins and quick breads. This recipe can be easily doubled or tripled.

Ingredients

2 tablespoons fresh lemon juice
   (1 small lemon)
1 cup confectioner's sugar

Yield: About ¹/₂ cup

1. Juice the lemon and add the juice to a small bowl along with the sugar. Stir until well combined.

2. Continue to stir until the mixture is smooth and thick enough to drip in long ribbons from the whisk or spoon. If it's too thin, add a few more tablespoons sugar; if it's too thick, add more juice – one drop at a time. Use immediately or store in an airtight container.

Stuff You'll Need

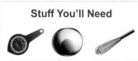

My, you're a saucy sauce!

Dessert sauces can add flavor and richness to just about any baked treat. Adding the right fruit sauce to a piece of cake can elevate it to delicious new heights, while covering a brownie in hot fudge can make any chocolate lover weak in the knees. (And you thought hot fudge was just for ice cream sundaes!) And drizzling a little butter sauce over buttery pound cake or coffeecake will make it even "butterier." (I love making up words!)

Basic Steps for Making Stovetop Dessert Sauces

1. Heat slowly

Most sauces require ingredients to be melted or broken down. This has to be done slowly over low heat so they don't burn. Once the ingredients have been blended, they often need to be boiled or cooked over medium heat and constantly stirred until thickened to the right consistency.

2. Stir constantly

Stirring is required not only to dissolve sugars and blend ingredients, but also to keep sauces from sticking to or boiling over the pot. As sauces boil, it is important to stir them quickly and constantly with a spoon, whisk, or even a rubber spatula.

Storing Dessert Sauces

▶ To store most dessert sauces, place them in airtight containers and refrigerate. Most will keep for three to four weeks. In the freezer, they can last for three to four months.

▶ Before storing a freshly cooked sauce, cool it completely.

▶ To reheat a refrigerated sauce, simmer it in a saucepan over low heat. You can also heat it in the microwave (be sure to use a microwave-safe container).

Fudge Sauce

Although this sauce is traditionally added to ice cream sundaes, it's also delicious drizzled over brownies, muffins, cream puffs, and slices of your favorite cake.

Ingredients

1 cup semi-sweet chocolate morsels
1 cup sweetened condensed milk
1 tablespoon butter
1 teaspoon vanilla extract

Yield: About 2 cups

1. Place the chocolate morsels and milk in a medium pot over medium heat. Stirring frequently, bring the mixture to a gentle boil. Continue to stir until the morsels have melted.

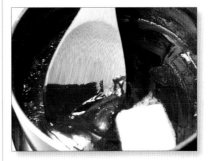

2. Remove the pot from the heat and let the mixture cool for 2 or 3 minutes, then add the butter and vanilla. Stir the sauce until well blended. Use warm or hot.

Stuff You'll Need

Caramel Sauce

1. Place the sugars, cream, and butter in a medium pot over medium heat. Stirring briskly, bring to a gentle boil. Continue stirring for another minute.

This sauce is fantastic on ice cream, cheesecake, English puddings, apples, and anything that goes with caramel.

Ingredients

2. Remove the pot from the heat and allow the mixture to cool for a minute, then stir in the vanilla extract. Use warm or hot.

$^1/_2$ cup granulated sugar
$^1/_2$ cup firmly packed brown sugar
$^1/_2$ cup heavy cream
$^1/_4$ cup butter ($^1/_2$ stick)
1 teaspoon vanilla extract

Yield: About 1 cup

Stuff You'll Need

Raspberry Sauce

1. Place all the ingredients in a medium pot over medium-low heat and stir until well blended.

This sauce is amazing with rich chocolate desserts, ice cream, and cheesecake.

Ingredients

2 cups fresh or frozen raspberries
2 tablespoons granulated sugar
2 teaspoons cornstarch
$^1/_2$ cup water

2. While stirring, simmer the mixture for 2 minutes or until the raspberries break down and the sauce starts to thicken. Remove from heat and let cool. Use warm or cold.

Yield: About 1$^1/_2$ cups

Stuff You'll Need

Butter Sauce

Here's my favorite buttery dessert sauce, which absorbs into cakes and coffeecakes, making them richer and moister.

Ingredients

1/4 cup butter (1/2 stick)
2 tablespoons water
1 1/2 teaspoons vanilla extract
1/2 cup granulated sugar

Yield: About 3/4 cup

1. Place the butter, water, and vanilla in a small saucepan over medium heat, and stir until the butter is melted.

2. Add the sugar and continue to stir until fully dissolved. Use hot or warm.

Stuff You'll Need

Fill 'er up!

Can you imagine an éclair without the custard, a jelly doughnut without the jelly, or a cannoli shell without the luscious cream? To me, there's nothin' better than pastries filled with other delicious goodies like fruits, creams, and custards. Most fillings are either prepared on the stovetop or whipped into shape without being cooked.

Basic Techniques for Making Fillings

Storing Dessert Fillings

▶ Cheese and cream-based fillings can be refrigerated in an airtight container up to two days or frozen for several weeks. Fruit-based fillings will keep up to a week in the refrigerator or several months in the freezer.

Stovetop cooking
Using a stove, a saucepan, and a whisk or spoon, you can make several different types of fillings for a variety of desserts. These fillings are often thickened with ingredients like egg yolks, flour, or cornstarch, which require heat to activate the binding agents.

Whipping
Many uncooked pastry fillings are whipped with the aid of an electric mixer. Their primary ingredient is typically heavy cream or a soft cheese like ricotta, which is often folded with other flavorful ingredients.

▶ Fillings can, and will, soften pastry dough and shells. For this reason, it is best to consume most filled desserts shortly after they are made – within a day or two.

▶ The best way to store filled pastries is in an airtight container in the freezer.

Apple Filling

This filling is a favorite in strudels and turnovers.

Ingredients

2 large Granny Smith or McIntosh
   apples, peeled and cored
1 teaspoon fresh lemon juice
1/4 cup firmly packed brown sugar
1 tablespoon all-purpose flour
1/4 teaspoon ground cinnamon
1/4 cup chopped walnuts (optional)

Yield: About 2 cups

1. Cut the apples into thin slices, then cut the slices in half. Place in a medium pot along with the remaining ingredients, and stir to coat the apples.

2. Bring the mixture to a boil over medium-high heat, then reduce the heat to low. Stirring occasionally, simmer 5 minutes or until the apples are soft, but not mushy. Use according to the specific recipe.

Stuff You'll Need

Blueberry Filling

I can't tell if blueberries are blue or if they're violet, which to me is more of a purple. Well I guess they taste blue and that's all that matters.

Ingredients

1 cup fresh or frozen blueberries
1/4 cup granulated sugar
1 teaspoon cornstarch
1 tablespoon fresh lemon juice or water

Yield: About 1 cup

Stuff You'll Need

1. Place all the ingredients in a medium pot and stir to coat the blueberries.

2. Bring the mixture to a boil over medium-high heat, then reduce the heat to low. Stirring occasionally, simmer 3 to 5 minutes or until the sauce has thickened. Use according to the specific recipe.

Nut Filling

Many recipes for tarts, turnovers, and other filled pastries call for a nut filling. This one is basic and delicious.

Ingredients

1 tablespoon butter
2 cups coarsely chopped nuts*
1 cup firmly packed brown sugar
1/4 cup water
2 tablespoons light corn syrup

* Pecans, hazelnuts, walnuts (or a combination of each) are recommended.

Yield: About 2 cups

Stuff You'll Need

1. Melt the butter in a medium pot over medium heat, then add the nuts. Stirring often, cook the mixture 2 minutes or until the nuts are fragrant.

2. Add the brown sugar, water, and corn syrup, then reduce the heat to low. Stirring occasionally, simmer about 5 minutes or until the nuts are coated with a sticky caramel-like sauce. Use according to the specific recipe.

Lemon Custard

Use this filling in tarts, pies, and any pastry that will benefit from a blast of lemon.

Ingredients

1/2 cup fresh lemon juice (3 to 4 large lemons)
4 egg yolks*
1 cup granulated sugar
5 tablespoons butter
1 tablespoon lemon zest or finely chopped lemon peel

* For egg separating instructions, see page 51.

Yield: About 1 1/2 cups

1. Juice the lemons and add the juice to a medium pot along with the remaining ingredients. Stir until well blended.

2. While stirring with a whisk, bring the ingredients to a boil over medium-high heat. Reduce the heat to low and simmer, stirring rapidly until the mixture starts to thicken. Continue stirring another minute, then remove from the heat. Use according to the specific recipe.

Stuff You'll Need

Chocolate Ganache

I use this easy-to-make rich chocolate filling for many recipes, including tarts, tartlets, and pies. For instructions on how to turn it into a luscious frosting, see the Important Tips box below.

Ingredients

$^{1}/_{2}$ cup heavy cream
2 cups semi-sweet chocolate morsels

Yield: About 2 cups

Important Tips

▶ If you are using bar chocolate instead of morsels, chop it up so it melts quickly.

▶ To turn this recipe into a frosting, use 1 cup heavy cream. Unlike most frostings, which are thick and fluffy, this one will be more like a thick glaze. Spread it while warm on the cake.

Stuff You'll Need

1. Heat the cream in a small saucepan over medium heat until it reaches a medium boil.

2. Place the chocolate morsels in a medium heatproof bowl and pour the boiling hot cream on top. Whisk until smooth. Use according to the specific recipe.

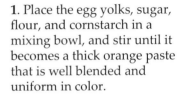

Pastry Cream

Although this stovetop custard is great on its own, it also makes a perfect filling for pies, tarts, and a variety of pastries.

Ingredients

3 egg yolks*
¼ cup granulated sugar
2 tablespoons flour
2 tablespoons cornstarch
1¼ cups whole milk (do not use reduced-fat)
2 teaspoons Grand Marnier (optional)

* For egg separating instructions, see page 51.

Yield: About 2 cups

Important Tip
To avoid lumps, whisk the pastry cream very quickly and briskly when it starts to thicken.

Stuff You'll Need

1. Place the egg yolks, sugar, flour, and cornstarch in a mixing bowl, and stir until it becomes a thick orange paste that is well blended and uniform in color.

2. Add the milk and whisk until well blended. Transfer the mixture to a medium pot over medium-high heat.

3. Stirring constantly with a whisk, bring the mixture to a boil, then reduce the heat to low. Continuing to stir, simmer the mixture until it starts to thicken. Remove from the heat and let cool a bit before adding the Grand Marnier (if using). Use according to the specific recipe.

Cannoli Cream

Mama mia! You didn't think I'd forget the cannoli cream. Pack it into cannoli shells (which you can buy premade) or puff pastry shells. Also makes a great frosting!

Ingredients

2 cups ricotta cheese
$1/2$ cup granulated sugar
2 teaspoons vanilla extract
$1/2$ cup mini chocolate morsels

Yield: About 3 cups

Stuff You'll Need

1. Place the ricotta cheese, sugar, and vanilla in a medium bowl and beat with an electric mixer on medium speed until smooth.

2. Fold in the chocolate morsels until well combined. Use according to the specific recipe.
.

Mascarpone Cream

What the heck is mascarpone? Why, it's the soft, creamy Italian cheese that is used to make many delicious sauces and fillings, like the one for tiramisu!

Ingredients

1 cup heavy cream
$1/2$ cup mascarpone cheese
$1/2$ cup granulated sugar
2 teaspoons vanilla extract

Yield: About 2 cups

Stuff You'll Need

1. Place the cream in a medium bowl and beat with an electric mixer on medium speed until soft peaks form.

2. Add the mascarpone, sugar, and vanilla. Continue to beat until the ingredients are just blended and the mixture is smooth and thick. Do not overbeat! Use according to the specific recipe.

White Chocolate Mousse

Delicious as a dessert on its own, this luscious mousse makes a wonderful filling for puff pastry. Also makes a great frosting!

Ingredients

1½ cups heavy cream
1 teaspoon vanilla extract
6 ounces white chocolate

Yield: About 2 cups

Important Tips

▶ For this recipe, you'll want to just melt the chocolate, not cook it. Use either a double boiler or a saucepan over very low heat.

▶ Melted white chocolate will harden very quickly as it cools, so don't wait too long before folding it into the whipped cream. It should be warm, but not hot.

Stuff You'll Need

1. Place the cream and vanilla in a medium bowl and beat with an electric mixer on medium speed until stiff peaks form. Set aside.

2. Place the white chocolate in a medium pot over *very low* heat. Stir with a whisk until melted, then transfer to a large bowl.

3. When the chocolate has cooled to warm, top it with half the whipped cream and gently fold until blended. Fold in the remaining whipped cream until well combined. Refrigerate at least two hours before serving as is or using as a filling.

Mousse au Chocolat

This recipe for authentic French mousse comes from my friend who lives in France. This is the real thing . . . and when you taste it, you'll know what it feels like to float on a French chocolate cloud. It's an amazing dessert on its own, but you can use it as a luscious pastry filling.

Ingredients

3 eggs, separated*

1/4 cup butter (1/2 stick)

8 ounces dark chocolate

2 tablespoons water

Pinch salt

* For egg separating instructions, see page 51.

Yield: About 2 cups

Important Tips

▶ Because raw eggs are used in this recipe, be sure they are pasteurized to avoid possible food poisoning.

▶ Use the best chocolate you can find. If possible, use Swiss or Belgian chocolate, which is sold in grams. The 8 ounces in this recipe is equivalent to 225 grams.

Stuff You'll Need

1. Separate the eggs. Put the whites in a medium bowl, and the yolks in a large bowl. Add a pinch of salt to the egg whites and beat with an electric mixer on medium speed until stiff peaks form. Set aside.

2. Cut up the butter, break up the chocolate, and place in the top of a double boiler over medium-low heat or in a medium saucepan over *very low* heat. Add the water and stir until the butter and chocolate are fully melted. Set aside to cool for 3 to 5 minutes.

3. Add the cooled chocolate mixture to the egg yolks and beat with an electric mixer on high speed for 2 minutes. The mixture should increase in volume and be a little foamy.

4. Add about 3 heaping tablespoons of the beaten egg white to the chocolate mixture, and gently fold until blended.

5. Add the remaining egg whites and gently fold until the mixture is well combined. Refrigerate at least two hours before serving as is or using as a filling.

On top of everything else. . .

Now that you've made a dessert that is absolutely delicious, you can send it "over the top" by giving it the perfect crown. On the following pages, you'll find a variety of luscious toppings, including a collection of flavored whipped creams, a nutty pecan blend that adds texture and crunch to baked goods, and a simple glaze to preserve your fruit-covered pies and tarts.

Basic Techniques for Making Toppings

Whipping

You can prepare the whipped cream toppings in this section by hand with a whisk, but an electric mixer will do the job quicker and more efficiently. Begin mixing the cream on low speed for about a minute, then increase the speed to high and beat for several minutes until stiff peaks form.

Folding

Flavorful extracts and sugars are often added to cream before it is whipped. Other flavorful ingredients, like fruit sauces and melted chocolate, are folded into the cream after it's whipped. Be sure to fold ingredients gently to keep the creamy mixture light and airy. (For folding instructions, see page 57.)

Stovetop cooking/heating

Some dessert toppings need to be cooked or heated to dissolve ingredients, thicken mixtures, or both. Be sure to follow recipe directions regarding the heat intensity, the amount of stirring required, and the length of time that's needed to heat or cook the topping.

Whippy Cream

Whipped cream is probably one of the most popular dessert toppings because it goes with just about everything! Be sure to check out the variations to this basic recipe. And experiment with different extracts and sauces to come up with your own flavorful toppings.

1. Place the ingredients in a medium bowl and beat with an electric mixer on low speed for about a minute.

2. Increase to high speed and beat until stiff peaks form. Use immediately or cover and refrigerate up to two days.

Ingredients

1 cup heavy cream, cold
1 teaspoon confectioner's sugar
$1/4$ teaspoon vanilla extract (optional)

Yield: About 2 cups

Important Tips

▶ To whip cream to its ultimate "whippiness," use cold beaters and a cold mixing bowl. Just put them in the refrigerator for about fifteen minutes. Then add the cold heavy cream and whip away!

▶ Don't overbeat, or the whipped cream will turn to butter!

Stuff You'll Need

Try These Variations!

Choco Whippy Cream

Add: 2 ounces semi-sweet chocolate

Melt the chocolate in a small saucepan over low heat, then let it cool. Fold the melted chocolate into the whipped cream until it is uniform in color.

Berry Whippy Cream

Add: Blueberry Filling, page 90

Fold the blueberry filling into the whipped cream until it is uniform in color.

Coffee Whippy Cream

Add: 1 tablespoon prepared expresso
(or 1 teaspoon instant coffee)
2 tablespoons confectioner's sugar

Before whipping the cream, add the espresso and additional sugar to Step 1 above.

Streusel Topping I

Streusel toppings are used in a number of recipes for baked goods, like coffeecakes, muffins, and quick breads.

Ingredients

$1/2$ cup all-purpose flour
$1/2$ cup granulated sugar
$1/4$ cup cold butter ($1/2$ stick), cut up

Yield: About $1^1/2$ cups

Stuff You'll Need

1. Place the ingredients in a medium bowl. Using a pastry blender (or 2 knives in a criss-cross motion), cut the butter into the dry ingredients until a crumbly mixture is achieved.

2. Use the topping according to the specific recipe instructions.

Streusel Topping II

Here is another streusel topping with just a hint of cinnamon.

Ingredients

$2/3$ cup granulated sugar
$1/2$ cup flour
$1/2$ teaspoon ground cinnamon
$1/3$ cup cold butter, cut up

Yield: About $1^1/2$ cups

Stuff You'll Need

1. Place the ingredients in a medium bowl. Using a pastry blender (or 2 knives in a criss-cross motion), cut the butter into the dry ingredients until a crumbly mixture is achieved.

2. Use the topping according to the specific recipe instructions.

Pecan Topping

This topping adds nutty crunch to pound cakes and coffeecakes. Delicious over ice cream, too.

Ingredients

¹/₄ cup butter (¹/₂ stick)
3/4 cup firmly packed brown sugar
1 cup chopped pecans

Yield: About 1¹/₄ cups

Stuff You'll Need

1. Melt the butter in a small saucepan over low heat.

2. Add the brown sugar and pecans, and stir until the nuts are well coated. Stirring frequently, continue cooking about 2 minutes or until the sugar has dissolved. Use according to specific recipe instructions.

Fruit Glaze

Brush this simple glaze on pies, tarts, and pastries that have fresh fruit on top. It will help preserve the fruit for a few days.

Ingredients

¹/₄ cup apricot jelly for light fruits,
   or red currant jelly for dark fruits
1 tablespoon water

Yield: About ¹/₄ cup

Stuff You'll Need

1. Place the ingredients in a small pan over low heat. Stirring frequently, heat the mixture about 1 minute or until it has a smooth, spreadable consistency. Transfer to a small bowl and let cool to room temperature.

2. Using a pastry brush, coat the fresh fruit topping with a layer of the glaze.

Is it Icing or Frosting?

What's the difference between icing and frosting? Frosting is typically beaten or whipped, thick, and used to fill or spread on cakes and cupcakes. Icing is thinner than frosting, and usually drizzled over or spread on cookies, coffeecakes, and pastries. Icing also hardens, while frosting tends to remain soft. Here are some interesting facts about toppings and fillings for many baked goods.

How Icing Got Its Name

Originally, cakes were served plain without frosting or icing. The first cake "toppers" were simple sprinklings of sugar. Later, egg whites were incorporated with sugar and the mixture was boiled and then poured over the cake. When the mixture cooled, it hardened into a shiny topping that resembled ice.

Fit for a King?

Royal icing is a pure white icing that hardens to a beautiful smooth finish. It is made with confectioner's sugar, egg whites, and lemon juice that are beaten together until thick and stiff. This icing is often used to frost cakes – wedding cakes in particular. When it dries, it becomes almost airtight, which means the cake it covers will keep for a long time. Royal icing can also be piped from a pastry bag into beautiful flowers, borders, and other cake decorations, and it is the perfect glue for holding together gingerbread houses.

That's a Lot of Frosting!

In 2007, the largest wedding cake was unveiled at the Mohegan Sun Hotel and Casino in Connecticut for the New England Bridal Showcase. The seventeen-foot-tall, 15,000-pound monster was covered with 4,810 pounds of buttercream frosting.

Thank You, Fannie

The first modern buttercream frosting recipes were introduced in the early 1900s by Fannie Farmer – an American culinary expert, teacher, and cookbook author.

Chocolate Mayonnaise

Mousse is the French word for "foam." It has a light, airy texture that is created by folding whipping ingredients like egg whites or heavy cream with a heavier base mixture. Originally, mousse was made with savory ingredients like meat and fish. Then in the late 1800s, French artist Henri Toulouse Lautrec came up with the brilliant idea of making the dish with chocolate instead. *Magnifique!* He called his culinary invention *mayonnaise de chocolat*, which eventually came to be known (and loved) as *mousse de chocolat* or chocolate mousse.

From Custards to Pie Fillings

Two popular pie fillings actually started out as custards during the early days in America. After removing the seeds and fibers from the inside of a pumpkin, pilgrims filled it with cream and baked it whole. The creamy custard-like mixture that formed was eventually used as a filling for pumpkin pies. Lemon custard, which was invented by the Quakers, evolved into the filling for lemon meringue pie.

5. Cookie Mania!

Cookie Drops 104
   Chocolate Chip Cookies, 106
   Peanut Butter Cookies, 108
   Oat-Rageous Oatmeal
     Cookies, 110
   Oat-Butterscotch Cookies, 111
   Coconut Macaroons I, 112
   Coconut Macaroons II, 113

Nutty Cookies 114
   Flourless Chocolate
     Nut Cookies, 115
   Persian Walnut Cookies, 116
   Mexican Wedding Cakes, 117
   Walnut Puffs, 118

Biscotti Party 120
   Chocolate Almond Biscotti, 122
   White Chocolate
     Macadamia Biscotti, 124

Cool Cookies 126
   Sugar Cookies, 128
   Ginger Snappies, 130
   Almond Crispies, 131
   Mama's Shortbread, 132

The secret ingredient is . . .

I may be biased, but in my opinion, my grandmother was the best cookie baker – ever! She could have beaten anyone in a cookie-baking contest any day of the week. When I was very young, Grandma let me in on what she believed was her secret for making great cookies every time. She said the key to cookie success is . . . (*drum roll, please*) using softened butter.

When I first starting baking, I chose to ignore Grandma's advice. I didn't feel like taking the time to let the butter soften, so I'd quickly melt it in a pot on the stove, leave it hard, or use whipped varieties. These different butter states – whether too liquid or too solid – affected the consistency of the dough. As a result, the cookies were still edible, but always a little "off." Of course, using softened butter isn't the only trick to making great cookies, which is why this chapter is filled with lots of other helpful tips to ensure cookie-baking success every time.

And wait until you check out the variety of easy-to-make recipes, which are among my all-time favorites. Starting out are some classic "drop" cookies including Chocolate Chip, Out-Rageous Oatmeal, and Coconut Macaroons. I'll show you how to make crisp, delicious biscotti cookies – perfect for dunking into a cup of coffee or pairing with a scoop of ice cream. You'll also find recipes for cool "refrigerator cookies" including Mama's Shortbread, Ginger Snappies, classic Sugar Cookies, and much more. You're going to find it easy to keep your cookie jar filled!

So let's soften some butter, roll up our sleeves, and make some sweet cookies!

Making drop cookies is as easy as falling off a spoon.

Drop cookies are really popular. They're easy to make, easy to carry, and easy to store. Plus they can be soft and chewy or "crispity" and "chrunchity." Sometimes, nothing taste better than one of these homemade cookies and a glass of milk. This section is dedicated to four of my favorites – chocolate chip, peanut butter, oatmeal, and macaroons.

Basic Steps for Making Drop Cookies

1. Cream
The first step for most drop cookie recipes involves beating together sugar with a fat, like butter, margarine, or shortening, which creates air pockets in the fat to help make the cookies light. Extracts can also be included in this process, and eggs are often blended into the creamed mixture.

2. Stir
After creaming the butter and sugar, it's time to grab a wooden spoon and stir in the dry ingredients – typically a mixture of flour, salt, baking powder and/or baking soda – to form a smooth sticky dough.

3. Add extras
Once the dough is ready, many drop cookie recipes include "add-ins" – like chocolate morsels, nuts, candy, and/or coconut – which are mixed into the dough until they are well distributed. These add-ins can be part of the basic recipe or used to make delicious variations.

Add-Ins

Drop cookies are good. Drop cookies with add-ins are better.

▶ **Morsels/Chips/Chunks**

Butterscotch
Milk chocolate
Peanut butter
Semi-sweet chocolate
White chocolate

▶ **Dried Fruit**

Coconut, flaked/shredded
Dates, chopped
Raisins, golden and brown

▶ **Candy**

Chocolate bars, chopped
Coated chocolate (M&M's)
Coated peanut butter
 (Reese's Pieces)

▶ **Nuts**

Almonds, Cashews,
Hazelnuts, Macadamias
Peanuts, Pecans
Pistachios, Walnuts

Helpful Tips

▶ Softened butter is an ingredient in most drop cookies. It should be soft, but still a little firm (see page 51). Keep in mind that if the butter is too cold, it won't incorporate properly into dough. If it's melted, the cookies won't hold their shape when baked.

▶ For best results when creaming ingredients, use an electric mixer on low (or medium-low) speed. Beat the mixture for about two minutes or until it is light and fluffy. Before I had an electric mixer I used to cream the ingredients with a whisk by hand. It took much longer and didn't do as good a job.

▶ It isn't necessary to use an electric mixer to blend the dry ingredients into the creamed mixture. Some swift strokes with a wooden spoon will do the trick.

▶ Stir chips, nuts, or other add-ins into the dough during the final stage. The dough should be the right consistency before adding these items.

▶ When dropping dough on the cookie sheet, leave an inch or so of space between them. This will allow for the dough to expand during baking.

Storing Drops

▶ Be sure to cool the cookies completely before storing them in an airtight container. Most varieties will stay fresh up to a week. They will keep for a few weeks in the refrigerator, and a few months in the freezer.

▶ If you plan to stack the cookies, first line the bottom of an airtight container with wax paper or parchment paper. Then separate each cookie layer with another sheet of paper.

Cool Idea

I never plan on eating more than a few cookies at a time. So I usually make a dozen or less, then put the remaining dough in a plastic bag and store it in the refrigerator, where it will keep for up to two weeks. That way, I can enjoy freshly baked cookies every time!

Chocolate Chip Cookies

Chocolate chip cookies are probably the most popular cookie in America. They are crunchy, sweet, and contain chocolate. They also store and travel well. Need I say more?

Ingredients

1 cup butter (2 sticks), softened
$3/4$ cup firmly packed brown sugar
$3/4$ cup granulated sugar
1 teaspoon vanilla extract
2 eggs
$2^1/4$ cups all-purpose flour
1 teaspoon baking soda
1 teaspoon salt
2 cups semi-sweet chocolate morsels
1 cup coarsely chopped walnuts
  (optional)

Yield: About 3 dozen cookies

1. Place the butter, sugars, and vanilla in a large mixing bowl. Cream with an electric mixer on low speed for 2 to 3 minutes or until light and fluffy. Add the eggs and continue to beat until well blended.

2. Combine the flour, baking soda, and salt in a medium bowl. Add this flour mixture to the creamed mixture a half-cup at a time, and stir with a wooden spoon to form a smooth, sticky dough.

3. Add the chocolate morsels and nuts (if using) to the dough, and stir until well distributed.

4. Drop rounded teaspoons of dough onto an ungreased cookie sheet, leaving at least an inch of space between them.

Stuff You'll Need

5. Bake in a preheated 350°F oven for 10 to 12 minutes, or until light golden brown. Cool for a minute before removing the cookies from the sheet with a spatula. Transfer to a wire rack to finish cooling.

Try These Variations!

The ways you can customize this recipe are practically endless. In addition to the two variations at right, you might want to check out the combinations below.

Other combinations:

▶ Milk chocolate morsels and hazelnuts

▶ White chocolate morsels and macadamia nuts

▶ Semi-sweet chocolate morsels and pecans

Chocolate-Chocolate Chip Cookies

Add

▶ ¹/₄ cup unsweetened cocoa

Add the cocoa in Step 2 of the recipe.

Candy Chocolate Chip Cookies

Substitute

▶ 1 cup candy coated chocolate (like M&M's)

Instead of chocolate morsels, add candy-coated chocolate in Step 3 of the recipe.

Peanut Butter Cookies

Boy oh boy, do I love peanut butter! And when it comes to peanut butter cookies, these are the best! Instead of dropping the dough directly onto a cookie sheet, I usually roll it into balls. Then I flatten the balls with a fork to create this cookie's classic criss-cross pattern. Do you know what this pattern is supposed to look like? Peanut shells, of course!

Ingredients

$1/2$ cup butter (1 stick), softened
$1/2$ cup firmly packed brown sugar
$1/2$ cup granulated sugar
$1/2$ teaspoon vanilla extract
1 egg
1 cup peanut butter
$1 3/4$ cups all-purpose flour
$1/2$ teaspoon baking soda

Yield: About 24 to 30 cookies

Important Tip

You can use smooth, crunchy, organic, low-fat, or any other type of peanut butter you want for these cookies. It's all good!

Stuff You'll Need

1. Place the butter, sugars, and vanilla in a large mixing bowl. Cream with an electric mixer on low speed for 2 to 3 minutes or until light and fluffy. Add the eggs and peanut butter and continue to beat until well blended.

2. Combine the flour and baking soda in a medium bowl. Add this flour mixture to the creamed mixture a half-cup at a time, and stir with a wooden spoon to form a smooth, sticky dough.

3. Roll heaping teaspoons of dough into balls with your hands and place them on an ungreased cookie sheet about 2-inches apart. Flatten the balls with a fork, creating a criss-cross pattern on top.

4. Bake in a preheated 350°F oven for 10 to 12 minutes or until light golden brown. Cool for a few minutes before removing the cookies from the sheet with a spatula. Transfer to a wire rack to finish cooling.

Try These Variations!

Here are a few add-ins to make your peanut butter cookies even more special.

Add ins:

▶ Peanut butter chips

▶ Chocolate morsels

▶ Candy-coated chocolate (like M&M's)

Peanut-Peanut Butter Cookies

Add

▶ 1 cup skinless roasted peanuts

Add the peanuts in Step 2 of the recipe.

Peanut Butter 'n Pieces Cookies

Add

▶ 1 cup candy-coated peanut butter (like Reese's Pieces)

Add the candy-coated pieces in Step 2 of the recipe.

Oat-Rageous Oatmeal Cookies

Oats add mild flavor and texture to many baked goods. What I really love about this cookie recipe is that it lends itself to lots of variations.

Ingredients

$\frac{1}{2}$ cup butter (1 stick), softened

$\frac{1}{2}$ cup firmly packed brown sugar

$\frac{1}{2}$ cup granulated sugar

1 teaspoon vanilla extract

1 egg

1 cup all-purpose flour

$\frac{1}{2}$ teaspoon baking soda

$\frac{1}{2}$ teaspoon baking powder

$\frac{1}{2}$ teaspoon salt

1 cup old-fashioned rolled oats

Yield: About 3 dozen cookies

1. Place the butter, sugar, and vanilla in a large mixing bowl. Cream with an electric mixer on low speed for 2 to 3 minutes or until light and fluffy. Add the egg and continue to beat until well blended.

2. Combine the flour, baking soda, baking powder, and salt in a medium bowl. Add this flour mixture to the creamed mixture a half a cup at a time, and stir with a wooden spoon to form a smooth, sticky dough. Add the oats and stir until well distributed.

3. Drop rounded teaspoons of dough onto a greased cookie sheet, leaving at least an inch of space between them.

Stuff You'll Need

4. Bake in a preheated 350°F oven for 10 to12 minutes or until light golden brown. Cool for a minute before removing the cookies from the sheet with a spatula. Transfer to a wire rack to finish cooling.

Try These Variations!

In addition to the variations at right, check out the following add-ins for this oatmeal cookie. Bet you can think of lots more.

Add Ins:

▶ Peanut butter morsels

▶ Chocolate morsels

▶ Chocolate chunks

Oatmeal-Raisin Cookies

Add

▶ 1 cup brown or golden raisins

Add the raisins in Step 2 of the recipe along with the oats.

Coconut-Oatmeal Cookies

Add

▶ 1 cup sweetened shredded coconut

Add the coconut in Step 2 of the recipe along with the oats.

Try This Variation!

Oat-Butterscotch Cookies

I bought a bag of butterscotch morsels one day and decided to try them with an oatmeal cookie recipe. Here is the very sweet result of that experiment.

Ingredients

$3/4$ cup butter ($1^1/2$ sticks), softened
$3/4$ cup firmly packed brown sugar
$3/4$ cup granulated sugar
1 teaspoon vanilla extract
2 eggs
$1^1/4$ cups all-purpose flour
1 teaspoon baking soda
$1/2$ teaspoon salt
3 cups rolled oats
$1^2/3$ cups butterscotch morsels

Yield: About 4 dozen cookies

1. Follow Steps 1 and 2 of the Oat-Rageous Oatmeal Cookie recipe on page 110. Add the butterscotch chips to the dough in Step 2 along with the oats.

2. Drop rounded teaspoons of dough onto an ungreased cookie sheet, leaving at least an inch of space between them.

3. Bake in a preheated 350°F oven for 10 to 12 minutes or until golden brown. Cool for a minute before removing the cookies from the sheet with a spatula. Transfer to a wire rack to finish cooling.

Coconut Macaroons I

1. Place the coconut, flour, and salt in a large bowl and stir until well combined

These macaroons are simply delicious. Although you can drop the dough from a spoon onto the cookie sheet, I recommend rolling it into balls instead. If you roll the dough, here's a word of advice – be near a faucet with hot water. The dough is very sticky and the condensed milk will stick to your hands, so you have to constantly wash them (your hands, not the cookies).

2. Add the condensed milk and vanilla, and stir until the coconut is well coated.

Ingredients

2$\frac{1}{2}$ cups sweetened flaked coconut
$\frac{1}{3}$ cup all-purpose flour
$\frac{1}{8}$ teaspoon salt
$\frac{2}{3}$ cup sweetened condensed milk
1 teaspoon vanilla extract

Yield: 15 to 20 cookies

3. Line a cookie sheet with parchment paper. Roll heaping teaspoons of dough into balls with your hands, and place them on the cookie sheet at least 2 inches apart.

Stuff You'll Need

4. Bake in a preheated 350°F oven for 12 to 15 minutes or until the tips of the coconut begin to turn golden brown. Let the cookies cool on the cookie sheet.

Coconut Macaroons II

This recipe uses whipped egg whites instead of condensed milk, which makes them extra light.

Ingredients

¹/₂ cup granulated sugar
¹/₄ cup all-purpose flour
¹/₄ teaspoon salt
2 cups sweetened flaked coconut
3 egg whites*
1 teaspoon almond extract

* For egg separating instructions, see page 51.

Yield: 18 to 20 cookies

Stuff You'll Need

1. Place the sugar, flour, salt, and coconut in a large bowl and stir well. Place the egg whites in a medium bowl and beat with an electric mixer until stiff peaks form. Add the beaten egg whites and almond extract to the coconut mixture and stir until the coconut is well coated.

2. Drop rounded teaspoons of dough onto a greased cookie sheet at least 2 inches apart. Bake in a preheated 350°F oven for about 15 minutes or until the tips of the coconut begin to turn golden brown. Let the cookies cool on the cookie sheet.

Try These Variations!

Chocolate Macaroons	Chocolate Chip Macaroons	Diabetic Coconut Macaroons

Add

▶ ¹/₂ cup unsweetened cocoa powder

Follow the directions for Coconut Macaroons I (page 112) and add the cocoa in Step 2.

Add

▶ 1 cup mini chocolate morsels

Follow the directions for Coconut Macaroons II (above) and add the chocolate morsels in Step 2.

Substitute

▶ ³/₄ cup Splenda
▶ 2 cups unsweetened coconut

Follow directions for Coconut Macaroons II, but use Splenda instead of sugar, and unsweetened coconut instead of sweetened.

These cookies are totally nuts!

I'm nuts for nutty cookies! They're great. Nuts add both delicious taste and texture. Lots of recipes have nuts as add-ins, but the ones in this section actually use finely ground nuts instead of or as part of the flour. The "powdery" mixture contains natural nut oils that help create pockets of air in the dough during baking. The result? Cookies that are extra light.

Basic Step for Nut Cookies

Grind

Although you can buy nuts that are already ground, you can also grind them yourself in a food processor, blender, or coffee grinder. To grind nuts evenly, "pulse" them, rather than let the appliance run continuously. And be careful not to "overgrind," as the mixture will turn into butter.

Helpful Tips

▶ Because of their high-fat content, nuts become stale quickly, so be sure to taste them before using. The flavor of a stale nut will ruin any type of dish – guaranteed!

▶ If you use a coffee grinder to grind the nuts, be sure to wash it well before using (unless you want to end up with coffee-flavored cookies).

▶ For nut cookies that are coated with confectioner's sugar (like the Walnut Puffs on page 118 and the Mexican Wedding Cakes on page 117), be sure they are completely cool before rolling them in the sugar. If the cookie is hot (or even warm), the powdery white sugar will begin to melt, become sticky, and turn an unappealing gray.

Storing Nut Cookies

▶ Once baked, cookies with nuts tend to get stale. For this reason, it is best to freeze or refrigerate any leftovers. When properly stored in airtight containers, nutty cookies will last about two weeks in the refrigerator; in the freezer, they'll last for several months. For the fullest flavor, be sure to let the frozen cookies thaw completely before eating

▶ When storing cookies that are coated with confectioner's sugar, first line the bottom of an airtight container with wax paper or parchment. Separate each layer with another sheet of paper.

▶ Be sure to cool the cookies completely before storing.

Flourless Chocolate Nut Cookies

It's hard to believe these cookies are flourless. They are also unleavened, which makes them perfect for some holidays like Passover.

Ingredients

1$\frac{1}{2}$ cups finely ground walnuts

3 cups confectioner's sugar

$\frac{1}{2}$ cup unsweetened cocoa powder

$\frac{1}{4}$ teaspoon salt

4 large egg whites*

1 tablespoon vanilla extract

* For egg separating instructions, see page 51.

Yield: About 2 dozen cookies

Important Tip

The longer you bake these cookies, the crispier they will become. At 15 minutes, they will be crisp on top and chewy like a brownie in the center. At 20 minutes, they will be crisp all the way through.

Stuff You'll Need

1. Place the nuts in a large bowl along with the confectioner's sugar, cocoa, and salt. Stir until well combined.

2. Add the egg whites and vanilla to the bowl and beat with an electric mixer on medium-high speed for about 2 minutes or until the mixture is thick and foamy.

3. Line a cookie sheet with parchment paper. Drop tablespoons of the batter-like dough onto the sheet into 2-inch rounds. Allow at least an inch of space between them.

4. Bake in a preheated 350°F oven for 15 to 20 minutes or until the tops are slightly cracked. Let the cookies cool on the cookie sheet.

Persian Walnut Cookies

Lemon zest and cardamom give these nutty cookies their distinctive Middle Eastern flavor. If, however, you prefer cookies that are plainer – mild and sweet – simply leave these ingredients out. Delicious both ways!

Ingredients

4 egg yolks*
1/4 cup granulated sugar
1 teaspoon vanilla extract
1 1/2 cups finely chopped walnuts
1/2 teaspoon lemon zest (optional)
1/4 teaspoon ground cardamom
   (optional)

* For egg separating instructions, see page 51.

Yield: About 18 to 20 cookies

Important Tip

Since the dough for this recipe is basically nuts covered with sugary syrup, it tends to really spread out during baking. When spooning mounds of dough on the cookie sheet, leave at least 2 inches of space between them.

Stuff You'll Need

1. Place the egg yolks, sugar, and vanilla in a medium mixing bowl. Beat with an electric mixer on low speed for 5 minutes or until the mixture is pale and has the texture of thick syrup.

2. Add the walnuts, lemon zest, and cardamom (if using) and stir well. The egg mixture will tend to separate from the nuts and seep to the bottom of the bowl. So re-stir the mixture occasionally to keep the nuts coated before placing on the cookie sheet.

3. Drop rounded teaspoons onto a parchment-lined cookie sheet, leaving at least 2 inches of space between them.

4. Bake in a preheated 350°F oven for 25 to 30 minutes or until the tops are dry and slightly cracked. Let the cookies cool on the cookie sheet.

Mexican Wedding Cakes

Light and airy, these delicious vanilla-flavored pecan cookies are covered in sweet confectioner's sugar. Try substituting the vanilla with maple extract . . . it's maple-icious!

Ingredients

1 cup butter (2 sticks), softened
$1/4$ cup granulated sugar
2 teaspoons vanilla extract
2 cups finely ground pecans
$1/2$ teaspoon salt
2 cups all-purpose flour
1 cup confectioner's sugar

Yield: About 3 dozen cookies

1. Place the butter, sugar, and vanilla in a large mixing bowl. Cream with an electric mixer on low speed for 2 to 3 minutes or until light and fluffy.

2. Stir the pecans and salt into the creamed mixture with a wooden spoon. Add the flour a half cup at a time, and stir to form a soft, slightly sticky dough.

3. Roll the dough into $1^1/4$-inch balls, and place on an ungreased cookie sheet about an inch apart. Bake in a preheated 350°F oven for 25 to 30 minutes or until lightly browned (some may be slightly cracked).

4. Cool for a minute before removing the cookies from the sheet with a spatula. Transfer to a wire rack and allow to cool completely. Roll the cooled cookies in confectioner's sugar until well coated.

Stuff You'll Need

Walnut Puffs

These cookies and the Mexican Wedding Cakes on page 117 are among my absolute favorites. Both are egg-free and contain no leavening ingredients. Take one bite for a delicious melt-in-your mouth explosion.

Ingredients

2 cups finely ground walnuts
1 cup butter (2 sticks), softened
$1/3$ cup firmly packed brown sugar
$1/2$ teaspoon maple extract
2 cups all-purpose flour
$1/2$ teaspoon salt
1 cup confectioner's sugar

Yield: About 3 dozen cookies

Important Tip

The temperature of the butter is especially critical for this recipe. Be sure it's softened!

Stuff You'll Need

1. Finely grind the walnuts and set aside.

2. Place the butter, brown sugar, and maple extract in a large mixing bowl. Cream with an electric mixer on low speed for 2 to 3 minutes or until light and fluffy.

3. Stir the walnuts and salt into the creamed mixture, then add the flour a half cup at a time, and stir to form a soft, slightly sticky dough.

4. Roll the dough into $1^1/4$-inch balls, and place on an ungreased cookie sheet about an inch apart. Bake in a preheated 350°F oven for 25 to 30 minutes or until lightly browned (some may be slightly cracked).

5. Cool for a minute before removing the cookies from the sheet with a spatula. Transfer to a wire rack and allow to cool completely. Roll the cooled cookies in confectioner's sugar until well coated.

Twice baked is twice as nice.

Biscotti cookies are baked twice, which makes them drier than most other cookies – it also makes them last longer. Excellent for dunking in coffee, serving with ice cream, or simply enjoying on their own, biscotti are truly special (and addictive)! Once you're hooked, you're likely to always have some in your cookie jar.

Basic Steps for Making Biscotti

1. Shape and bake

After making the dough, place it right on the cookie sheet and shape it into a loaf with your hands. Because this dough is characteristically sticky, line the cookie sheet with parchment paper or aluminum foil that has been coated with cooking spray. Bake the loaf according to the recipe instructions.

2. Cut

Once the baked loaf is cool enough to handle, transfer it to a cutting board. Cut it into diagonal slices that are between $1/2$ and $3/4$ inch thick. A long serrated knife is best for this job, especially if the loaf contains whole nuts. Place the slices on an ungreased cookie sheet.

3. Bake again

To take the remaining moisture out of the cut cookies, pop them back into the oven for a few minutes (according to the recipe). This final baking stage makes them extra crunchy and excellent for long-term storage.

Helpful Tips

Biscotti can be a little tricky. Here are a few important tips to help you make perfect batches time and time again.

▶ Lining the cookie sheet with parchment paper (or foil that has been coated with cooking spray) serves two purposes. Most obvious, it prevents the loaf from sticking to the pan. Second, it allows you to use the paper to lift the baked loaf and transfer it easily (and intact) to a cutting board.

▶ For the traditional biscotti-making method (as in the Chocolate Almond Biscotti on page 122), be sure to spend the time and beat the eggs to the right consistency. The egg mixture should thicken somewhat and stream slowly from the beaters.

▶ Stir chips, nuts, or other add-ins into the dough during the final stage. The dough should be the right consistency before adding these items.

▶ To keep the cookies similar in size, lightly score the top of the loaf before cutting.

▶ With a long serrated knife, use a firm, slight sawing motion to cut through the loaf. This is particularly important when the loaf contains hard nuts like almonds (especially whole ones).

Storing Biscotti

▶ Biscotti keep fresher much longer than regular cookies. Stored in an airtight container, they will keep up to six weeks. In the freezer, they can last for many months.

▶ Be sure to cool the cookies completely before storing.

A Classic Italian Tradition

In Italian, *biscotti* means "biscuits," which for most English-speaking countries outside of North America is another term for "cookies." More specifically, the word actually means "twice cooked/baked." Because this cookie is baked twice, it is basically a dehydrated food, which means it can be stored for long periods of time.

The origins of biscotti can be traced back to ancient Rome, where this cookie served as a staple food that helped sustain travelers on long journeys. Biscotti was particularly handy during periods of war, when the Roman legions would take plenty of *biscoctus* with them on their long sieges. Unfortunately, they didn't have any coffee to dunk the hard cookies in. Between that and poor oral hygiene, it's no wonder they were always so darn cranky!

In addition to lasting a long time, biscotti is also resistant to mold, which may be why Christopher Columbus took it along on his sea voyages.

Chocolate Almond Biscotti

The crunch of almonds combined with the rich taste of chocolate makes this traditional biscotti one of the most popular varieties.

Ingredients

4 squares (1 ounce each) semi-sweet baking chocolate

2 eggs

1 cup granulated sugar

$1/4$ cup vegetable oil

1 teaspoon vanilla extract

$1^1/2$ cups coarsely chopped blanched almonds

2 cups all-purpose flour

$1/2$ teaspoon baking soda

$1/2$ teaspoon baking powder

$1/2$ teaspoon salt

Yield: About 2 dozen cookies

Stuff You'll Need

1. Coarsely chop the chocolate and set aside.

2. Place the eggs, sugar, oil, and vanilla in a large mixing bowl. Beat with an electric mixer on medium speed for 5 minutes or until the mixture thickens and streams slowly from the beaters (as shown).

3. Combine the flour, baking soda, baking powder, and salt in a medium bowl. Add the flour mixture to the egg mixture a half cup at a time, and stir with a wooden spoon to form a soft, sticky dough. Add the almonds and stir until well distributed.

4. Line a cookie sheet with parchment paper or aluminum foil that's been coated with cooking spray. Form the dough into a 15-x-3-inch loaf on the cookie sheet with your hands. Bake in a preheated 350°F oven for 25 minutes or until lightly browned.

5. Let the loaf sit about 15 minutes or until it is cool enough to handle, then transfer to a cutting board. Using a long serrated knife, cut the loaf diagonally into $3/4$-inch slices.

6. Arrange the slices on an ungreased cookie sheet and bake in a 350°F oven for 10 to 15 minutes or until toasted. Allow the cookies to cool right on the cookie sheet.

Important Tip

The most crucial part of this recipe is getting the egg mixture to the right consistency – should be somewhat thick. Be sure to beat it for at least 5 minutes. I use a timer to make sure I give it the full amount of time (the minutes go by pretty slowly when using an electric mixer).

White Chocolate Macadamia Biscotti

Here is a chewier Americanized version of biscotti. Some people prefer this to the more authentic tooth-cracking cookie. Me? I luv 'em both!

Ingredients

1/2 cup butter (1 stick), softened
3/4 cup granulated sugar
1 teaspoon vanilla extract
1/2 teaspoon almond extract
2 eggs
2 cups all-purpose flour
1 1/2 teaspoons baking powder
1/4 teaspoon salt
1 cup white chocolate morsels
1/2 cup chopped macadamia nuts

Yield: About 2 dozen cookies

Important Tip

If you prefer drier, crispier cookies, continue baking up to 10 minutes longer than the recipe indicates. The longer they bake, the crispier they'll be.

Stuff You'll Need

1. Place the butter, sugar, and vanilla and a large mixing bowl. Cream with an electric mixer on low speed for 2 to 3 minutes or until light and fluffy. Add the eggs and continue to beat until well blended.

2. Combine the flour, baking powder, and salt in a medium bowl. Add this flour mixture to the creamed mixture a half cup at a time, and stir with a wooden spoon to form a soft, sticky dough. Add the macadamia nuts and white chocolate morsels and stir until well distributed.

3. Line a cookie sheet with parchment paper or aluminum foil that's been coated with cooking spray. Form the dough into a 15-x-3-inch loaf on the cookie sheet with your hands. Bake in a preheated 350°F oven for 25 minutes or until lightly browned.

4. Let the loaf sit about 15 minutes or until it is cool enough to handle, then transfer to a cutting board. Using a long serrated knife, cut the loaf diagonally into 3/4-inch slices.

5. Arrange the slices on an ungreased cookie sheet.

6. Return the cookies to the oven for 10 to 15 minutes or until lightly toasted. Allow them to cool right on the cookie sheet.

Try This Variation!

With this recipe, you can use lots of delicious add-ins.

Other Combinations:

▶ Semi-sweet chocolate morsels and almonds

▶ Milk chocolate morsels and hazelnuts

▶ Butterscotch morsels and semi-sweet chocolate morsels

Almond Biscotti

Substitute

▶ 1 cup whole almonds

Substitute the almonds for the white chocolate and macadamia nuts in Step 2 of the recipe.

Refrigerator cookies are like, totally . . . cool!

Refrigerator cookies, or "roll cookies" as they are also known, are made from dough that is so soft and sticky it has to be refrigerated before being shaped and baked. The coolest thing about these cookies is that you can form and cut the dough into many different shapes.

Basic Steps for Making Refrigerator Cookie Dough

1. Cream

The first step for most refrigerator cookie recipes involves beating together sugar with a fat, like butter, margarine, or shortening, which creates air pockets in the fat to help make the cookies light. Extracts can also be included in this process, and eggs are often blended into the creamed mixture.

2. Stir

After creaming the butter and sugar, it's time to grab a wooden spoon and stir in the dry ingredients – typically a mixture of flour, salt, baking powder and/or baking soda – to form a smooth, soft, and very sticky dough.

3. Refrigerate

Refrigerator cookies have a high butter to flour ratio, so chilling the dough brings the butter back to a more solid form. This makes the dough easier to handle, roll, shape, and form. Before refrigerating, wrap the prepared dough in plastic wrap, or place it in a covered container or plastic storage bag.

Basic Method for Forming Refrigerator Cookies

1. Unwrap the chilled dough
Place the dough on a clean flat surface that has been sprinkled with flour. If the dough is very hard, let it sit a minute to soften a bit.

2. Flatten
Roll out the dough evenly to an approximate 1/4-inch thickness. You can flatten it with a rolling pin, a bottle, or even your hands.

3. Cut out shapes
One way to cut out shapes in the dough is with a cookie cutter. You can also use a sharp knife, a pastry cutter, or the rim of a drinking glass.

Helpful Tips

▶ To prevent the dough from sticking to the rolling pin, rub it with a little flour. But don't add any additional flour to the dough, as this will change its texture.

▶ Be sure to refrigerate the dough for the required time, or it may be too sticky to roll out or to shape. Refrigerating past the suggested time is fine; however, the dough may become too stiff to work with. If this happens, just let it sit out a room temperature for a short while.

▶ When flattening dough, you can roll it out directly on a clean flat surface or on a clean sheet of wax paper. (Both should be lightly sprinkled with flour.) I prefer rolling on the wax paper, which I find neater and easier. I also use the flexibility of the paper to remove the cut-out dough shapes more efficiently.

▶ Instead of refrigerating the dough, you can prepare the cookies like drop cookies (page 104). Drop rounded teaspoons of the dough (it will be sticky) on a parchment-lined cookie sheet at least an inch apart, and bake according to the recipe.

Try These Shaping Methods, Too!

Roll into balls and flatten
Instead of flattening out the dough with a rolling pin, you can roll it into balls, place the balls on a cookie sheet, and then flatten them with the bottom of a drinking glass.

Slice from a roll
Before refrigerating the dough, form it into a long roll (about 2 inches in diameter is standard). Once the roll is chilled, cut it into uniform 3/8- to 1/2-inch-thick slices.

Storing Cool Cookies

▶ Be sure to cool the cookies completely before storing them in an airtight container. Most varieties will stay fresh up to a week. They will keep for a few weeks in the refrigerator, and a few months in the freezer.

Sugar Cookies

As their name implies, these cookies are sugary sweet. This basic recipe produces cookies that are crisp, light, and delicious. Although they are great as is, check out Chapter 14 for lots of decorating ideas.

Ingredients

1 cup butter (2 sticks), softened
$^2/_3$ cup granulated sugar
1 teaspoon vanilla extract
1 egg
2$^1/_4$ cups all-purpose flour
$^1/_2$ teaspoon salt

Yield: About 3 dozen cookies

Important Tip

To make drop cookies with this recipe, don't refrigerate the dough. Drop rounded teaspoons onto an ungreased cookie sheet and follow the baking instructions in Step 6.

Stuff You'll Need

1. Place the butter, sugar, and vanilla in a large mixing bowl. Cream with an electric mixer on medium speed for 2 to 3 minutes or until light and fluffy. Add the egg and continue to beat until well blended.

2. Combine the flour and salt in a medium bowl. Add the flour mixture to the creamed mixture a half cup at a time, and stir with a wooden spoon to form a smooth dough that is not too stiff.

3. Loosely form the dough into a ball or loaf and either cover with saran wrap or place in a plastic storage bag. Refrigerate 2 to 3 hours or until chilled and firm.

4. Lightly sprinkle a clean flat surface with flour. Place the dough on top and flatten with a rolling pin to a $^1/_4$-inch thickness.

5. Using a cookie cutter or the rim of a glass, cut shapes into the flattened dough. Place on an ungreased cookie sheet about an inch apart. Gather up the excess dough and roll it out again to make more cookies.

6. Bake in a preheated 350°F oven for 8 to 10 minutes or until the edges are slightly browned. Cool for a minute before removing the cookies from the sheet with a spatula.

Try This Variation!
Sugar Tots

For this Sugar Cookie variation, you don't have to chill the dough.

Add

▶ Fruit jams or preserves

▶ Pecan or walnut halves

Yield: About 30 to 36 cookies

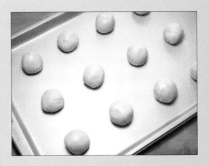

1. Prepare the dough according to Steps 1 and 2 of the recipe. Roll heaping teaspoons of the dough into balls and place on an ungreased cookie sheet at least an inch apart.

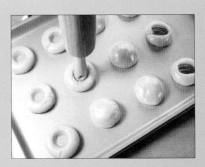

2. Using your thumb or the end of a rolling pin, press a well into each ball. Spoon some jam into the wells or press a nut into the center.

3. Bake in a preheated 350°F oven for 10 to 12 minutes or until the cookies are a light golden brown.

Ginger Snappies

I am not a big fan of ginger, but I love ginger snappies. They're really addicting, so be careful!

Ingredients

³/₄ cup butter (1¹/₂ sticks), softened
¹/₂ cup granulated sugar
¹/₂ cup firmly packed brown sugar
¹/₄ cup molasses
1 teaspoon vanilla extract
1 egg
2 cups all-purpose flour
¹/₂ teaspoon baking soda
2 teaspoons ground cinnamon
2 teaspoons ground ginger
¹/₄ teaspoon salt

Yield: About 2 dozen cookies

Important Tip

Because of the sticky molasses in this recipe, the dough must be refrigerated!

Stuff You'll Need

1. Place the butter, sugars, molasses, and vanilla in a large mixing bowl. Cream with an electric mixer on medium speed for 2 to 3 minutes or until light and fluffy. Add the egg and continue to beat until well blended.

2. Combine the flour, baking soda, cinnamon, and ginger. Add this to the creamed mixture a half cup at a time, and stir with a wooden spoon to form a soft, sticky dough. Cover and refrigerate for 3 hours.

3. Roll the chilled dough into balls about an inch in diameter, then roll them in granulated sugar until fully coated.

4. Place the balls on a parchment-lined (or greased) cookie sheet about 2 inches apart. Flatten them with the bottom of a glass.

5. Bake in a preheated 350°F oven for 10 to 12 minutes or until lightly browned. Cool for a few minutes before removing the cookies from the sheet with a spatula. Transfer to a wire rack to finish cooling.

Almond Crispies

These cookies are aptly named. The shortening gives them a pastry-like lightness and "crispitiness."

Ingredients

$1/2$ cup shortening

$3/4$ cup granulated sugar

1 teaspoon almond extract

2 eggs, separated*

$1/4$ cup milk

2 cups all-purpose flour

$1/2$ cup ground almonds

$1\ 1/2$ teaspoons baking soda

1 teaspoon cream of tartar

$1/8$ teaspoon salt

* For egg separating instructions, see page 51.

Yield: About 3 dozen crispies

Important Tip

Keep a close eye on these cookies near the end of baking time. They burn very quickly!

Stuff You'll Need

1. Place the shortening, sugar, and almond extract in a large mixing bowl. Cream with an electric mixer on medium speed for 2 to 3 minutes or until light and fluffy. Add the egg yolks and milk, and continue to beat until well blended.

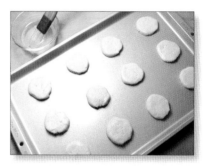

2. Combine the remaining ingredients in a medium bowl. Add this mixture to the creamed mixture a half cup at a time, and stir with a wooden spoon to form a soft, sticky dough.

3. Divide the dough in half. Form two 12-inch rolls about 2 inches in diameter. Wrap and refrigerate until chilled and firm, then cut the logs into $3/8$-thick slices.

4. Place the slices on a lightly greased cookie sheet. Beat the egg whites, then brush some on each slice with a pastry brush.

5. Bake in a preheated 350°F oven for 10 to 12 minutes, or until the edges are light golden brown. Cool for a minute, then transfer the cookies to a wire rack to finish cooling.

Mama's Shortbread

Here's a cookie with just four (count 'em four) ingredients. Shortbread is so easy to make, yet it's rich, buttery, and crunchy to boot!

Ingredients

1 cup butter (2 sticks), softened
$1/2$ cup confectioner's sugar
1 teaspoon vanilla extract
2 cups all-purpose flour

Yield: About 2 dozen cookies

Stuff You'll Need

1. Place the butter, sugar, and vanilla in a large mixing bowl. Cream with an electric mixer on medium speed for 2 to 3 minutes or until light and fluffy.

2. Add the flour to the creamed mixture a half cup at a time, and stir with a wooden spoon to form a soft, sticky dough.

3. Either place the dough in a covered container or cover it with plastic wrap. You could also seal it in a plastic storage bag. Refrigerate at least 1 hour or until chilled and firm.

4. Lightly sprinkle a clean flat surface with flour. Place the dough on top and flatten with a rolling pin to a $1/4$-inch thickness.

5. Using a cookie cutter or the rim of a glass, cut shapes into the flattened dough. Place on an ungreased cookie sheet about an inch apart. Gather up the excess dough and roll it out again to make more cookies.

6. Bake in a preheated 350°F oven for 10 to 12 minutes or until the edges are light golden brown. Cool for a minute before removing the cookies from the sheet with a spatula. Transfer to a wire rack to finish cooling.

Try This Variation!

Here's an even easier way to form shortbread cookies.

1. Instead of rolling out the dough in Step 4, press it into a 9-inch pie or cake pan. Score the dough with a sharp knife so the cookies will be easy to cut once baked. And poke holes in the dough with a fork to keep it from blistering as it bakes.

2. Bake in a preheated 350°F oven for 18 to 20 minutes or until light golden brown. Let cool for 5 minutes, then cut along the scored lines and remove the cookies from the pan.

Kooky for Cookies

Whether they are plain or fancy, soft and chewy, or crisp and crunchy, cookies are always a welcome treat. They are loved and appreciated throughout the world.

A Cookie by Any Other Name

By definition, a cookie is a small flat or slightly raised cake. It doesn't have to be sweet or crunchy. The word cookie is derived from the Dutch word *koekje*, which means "small cake." In Germany, cookies are *keks*; in Spain they are *galletas*; and in Italy, the general term is *biscotti*.

Chocolate Chip, the "All-American Cookie"

The chocolate chip cookie was the accidental creation of Ruth Wakefield, owner of the Toll House Inn in Massachusetts. While attempting to make chocolate cookies for her guests at the Inn, Ruth ran out of baking chocolate when mixing the batter. So she broke some Nestle's semi-sweet chocolate bars into pieces, thinking they would melt into the batter. They didn't – and chocolate chip cookies were born! (She called them Toll House Crunch Cookies.) As the popularity of the cookie grew, so did the sale of Nestle's chocolate. Ruth eventually allowed Nestle to print her recipe on its packaging. In return, she received a lifetime supply of chocolate chips.

Animal Crackers in My Soup

In 1903, Nabisco introduced the animal cracker – the first commercial cookie sold in the United States. An immediate hit, the bite-sized cookies came packaged in unique brightly colored boxes that looked like circus cages filled with animals. Once empty, the boxes were designed to be used as Christmas tree ornaments, which is why a string runs across the top. Over the years, there have been nearly forty different animal-shaped cookies. Currently, about 40 million boxes of animal crackers are produced every year. The cookies are baked at a rate of 12,000 per minute in an oven that is the length of a football field. Over 15,000 cartons and 300,000 cookies are produced in a single day. More than 8,000 miles of string are used each year for the packaging.

I Ate Over 300 Cookies Last Year!

Americans eat an estimated 2 billion cookies a year. That's about 300 per person! Cookies manufactured in the United States are also popular around the world.

The Japanese Love Their Fish!

Eel cookies are popular in Japan. These tasty treats are made with eel bones, eel extract, and garlic. I wonder if they serve them with milk? Eel milk perhaps?

Door-to-Door Cookies

The Girl Scouts have been selling cookies since 1917. Thin Mints are the most popular variety, accounting for 25 percent of sales. Although many Girl Scouts still sell their cookies door to door, it has become an increasingly popular trend to sell from tables and booths that are set up in high-traffic areas. In 2008, a fifteen-year-old from Dearborn, Michigan, sold an amazing 17,328 boxes of cookies! Of course 17,000 of them went to her parents, grandparents, and other relatives (just kidding!).

Brownies Are Square, Man! 136
   Bitchin' Brownies, 138
   Chocoroon Brownies, 140
   Soufflé Brownies, 142
   Beautiful Blondies, 144

Belly Up to the Bar 146
   E-Zay Lemon Squares, 148
   Chocolate Pecan Bars, 150
   Pumpkin Cheesecake Bars, 152
   5-Layer Choconut Bars, 154
   Chocoberry Oaties, 156

Squares don't hang out in bars

What do brownies, lemon squares, and chocolate pecan bars have in common? They are all baked in square or rectangular pans, and then cut into individual squares or rectangular bar shapes. But while their shapes may be similar, baked goods that fall into this "catchall" category can be very different. A brownie, for instance, is more like a cake, while a chocolate pecan bar is more like a cookie. And a lemon square is like a luscious mini pastry. Ready for some good news? This chapter has 'em all.

The first place I'll be taking you is "Brownie Town" (sometimes referred to as "Squaresville"). There are two types of brownies that reside there. The first is the traditional (*yee-haw!*) American-style brownie, which is like a rich, dense cake. The second is a special (*ooh-la-la!*) French-style brownie that uses beaten eggs to make them extra light.

After leaving "Brownie Town," we'll be hittin' some bars. Cookie bars, cheesecake bars, oat bars . . . mmmm. Although some of the luscious treats in this section may be referred to as bars, they can be called squares as well. It all depends on how you cut 'em. And what a great selection of recipes there are. Cheesecake enthusiasts will flip for the light and luscious Pumpkin-Cheesecake Bars, while cookie lovers are sure to enjoy the 5-Layer Choconut Bars – straight from my grandma's recipe files. You'll find these jewels and a whole lot more.

So let's stay up late and try out a few bars tonight. Just watch out for that sugar hangover in the morning!

Check out these brownies, Daddy-O!

I think brownies are real cool – no, I mean hot! For the novice baker, brownie recipes are especially great. They're really easy to prepare and practically foolproof. They also lend themselves to a wide range of variations. The same goes for blondies, which are like brownies in shape and texture, but flavored with brown sugar instead of chocolate. Man, I think you're really gonna dig these squares!

Basic Steps for Making Brownies and Blondies

1. Cream

The first step for making most brownies involves beating together sugar with a fat, like butter, margarine, or shortening, which creates air pockets in the fat to help make the brownies light. Extracts can also be included in this process, and eggs are often blended into the creamed mixture.

2. Stir

After creaming the mixture, it's time to grab a wooden spoon and stir in the dry ingredients – typically a mixture of flour, salt, baking powder and/or baking soda – to form the batter.

3. Add extras

Once the batter is ready, many brownie recipes include "add-ins" – like chocolate morsels, nuts, candy pieces, and/or coconut. These add-ins, which are mixed into the batter until they are well distributed, can be part of the recipe itself or used to make delicious brownie variations.

Helpful Tips

▶ Since chocolate is the main flavoring in brownies, try to use good-quality chocolate or cocoa powder (unsweetened). Better-quality chocolate results in better-quality brownies.

▶ Use the size pan that is called for in the recipe instructions. Variations can throw off baking times and affect texture. If the pan is too large, the brownies will come out thin, dry, and hard; if the pan is too small, the batter will rise too high and result in brownies that are too "cakey."

▶ If using a glass baking pan rather than a metal one, lower the oven temperature 25°F.

▶ Brownies tend to stick to the baking pan. For this reason, it is important to grease and flour the pan (even a nonstick type) before adding the batter. Or you can line the bottom of the pan with parchment paper (see page 59 for details). Be aware, however, that even if you use parchment, you'll still have to grease and flour the sides of the pan.

▶ Begin testing your brownies for doneness shortly before the time that's indicated in the recipe. The perfect moment of doneness is the first moment a toothpick inserted into the center of the brownies comes out clean. Underbaked brownies tend to be wet in the center (especially those in the middle of the pan), while overbaked brownies are likely to be dry and hard.

▶ Before cutting those freshly baked brownies, be sure to give them plenty of time to cool, especially if they contain moist add-ins like chocolate morsels. If you cut brownies while warm, they won't hold together well.

▶ When it comes to serving size, a standard brownie is generally a 2-inch square (approximately). The recipe yields in this chapter are based on that size.

Storing Brownies

▶ Allow brownies to cool completely before storing

▶ Cover a pan of leftover uncut brownies with foil or place the entire pan in a resealable plastic storage bag. They should keep for a few days. (Refrigerate if they contain cream cheese or other perishable ingredient.) To keep cut brownies fresher longer, store them in an airtight container in the refrigerator, where they will keep up to a week. In the freezer, they will keep up to three months.

▶ Before freezing brownies, it is best to wrap them individually in plastic wrap before placing them in a freezer bag or an airtight container.

Add-Ins

Brownies and blondies are good on their own. With add-ins, they're even better!

▶ **Nuts**

Almonds, Cashews,
Hazelnuts, Macadamias,
Peanuts, Pecans,
Pistachios, Walnuts

▶ **Morsels/Chips/Chunks**

Butterscotch
Milk chocolate
Peanut butter
Semi-sweet chocolate
White chocolate

▶ **Candy**

Chocolate bars, chopped
Coated chocolate (M&M's)
Coated peanut butter
(Reese's Pieces)

▶ **Dried Fruit**

Coconut, flaked/shredded
Dates, chopped
Raisins, brown and golden

Bitchin' Brownies

These are true blue all-American brownies. Enjoy them as is or with added goodies like nuts or chocolate morsels. Try them warm topped with vanilla ice cream – nirvana!

Ingredients

¹/₂ cup butter (1 stick), softened
1 cup granulated sugar
1 teaspoon vanilla extract
2 eggs
1 cup all-purpose flour
¹/₃ cup unsweetened cocoa powder
¹/₄ teaspoon baking powder
¹/₄ teaspoon salt

Yield: 16 brownies

1. Place the butter, sugar, and vanilla in a large mixing bowl. Cream with an electric mixer on low speed for 2 to 3 minutes or until light and fluffy. Add the eggs and continue to beat until well blended.

2. Combine the flour, cocoa, baking powder, and salt in a medium bowl. Add this flour mixture to the creamed mixture a half-cup at a time, and stir with a wooden spoon to form a smooth batter.

3. Pour the batter into a greased and floured 8-inch square baking pan, and smooth with a rubber spatula. Bake in a preheated 350°F oven for 30 minutes, or until a toothpick inserted into the center comes out clean.

Stuff You'll Need

4. Allow the brownies to cool at least 20 minutes before cutting into squares. Serve warm or at room temperature.

Try This Variation!

Marble Brownies

For this variation, a wonderfully rich cream cheese topping is swirled over the batter to create a marble effect.

Add

▶ 4 ounces cream cheese, at room temperature
▶ $1/4$ cup granulated sugar
▶ 1 egg
▶ 1 tablespoon flour

1. Prepare the batter according to Steps 1 and 2 of the recipe and spread it evenly in the baking pan. Next, place the cream cheese, sugar, egg, and flour in a medium bowl and beat until smooth.

2. Pour the cream cheese mixture on top of the batter and swirl it with a butter knife or rubber spatula to create the look of marble.

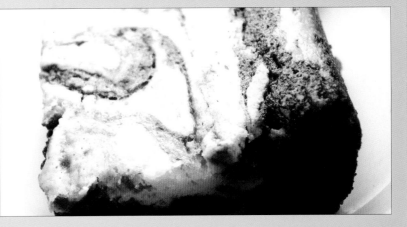

3. Bake in a preheated 350°F oven for 35 to 40 minutes or until a toothpick comes out clean when inserted into the center. Allow the brownies to cool for at least 20 minutes before cutting.

Try This Variation!

If Bitchin' Brownies aren't chocolaty enough for you, this double-chocolate variation should do the trick!

Chocolate-Chocolate Brownies

Add

▶ $3/4$ cup semi-sweet chocolate morsels

Mix the chocolate morsels into the batter at the end of Step 2 of the recipe.

Chocoroon Brownies

*If you're in the mood for a brownie **and** a macaroon, these fantastic Chocoroons are the perfect choice!*

Ingredients

¹/₂ cup butter (1 stick), softened
1 cup granulated sugar
2 teaspoons vanilla extract, divided
2 eggs
1 cup all-purpose flour
¹/₄ cup unsweetened cocoa powder
¹/₂ teaspoon cream of tartar
2 cups sweetened shredded coconut
³/₄ cup sweetened condensed milk

Yield: 16 chocoroons

Important Tips

▶ The coconutty bottom layer of these brownies is dense and sticky, so be sure to line the bottom of the pan with parchment paper.

▶ Chocoroons are hard to cut while in the pan. It's best to remove the cooled brownie in one piece and then cut it on a cutting board. First run a knife along the edge of the pan to loosen it, then lift it out with the help of a spatula (the parchment will help keep it together).

Stuff You'll Need

1. Place the butter, sugar, and 1 teaspoon of the vanilla in a large mixing bowl. Cream with an electric mixer on low speed for 2 to 3 minutes or until light and fluffy. Add the eggs and continue to beat until well blended.

2. Combine the flour, cocoa powder, and cream of tartar in a medium bowl. Add this flour mixture to the creamed mixture a half-cup at a time, and stir with a wooden spoon to form a smooth batter.

3. Place the coconut, condensed milk, and remaining vanilla extract in a separate medium bowl. Stir until well combined.

4. Line the bottom of an 8-inch square baking pan with parchment paper and grease the sides. Spread the coconut mixture evenly over the bottom with a rubber spatula.

5. Spread the chocolate batter over the coconut. Bake in a preheated 350°F oven for 30 minutes, or until a toothpick inserted in the center comes out clean. Let cool for an hour, then remove the entire brownie from the pan (see Important Tip at left). Cut into squares and serve.

Soufflé Brownies

These are the brownies I grew up with. They are richer, sweeter, and denser than most standard brownie varieties. They may be different from what you're used to, but we're talking brownies here – so you know they gotta be good!

Ingredients

¹/₂ cup butter (1 stick)
4 ounces semi-sweet baking chocolate
4 eggs
Pinch salt
2 cups granulated sugar
¹/₂ teaspoon vanilla extract
1 cup all-purpose flour
1 cup pecan or walnut halves (optional)

Yield: About 24 brownies

Important Tips

▶ Be sure to whip the eggs at least 5 minutes – the foamier the better.

▶ For this recipe, the less stirring the better. When adding ingredients to the batter in Steps 3 and 4, stir until almost blended. And stir gently.

Stuff You'll Need

1. Cut up the butter, break up the chocolate, and place in the top of a double boiler over medium-low heat, or in a medium saucepan over *very low* heat. Stir until melted, then remove from the heat and let cool.

2. Place the eggs and salt in a large mixing bowl. Beat with an electric mixer on high speed at least 5 minutes or until very foamy.

3. Add the cooled chocolate mixture to the eggs. Gently stir until almost blended.

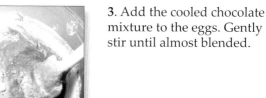

4. Sprinkle the flour over the batter and continue to stir until almost blended.

5. Add the pecans (if using). Continue to gently stir until the nuts are well distributed and the batter is uniform in color.

6. Pour the batter into a greased and floured 13-x-9-inch baking pan, and smooth with a rubber spatula. Bake in a preheated 350°F oven for 30 minutes or until a toothpick inserted into the center comes out clean.

7. Allow the brownies to cool at least 20 minutes before cutting into squares. Serve warm or at room temperature.

Beautiful Blondies

Blondies are like brownies, only without the chocolate. I used to make these when I was in my youth (or as they say in Brooklyn, "yout'") and didn't have a lot of baking ingredients around the house. Fortunately, I usually had the basic ingredients needed for this recipe, which often saved me when I had a desperate craving for sweets.

Ingredients

4 tablespoons butter ($1/2$ stick)
1 cup firmly packed brown sugar
1 egg
1 teaspoon vanilla extract
$1/2$ cup all-purpose flour
1 teaspoon baking powder
$1/4$ teaspoon salt

Yield: 16 blondies

Stuff You'll Need

1. Melt the butter in a small saucepan over a low heat.

2. Pour the hot melted butter into a large mixing bowl. Add the brown sugar and stir until completely dissolved. Add the egg and vanilla and continue to stir until well blended.

3. Combine the flour, baking powder, and salt in a small bowl. Add to the brown sugar mixture and stir to form a smooth batter.

4. Pour the batter into a greased and floured 8-inch square baking pan, and smooth with a rubber spatula.

5. Bake in a preheated 350°F oven for 25 to 30 minutes or until a toothpick inserted into the center comes out clean. Let cool at least 20 minutes before cutting into squares. Serve warm or at room temperature.

Try These Variations!

Be sure to try these delicious variations of Beautiful Blondies. Or have fun creating your own. Here are just some of the many add-ins I've used to make my blondies extra special.

Add-ins

▶ Butterscotch morsels

▶ White chocolate morsels

▶ Walnuts

▶ Macadamia nuts

▶ Pecans

Maple Walnut Blondies

Add

▶ ½ teaspoon maple extract

▶ 1 cup walnuts

Add the maple extract in Step 2 of the recipe, and the walnuts at the end of Step 3.

Coconut Blondies

Add

▶ 1 cup sweetened flaked coconut

Add the coconut at the end of Step 3.

You can take a bar out of a square, but you can't take a . . .

There's nothing better than a super-thick cookie – or a portable pie or cheesecake. The dessert bars (or squares, depending how you cut them) on the following pages are varied, but they have a few things in common – they're all prepared in square or rectangular pans, most have a bottom crust, and all are really delicious! Because they're very rich and flavorful, small portions are ideal. Of course, you can always have more than one!

Basic Steps for Making Dessert-Bar Pastry Crusts

1. Cut

The first step for making most of the pastry crusts in this section involves cutting cold butter into a flour mixture until it resembles a crumbly meal. Do this with a pastry blender, two knives in a criss-cross motion, or a wooden spoon with a stabbing motion. (For cutting instructions, see page 55.)

2. Form

Once the butter has been cut into the flour, gather up the moist pieces with your hands and press them together into a ball of dough. Don't squeeze, knead, or over press the dough, as this will result in a tough crust.

3. Shape

Using your hands, press the dough to an even thickness on the bottom of the baking pan. Prebake the bottom crust until the edges are lightly browned. If you don't bake it long enough, it will get soggy when the topping is added. And if you bake it too long, it will become brittle.

Basic Steps for Making Dessert-Bar Cookie Crusts

1. Crush
The first step for making the cookie crusts in this section involves crushing the cookies or graham crackers into crumbs. Place the cookies in a large plastic storage bag, then roll over the bag with a rolling pin. It's simple and mess-free. You can also use a food processor to do this.

2. Add
Melted butter is generally stirred into the crumbs to bind them together. When stirring these ingredients, be sure that all the crumbs are coated with butter. This will help form a solid crust that stays together.

3. Shape
Using you hands, pat the mixture to an even thickness on the bottom of the baking pan. You can leave the crust as is, or further compress it with the bottom of a glass. Compressing will result in an even firmer, flatter bottom crust.

Helpful Tips

▶ Always use the pan size that's indicated in the recipe instructions. Variations can throw off baking times and affect texture. If the pan is too large, the bars/squares may come out too thin and dry. If the pan is too small, the center may be undercooked; also, the bars/squares might be too thick and more "cakey" than they should be.

▶ Pay close attention to the temperature of the butter as instructed in the recipe, especially when preparing crusts. Butter can be melted, softened, or cold. The different consistencies affect the quality of the crust – the colder the butter, the lighter the crust.

▶ Because of the fluctuations in oven temperatures, begin checking the bars/squares for doneness a few minutes before the time suggested in the recipe.

▶ When prebaking a bottom pastry crust, be sure it bakes until the edges are lightly browned. If you don't bake it long enough, it will get soggy when the topping is added. And if you bake it too long, it will become brittle.

▶ Use a sharp knife for cutting.

▶ When it comes to the recipe yields in this chapter, the dessert bars are approximately 2-x-3 inches in size. The squares are 2-x-2 inches.

Storing Dessert Bars

▶ Dessert bars and squares and should be cooled and stored right in the baking pan.

▶ To keep them fresher longer, cut them as you need them.

▶ Cover the pan of uncut leftovers with foil or place the entire pan in a resealable plastic storage bag. They should keep for a few days. (Refrigerate if they contain cream cheese or other perishable ingredient.) To keep cut dessert bars/squares fresher longer, store them in an airtight container in the refrigerator, where they will keep up to a week. In the freezer, they will keep up to three months.

E-Zay Lemon Squares

Easy to make and fun to eat! For best results, use freshly squeezed lemon juice.

Ingredients

1 cup butter (2 sticks)
2 cups all-purpose flour
1 cup confectioner's sugar

Topping

4 eggs
2 cups granulated sugar
$\frac{1}{4}$ cup all-purpose flour
1 teaspoon baking powder
$\frac{3}{4}$ cup fresh lemon juice (about
  4 large lemons)

Yield: About 24 squares

Stuff You'll Need

1. Melt the butter in a small saucepan over medium-low heat. Set aside to cool.

2. Pour the melted butter in a large mixing bowl. Add the flour and sugar, and stir to form a smooth dough.

3. Press the dough evenly on the bottom of an ungreased 13-x-9-inch baking pan with your hands. Bake in a preheated 350°F oven for 15 minutes or until the edge of the crust has browned slightly. Remove from the oven and set aside to cool. (Leave the oven on.)

4. Place all the topping ingredients in a large mixing bowl. Beat with an electric mixer on high speed for at least 2 minutes or until the mixture is foamy.

5. Pour the lemon mixture over the cooled crust, and return to the oven for 30 minutes or until the center has set (it doesn't jiggle when you *gently* shake it).

6. Remove from the oven and let cool for about an hour. Sprinkle confectioner's sugar over the top.

7. Cut into squares or bars with a sharp knife. Serve warm (my favorite), at room temperature, or cold from the refrigerator.

Chocolate Pecan Bars

These bars are like big, thick "crispity" cookies.

Ingredients

1 cup butter (2 sticks), cold
1$\frac{1}{2}$ cups all-purpose flour
1 cup confectioner's sugar
$\frac{1}{3}$ cup unsweetened cocoa powder

Topping

14-ounce can sweetened
  condensed milk
1 egg
2 teaspoons vanilla extract
1$\frac{1}{2}$ cups finely chopped pecans

Yield: 18 bars

Stuff You'll Need

1. Cut the butter in small pieces. Combine the flour, sugar, and cocoa in large mixing bowl. Cut the butter into the dry ingredients until it resembles a crumbly meal. Gather the mixture with your hands and form it into a ball of dough.

2. Press the dough evenly on the bottom of an ungreased 13-x-9-inch baking pan with your hands. Bake in a preheated 350°F oven for 15 minutes or until the edge of the crust has browned slightly. Remove from the oven and set aside to cool. (Leave the oven on.)

3. To make the topping, place the condensed milk, egg, and vanilla in a large mixing bowl. Beat with an electric mixer on high speed for 2 minutes or until the mixture is foamy.

4. Add the pecans to the topping mixture and stir well.

5. Pour the topping over the crust, and return to the oven for 20 to 25 minutes or until the center has set (it doesn't jiggle when you *gently* shake it). Cool at least 20 minutes before cutting into bars. Serve at room temperature.

Pumpkin Cheesecake Bars

These are like little pieces of pumpkin heaven. The bars are creamy, rich, and delicious with a wonderful pumpkiny flavor.

Ingredients

$^1\!/_2$ cup ground pecans
1 cup all-purpose flour
$^1\!/_3$ cup firmly packed brown sugar
5 tablespoons cold butter

Topping

8-ounce package cream cheese, softened
$^3\!/_4$ cup granulated sugar
$^1\!/_2$ cup pumpkin purée
2 eggs
1 teaspoon ground cinnamon
1 teaspoon vanilla extract

Yield: 12 to 14 bars

1. Grind the pecans and transfer to a medium mixing bowl. Remove 2 tablespoons and set aside to use later in the recipe

2. Add the flour and brown sugar to the pecans and stir. Cut the butter in small pieces and add to the bowl. Cut the butter into the dry ingredients until it resembles a crumbly meal. Gather the mixture with your hands and form it into a ball of dough.

3. Press the dough evenly on the bottom of an ungreased 8-inch square baking pan with your hands. Bake in a preheated 350°F oven for 15 minutes or until the edge of the crust has browned slightly. Remove from the oven and set aside to cool. (Leave the oven on.)

4. Place all of the topping ingredients in a large mixing bowl. Beat with an electric mixer on high speed for about 2 minutes or until the mixture is smooth.

Stuff You'll Need

5. Pour the topping over the crust.

6. Sprinkle the reserved pecans over the topping, and return to the oven for 30 to 35 minutes or until the center has set (it doesn't jiggle when you *gently* shake it). Cool for 30 minutes, then refrigerate another 30 minutes or until well chilled.

7. Cut into bars with a sharp knife. Serve at room temperature or slightly chilled.

5-Layer Choconut Bars

I love each and every layer of this cookie/candy bar, which was one of my grandma's specialties. It's like having a multi-layer party in your mouth and everyone's invited!

Ingredients

1 cup crushed chocolate graham crackers
6 tablespoons butter, melted
$^1/_2$ cup semi-sweet chocolate morsels
$^1/_2$ cup white chocolate morsels
$^1/_2$ cup coarsely chopped pecans
1 cup sweetened condensed milk
$^1/_2$ cup sweetened shredded coconut

Yield: 12 bars

Important Tips

▶ The bottom of these bars gets real sticky, so be sure to line the pan with parchment paper.
▶ For best results, use a flat-bottomed glass to compress the bottom crust.

Stuff You'll Need

1. Crush the graham crackers and place the crumbs in a medium mixing bowl. Add the butter and stir until the crumbs are well coated.

2. Line the bottom of an 8-inch square baking pan with parchment paper. Add the graham cracker mixture and press it into an even layer with your hands. Using the bottom of a drinking glass, flatten the layer and compress it well.

3. Sprinkle the chocolate morsels over the bottom crust. Next, add the white chocolate morsels.

4. For the next layer, add the chopped pecans.

5. Pour the condensed milk evenly over the layered ingredients.

6. Top with the shredded coconut. Bake in a preheated 350°F oven for 20 minutes or until the top of the coconut has browned slightly.

7. Cool at least 30 minutes before cutting into bars with a sharp knife. Serve at room temperature.

Chocoberry Oaties

The mild tartness of dried cranberries is combined with rich chocolate in these luscious oat squares.

Ingredients

1/2 cup butter (1 stick)
1/2 cup firmly packed brown sugar
1/4 cup granulated sugar
1 tablespoon milk
1 teaspoon vanilla extract
1 egg
1 cup all-purpose flour
1 teaspoon baking soda
Pinch salt
1 cup uncooked quick or
   old-fashioned oats
1 cup semi-sweet chocolate morsels
1/2 cup dried cranberries (Craisins)

Yield: 16 squares

Stuff You'll Need

1. Melt the butter in a small saucepan over low heat. Set aside to cool for a minute.

2. Place the butter, sugars, milk, and vanilla in a large mixing bowl. Cream with an electric mixer on low speed for 2 to 3 minutes or until light and fluffy. Add the egg and continue to beat until well blended.

3. Combine the flour, baking soda, salt, and oats in a medium bowl. Add this mixture to the creamed mixture a half cup at a time, and stir with a wooden spoon to form a smooth sticky dough.

4. Add the chocolate and cranberries to the dough, and stir until well distributed.

5. Press the dough evenly on the bottom of a lightly greased 8-inch square baking pan.

6. Bake in a preheated 325°F oven for 30 to 35 minutes or until the top is lightly browned. Cool at least 30 minutes before cutting into squares with a sharp knife.

Try These Variations!

With this recipe you can make other delicious combos simply by changing the add-ins.

Fun combos

▶ Dried cranberries and pecans

▶ Chopped dates and chocolate chunks

▶ Raisins and milk chocolate morsels

White Chocolate 'n Pecan Oaties

Substitute

▶ 1 cup white chocolate morsels

▶ 1 cup coarsely chopped pecans

Instead of chocolate morsels and cranberries, add white chocolate morsels and pecans in Step 4 of the recipe.

Date-Nut Oaties

Substitute

▶ $1/2$ cup chopped dates

▶ 1 cup chopped walnuts

Instead of chocolate morsels and cranberries, add dates and walnuts in Step 4 of the recipe.

Cake and Pie to Go

As Americans, we are the snack food kings of the world. We are also people on the go-go-go, so we love any treat that's both portable and tasty. It's no wonder we perfected brownies and cookie bars!

The First Brownie

There are a number of conflicting stories regarding the origin of brownies. According to one, brownies are the variation of Scottish cocoa scones. According to another, they began as the accidental creation of a Maine housewife whose chocolate cake didn't rise properly. Another story claims that brownies were first made by a chef at Chicago's Palmer House Hotel. The chef was asked to create the dessert by a socialite who wanted it served to ladies who were attending the city's 1893 Colombian Exposition. She wanted it to be smaller than a piece of cake, portable, and able to be eaten by hand.

Brownie Eating As a Sport

The first sanctioned National Fudge Brownie Eating Championship took place in 2008 during the Northeastern Ohio Chocolate Festival. The title was given to the first "food warrior" to eat three pounds of brownies. The winner, Mark "The Human Vacuum" Lyle, downed the brownies in four minutes and sixteen seconds! (He has also earned titles in the competitive speed-eating of other foods, including chicken wings, corn on the cob, and ribs.)

Bell Bottoms and Lemon Squares

Lemon squares – a part-cookie, part-pastry version of lemon meringue pie (without the meringue) – became all the rage during the 1970s. Interest in these luscious treats was triggered when Lady Bird Johnson, wife of the President, mentioned that they were among her favorite desserts. Soon, recipes for lemon squares began appearing everywhere, and by the 1970s, virtually every home baker in America had one.

Blondes Don't Always Have More Fun

Blondies have been around since the 1700s – long before brownies (their "fame-hogging" brothers) arrived on the scene. Once chocolate became readily available and more affordable due to mass production, there was an explosion of products made with chocolate, including brownies. Blondies were suddenly relegated to a shadowy existence. They even suffered from loss of identity, as they were sometimes referred to as vanilla or butterscotch brownies, or blonde brownies. Poor little guys!

The First Cookie Bar

The first commercially manufactured bar cookie was made possible thanks to James Henry Mitchell, who invented a duplex dough-sheeting machine in 1982. That cookie, which is still popular today, is filled with fig jam and named after a Boston suburb named Newton. Can you guess which famous cookie it is?

The First Brownie Mix

A box of brownie mix has become a staple in American kitchens. The first mix was introduced in 1954 by Betty Crocker, followed shortly thereafter by Pillsbury in 1955 and much later in 1974 by another popular brand – Duncan Hines.

Humble Pie and Sweet Tarts 160

In Crust We Trust 162
    Forming Methods
        For Cookie Crusts, 162
        For Pastry Crusts, 164
        For Lattice Tops, 168
        For Tart Crusts, 170
    Crust Recipes
        Standard Cookie Crust, 172
        Flaky Pastry Pie Crust, 173
        Sweet Tart Crust, 174

No-Bake and Low-Bake Pies 176
    Peanut Butter Pie, 177
    Chocolate Cream Pie, 178
    Key Lime Pie, 179
    Choco-Banana Cream Pie, 180

Beautiful Baked Pies 182
    Nuts 4 Pecan Pie, 183
    Mom's Apple Pie, 184
    Lemon Meringue Pie, 186
    Triple Berry Pie, 187
    Georgia Peach Pie, 188

Cobblers, Crisps & Crumbles 190
    Peachy Blue Cobbler, 191
    Apple Crispy, 192
    Cherry-Apple Crumbly, 194

Sweet Tarts 196
    Strawberry Chocolate Tart, 197
    Fabulous Fruit Tart, 198
    Triple Nutty Tartlets, 200
    Canadian Butter Tartlets, 202

7. Easy as Pie

My, my, Miss American Pie!

Americans sure love their pie. As a nation, we eat more dessert pies than anywhere else in the world. We have restaurants and bake shops that are dedicated to pies; we hold contests for pie baking (and eating); and we even write songs about pies. "American as apple pie" is one of our favorite expressions. Why, we love pie so much, we sometimes jokingly refer to our mouths as "pie holes."

This chapter is all about pie and its *ooh-la-la* French cousin, the tart (*I'm still talking about pastries here*). We'll be starting at the bottom . . . with that all-important crust. Easy-to-follow instructions and helpful photos will show you how to "make and shape" all kinds of pie shells, from a light and flaky pastry crust to a variety of sweet and crunchy cookie crusts.

Next, you'll learn how to pair those crusts with luscious fillings, starting with a few that you don't even have to bake (you heard me right!). Of course, there are also traditional baked favorites like Mom's Apple Pie and classic Georgia Peach. And wait until you discover my wacky "upside-down" pies—a collection of cobblers, crisps, and crumbles—which have their crazy crusts on top of the fillings! Finally, you're going to fall in love with my fruit tarts, which are almost too beautiful to eat.

*Now you're going have to figure out if you want to fall in love with a tart, **not** bake a pie, or attempt an "upside-down" pie. So many choices, so little time . . .*

Humble Pies and Sweet Tarts

Mmmm, pie. Is there anything that compares to the heavenly aroma of Grandma's apple pie baking in the oven (or cooling on a windowsill)? And how could we laugh at those scary clowns if they didn't take a pie in the face once in a while? Did you know that the first pies were filled with meats, not sweets? And that early American settlers, who lacked the ingredients and tools to make traditional pies, came up with new pie versions that often included regional berries and fruits? Oh yeah, pie is happenin' all right!

Pies, Tarts, and Tartlets

Pies

Basically a pastry shell that contains a sweet or savory filling, the pie has been around for centuries. The mass production of sugar is what launched the popularity of sweet dessert pies. Pies can be open-faced with a single bottom crust, or covered with a top crust. Standard pies are 9 inches in diameter and 1¼ to 2 inches deep.

Tarts

Tarts are similar to open-faced pies, although they are not as deep—typically their crusts are no higher than an inch. Most dessert tarts are anywhere from 4 to 12 inches in diameter. Their crusts are usually prebaked before adding a filling, which is often a prepared custard, cream, or nut mixture. Fresh fruit is often arranged on top.

Tartlets

These small tarts are 2½ to 3 inches in diameter and easily prepared in standard muffin tins. Tinier mini tartlets measure 1½ to 2 inches in diameter and are made in mini muffin tins. Like standard tarts, tartlet crusts are usually prebaked before a prepared filling is added.

Helpful Tips

▶ For flaky pastry crusts, make sure the ingredients are cold. And be careful not to overwork the dough, as this will result in crusts that are hard and tough.

▶ Because pie fillings (especially for fruit pies) may boil over during baking, it's a good idea to place the pie pan on a cookie sheet to catch any drippings before they land on the oven floor. I usually cover the cookie sheet with foil, which both protects it (the boiling hot sugar and fruit juice can cause it to discolor) and makes cleanup much easier.

▶ To prevent the edge of the crust from overbrowning, carefully cover it with foil after the first fifteen minutes of baking.

▶ A prebaked pie crust tends to bubble up and blister as it bakes. To prevent this, after placing the dough in the pan, vent the dough by poking holes in it with a fork. Or you can cover the dough with a sheet of parchment paper and then add dried beans or rice to weigh the crust down as it bakes. Remove the parchment and "weight" about five minutes before the crust is done baking. Special pie weights made specifically for this purpose are also available.

▶ Unless the recipe specifies otherwise, bake pies on the middle rack of the oven.

▶ Before cutting a freshly baked pie (especially a fruit pie), allow it to cool to room temperature (at least 30 minutes), which allows the filling to set.

Storage Tips

▶ Pies and tarts are best eaten fresh. You can leave fruit pies at room temperature for a day. After that, they should be covered and refrigerated up to five days. Pies that contain eggs or dairy should be covered and refrigerated as soon as they are cool.

▶ Keep in mind that after three or four days, most pies become less appetizing—crusts get tough and chewy, fillings start to dry out, and cream toppings tend to get watery.

▶ To freeze a baked fruit pie, allow it to cool completely, then wrap it tightly in foil, place in a freezer bag, seal, and label. It will keep up to nine months. Do not freeze cream or custard pies.

"Upside-Down" Pies

Old-fashioned cobblers, crisps, and crumbles are closely related – they all contain fruit fillings and their crusts are baked on top. (This is why I call them "upside-down" pies.) They are often baked in deep-dish pans and very simple to make. Although fresh fruit is recommended, frozen fruit and even canned pie fillings work.

Cobblers always remind me of rustic fruit pot pies. The fruit is topped with a biscuit-like dough. The dough can completely cover the fruit (like a pot pie!) or it can be dropped in random spoonfuls over the top. When baked, these lumps of dough – which resemble cobblestones and may be how the dessert got its name – are surrounded by the hot bubbling fruit. Delicious!

The *crisp* is another deep-dish fruit creation that is traditionally sprinkled with a crunchy topping – often a combination of brown sugar, butter, flour, and chopped nuts or oats.

Crumbles are similar to crisps, only their topping is more of a crumbly streusel-style mixture.

Although you can enjoy these desserts at room temperature, I think they are best when eaten warm – and topped with a scoop of creamy vanilla ice cream or frozen yogurt. And if you happen to find yourself with any leftovers, store them right in the baking dish simply. Cover tightly with plastic wrap or foil and refrigerate up to three or four days.

Cobbler

Crisp

Crumble

Cookies in a crust?

Whoever came up with the idea of crushing cookies and then turning the crumbs into a pie crust should win an award. Not only are these crusts easy to assemble (a little melted butter is all you need to hold them together), you can also make them with lots of different cookies, including graham crackers, which, let's face it, are really cookies, not crackers! (Be sure to see the inset on page 163.)

Basic Steps for Forming Cookie Crusts

1. Crush
Begin by crushing the cookies. I find putting the cookies in a large plastic storage bag and then crushing them with a rolling pin is the easiest method (and requires no cleanup). Using a food processor is my next choice. Pulse the blades to form tiny crumbs, but don't let them turn to powder.

2. Stir
In order for the crumbs to hold together and form a crust, they must be stirred with warm (not hot) melted butter or margarine. First drizzle the butter evenly over the crumbs, and then stir until the crumbs have absorbed the butter and stick together when compressed.

3. Shape
Place the prepared crumb mixture into a pie pan. Shape the crust by pressing the crumbs evenly against the bottom and sides of the pan with your palm and fingers. (If you are able to press the crumbs to a flat, even thickness, you can skip the next two steps.)

4. Compress

After forming the basic cookie crust with your hands, use a flat-bottomed drinking glass to flatten the crumbs on the bottom of the pan. Compressing the crumbs will result in a firm crust that holds together well. It will also give the crust a more uniform thickness.

5. Smooth

To further shape the crust (and who doesn't appreciate a shapely crust?), smooth and flatten the crumbs on the sides and contours of the pan with a large metal spoon.

6. Bake (optional)

To prebake the crust for a no-bake pie, place it on the middle rack of a preheated 400°F oven for 8 to 10 minutes. Allow the crust to cool before adding the filling.

There's More to Cookie Crusts Than Honey Grahams

One of the beauties of cookie crusts is that you can make them from lots of different cookie varieties. Honey graham crackers make the classic crust for creamy cheesecakes, as well as pies like chocolate cream and key lime. For banana cream and frozen peanut butter pies, nothing is better than a crust made from chocolate graham crackers or dark chocolate wafers. Sugar cookies, vanilla wafers, and shortbread are other great choices for all sorts of no-bake and low-bake pies. And nothing is easier to make – see page 172 for a basic cookie crust recipe.

Vanilla Wafer Crust

Chocolate Cookie Crust

Chocolate Graham Cracker Crust

Pastry Crusts . . . Just like Ma use ta make.

Although you can buy premade refrigerated pie dough and frozen pie crusts at your local grocery store, why not try making your own? It isn't that difficult—even for the novice baker. It also allows you to save some money, create custom pie crust designs, and, most important, have the delicious taste that comes only from a homemade crust. What follows are the steps for turning flaky pastry dough (recipe on page 173) into a perfect pie crust.

Basic Steps for Forming a Bottom Pie Crust

1. Cut
The first step for making most pastry dough is cutting cold butter (or other fat) into a flour mixture until it resembles a crumbly meal. Do this with a pastry blender, two knives in a criss-cross motion, or a wooden spoon with a stabbing motion. (For cutting instructions, see page 55.)

2. Form
Gather the crumbly flour mixture with your hands and form it into a ball of dough. Roll the ball along the bottom of the bowl to collect any loose bits of the mixture. Be careful not to knead or overwork the dough or it will become tough.

3. Flatten and roll out
Place the dough on a sheet of wax paper that has been sprinkled with flour, and flatten it a bit with your palm. With a floured rolling pin, roll the dough outward from the center into an 1/8-inch-thick circle that is about 2 inches larger than the pie pan.

Basic Steps for Forming a Bottom Pie Crust

4. Measure

To make sure the circle of dough is large enough, place the pie pan face down in the middle. The dough should be about 2 inches larger than the pan on all sides. This excess is necessary to accommodate the depth of the pan and to create an edge for the crust.

5. Place and fit

Turn the pie pan right side up along with the dough and wax paper. Peel off the wax paper and gently pat the dough against the bottom and sides of the pan. Don't pull or stretch it. (If you didn't roll out the dough on wax paper, carefully fold it in half, lift it into the pan, and then unfold it.)

6. Trim

Once the dough is placed and fitted in the pan, trim away the excess that's hanging over the sides. To do this, run a sharp knife around the pan, using the edge as your cutting guide. Pie dough is fragile, so be gentle and patient as you trim.

7. Patch

If the dough tears or there is a gap in the crust, you can easily patch it. Press a scrap of dough into the problem area and shape it with your fingers to blend with the rest of the crust. If it doesn't stick, dab both the scrap and the crust with a little water before pressing them together.

8. Crimp

Although crimping the edge of the dough is optional for a single bottom crust, it does add a decorative touch. To create a simple scalloped edge, press the dough in equal intervals with your thumb or finger as shown above. Crimping the edge with the tines of a fork is another good option.

9. Vent (optional)

For pies with a no-bake filling, you'll need to prebake the crust. Before baking, it is important to vent the dough by poking holes in it with the tines of a fork as shown above. Otherwise the crust will blister and bubble up as it bakes. See the Helpful Tips on page 161 for more pie crust prebaking options.

Two times the crust is two times the fun!

A pie by definition is a filling surrounded by both a top and bottom crust – so if you want to make a "real" pie, you will have to know how to make a double crust. You already learned how to form a bottom crust on the previous pages. What follows are the simple steps for forming and adding a standard top crust. You can leave it as a solid topper or, depending on the type of pie, create one of the lattice-style crusts beginning on page 168.

Basic Steps for Adding a Top Crust

1. Divide
After preparing the dough and forming it into a ball (as shown in Steps 1 and 2 on page 164), divide it into two pieces, making one piece a little larger for the bottom crust. After you have prepared the bottom crust and added the filling, it is time to make the top crust.

2. Flatten and roll
Place the remaining ball of dough on a sheet of wax paper that has been sprinkled with flour, and flatten it a bit with your palm. With a floured rolling pin, roll the dough outward from the center into $1/8$-inch-thick circle that is about 1 inch larger than the pie pan.

3. Measure
To make sure the circle of dough is large enough to drape over the filling and cover the edges, place an empty pie pan (of the same size) face down in the middle. Make sure the dough is about 1 inch larger than the pan on all sides.

Basic Steps for Adding a Top Crust

4. Place and trim

Lift up the wax paper and circle of dough. Carefully drape the dough over the filling and peel off the wax paper. (If you did not roll out the dough on wax paper, fold it in half, lift it into the pan, and then unfold it.) To trim away the excess dough, run a sharp knife around the pan, using the edge as your guide.

5. Crimp

Crimping is important for double-crusted pies because it seals the top and bottom crusts together. If this is not done properly, the filling will seep out between the two crusts during baking. For a simple scalloped edge, press the dough in equal intervals with your thumb or finger as shown above. Crimping the edge with the tines of a fork is another option.

6. Vent

To allow steam to escape from the pie as it bakes and prevent the filling from boiling over and breaking through the top or the crimped edges, venting the top crust is necessary. Simply cut a few holes in the dough with a sharp knife—larger holes near the center and smaller holes or slits toward the edges.

How About Some Finishing Touches?

Once the top crust has been crimped and vented, you can pop it into the oven as is, or you can add a final touch. Using a pastry brush, coat the top with any of the following:

Beaten egg white

This will give the pie crust a beautiful glossy finish. Especially nice on fruit pies like apple and peach.

Egg wash

This mixture of beaten egg yolk and a tablespoon of cream or milk will give the crust a medium to dark-brown shine. I recommend it on berry pies.

Cream or milk

This simple ingredient will result in a medium to light golden crust.

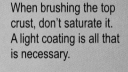

When brushing the top crust, don't saturate it. A light coating is all that is necessary.

You can also sprinkle some sugar crystals on top for added sweetness and crunch. A mixture of sugar and a little cinnamon is perfect for apple pies.

Basket weaving 101.

Once you've rolled out the dough for your top crust, you can cut it into strips and then lay the strips over the filling in a number of decorative ways. I'll show you how easy it is to make a simple lattice top, a more intricate basket weave, and a beautiful starburst design (shown above). The dough strips, which need to be flexible enough to bend, will turn dry and brittle when exposed to the air. So use them immediately after cutting.

Basic Steps for a Simple Lattice Top

1. Cut the strips

First, roll out the dough for the top crust (see Step 2 on page 166). Using a sharp knife and a straight edge, cut the dough into strips that are ½ to 1 inch wide. (As shown in the photo above, I use the long side of a cookie sheet as my straight edge.)

2. Place the first strips

Lay half the strips over the filling—put the longer strips across the middle of the pie and the shorter strips near the sides. Place them parallel to each other and about ½ inch apart, letting the ends hang over the edge of the pan.

3. Add the cross strips

Place the remaining strips over the bottom strips in a perpendicular criss-cross pattern. (You can also place them diagonally over the bottom strips to create a diamond pattern.) Trim the edges with a knife or scissors, then press the strips over the bottom crust to seal.

Basic Steps for a Basket Weave Top

1. Place the first strips
Cut the rolled-out dough (see Step 1 on the previous page) into 16 strips about $1/2$ inch wide. Lay 8 strips parallel to each other and equally spaced over the filling. Fold back every other strip halfway as shown in the photo above.

2. Add the cross strips
Lay your first cross strip across the center of the pie (it will run above the tops of the folded strips). Now unfold the strips, which will go over the cross strip. Next, fold back the strips that were originally flat and lay the next cross strip (see above). Repeat the process until you reach the end of the pie, then continue with the other half.

3. Trim the excess
With a sharp knife or pair of scissors, trim away the overhanging strips of dough. Press the strips over the bottom crust to seal.

Basic Steps for a Starburst Top

1. Place the first strips
Cut the rolled-out dough (see Step 1 on the previous page) into 8 strips about $5/8$ inch wide. Place the two longest strips over the filling to form a cross as shown in the photo above.

2. Place the remaining strips
Add the next two strips to divide the pie into eighths as shown above. Continue dividing the pie in equal spaces with the remaining strips. With a sharp knife or pair of scissors, trim away the overhanging strips of dough. Press the strips over the bottom crust to seal.

3. Cut out the center piece
Cut out a circle from a rolled-out piece of dough to press over the strips in the center of the pie (see photo at the top of the previous page). Use the rim of a drinking glass or a cookie cutter for this. If this center piece doesn't stick properly, wet the back a little before pressing it onto the strips.

Come here, you little tart.

Tarts are basically open-faced pies with a shallow crust. The crusts are usually prebaked and then filled with a prepared custard or cream, which is often topped with a decorative arrangement of fruit. Many of the fillings in Chapter 4 are great for tarts. The simple steps on the following pages will show you how to turn simple sweet pastry dough (recipe on page 174) into a perfect tart crust.

Basic Steps for Forming a Standard Tart Crust

1. Cut

The first step for making most tart dough is cutting cold butter (or other fat) into a flour mixture until it resembles a crumbly meal. Do this with a pastry blender, two knives in a criss-cross motion, or a wooden spoon with a stabbing motion. (For cutting instructions, see page 55.)

2. Form

Gather the crumbly flour mixture with your hands and form it into a ball of dough. Roll the ball along the bottom of the bowl to collect any loose bits of the mixture. Be careful not to knead or overwork the dough or it will become tough.

3. Flatten and roll out

Place the dough on a sheet of wax paper that has been sprinkled with flour, and flatten it a bit with your palm. With a floured rolling pin, roll the dough outward from the center into an 1/8-inch-thick circle that is about 1 inch larger than the tart pan.

4. Place

Lift up the wax paper, then carefully turn it over and place the dough in the tart pan. Peel off the wax paper. (If you didn't roll out the dough on wax paper, carefully fold the dough in half, lift it into the pan, and then unfold it.)

5. Shape and trim

Once the dough has been placed in the pan, use your fingers to gently pat it over the bottom and ease it into the scalloped edges. (The crust will shrink as it bakes and separate from the edge of the pan.) To trim the excess dough, press it over the sharp edges with your fingers or a rolling pin.

6. Vent

Most tarts contain a no-bake filling, so you will have to prebake the crust. Before baking, vent the dough by poking holes in it with the tines of a fork. Otherwise the crust will blister and bubble up as it bakes. See the Helpful Tips on page 161 for more crust prebaking options.

Making Tartlet Crusts in a Muffin Pan

Although you can use individual tartlet pans to prepare these tiny treats, I always make them in muffin pans. The recipe on page 174 yields enough dough to make twelve 3-inch tartlets and twenty-four 2-inch mini tartlets. I use a standard muffin pan for the larger ones and a mini-muffin pan for the smaller ones. Here are the steps for forming the crusts:

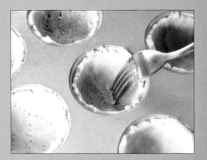

1. Divide

If you are making tartlets in a standard muffin pan, divide the dough into twelve balls that are about the same size. When making tiny tartlets in a mini-muffin pan, divide the dough into twenty-four balls.

2. Shape

To shape the crusts, place a ball of dough into each cup of the muffin pan. With your fingers, press the dough along the bottom and sides to form a cup shape. Tampers made specifically for this purpose are also available (and very convenient).

3. Vent

For tartlets with a no-bake filling, you'll need to prebake the crust. Before baking, it is important to vent the dough by poking holes in it with the tines of a fork. Otherwise the crust will blister and bubble up as it bakes.

Standard Cookie Crust

For this basic recipe, you can use just about any kind of cookie. Top choices include vanilla wafers, shortbread cookies, sugar cookies, and dark chocolate wafers or sandwich cookies (like Oreos) without the cream filling. Also high on the list are honey graham crackers and chocolate grahams.

Ingredients

4 tablespoons (½ stick) melted butter
1 cup cookie crumbs
1 tablespoon granulated sugar
   (optional)

Yield: 9-inch single pie crust

Stuff You'll Need

1. Melt the butter in a small saucepan over low heat. Set aside to cool a bit.

2. Place the cookie crumbs in a medium bowl. Add the butter and sugar (if using). Stir until the crumbs have completely absorbed the butter.

3. To form the crust, see the instructions on page 162.

4. If prebaking the crust, place it in a preheated 400°F oven for 8 to 10 minutes. Cool before filling.

Flaky Pastry Pie Crust

Rather than butter, this recipe calls for vegetable shortening, which produces a tender, flakier crust. It also yields enough dough for a 9-inch double-crust pie. For a single crust, make half the recipe.

Ingredients

2 cups all-purpose flour

$2/3$ cup Crisco or other solid vegetable shortening

$1/3$ cup cold water

Yield: 9-inch double pie crust

1. Place the flour, shortening, and water in a medium bowl. Cut the shortening into the flour until it resembles a crumbly meal. Press the mixture into a ball of dough with your hands.

2. Divide the dough into two pieces. To form the crust, see the instructions beginning on page 164. If you are not using the dough immediately, wrap it in plastic wrap and refrigerate up to a week.

Stuff You'll Need

3. If you are making a single crust that must be prebaked, place it in a preheated 425°F oven for 12 to 15 minutes or until light golden brown. Cool before filling.

Sweet Tart Crust

This recipe works for both large tarts and tartlets.

Ingredients

1¹/₂ cups all-purpose flour
¹/₄ cup granulated sugar
Pinch salt
¹/₂ cup cold butter (1 stick), cut into small chunks
1 egg, lightly beaten
¹/₄ teaspoon almond extract (optional)

Yield: 1 standard (12-inch) tart
12 medium (3-inch) tartlets
or 24 mini (2-inch) tartlets

1. Combine the flour, sugar, and salt in a large bowl. Add the butter, egg, and almond extract (if using). Using a pastry blender or wooden spoon, mix the ingredients until it resembles a crumbly meal.

2. Gather the crumbly flour mixture with your hands and form it into a ball of dough. Roll the ball along the bottom of the bowl to collect any loose bits of the mixture. Be careful not to knead or overwork the dough or it will become tough.

3. To form the crust for a standard tart or tartlets, see the instructions beginning on page 170.

4. To prebake the crust, place it in a preheated 350°F oven for 12 to 15 minutes or until light golden brown. Cool before filling.

Stuff You'll Need

Have your pie and eat it too!

Although this book is dedicated to baking, I had to include a few no-bake classics like chocolate cream and banana cream pie. All of the pies in this section have cookie crusts, which you can prebake before adding the filling if you want. Prebaked crusts are crispier and hold together a little better.

Basic Steps for Making No-Bake Pies

1. Prepare the crust

Instructions for forming cookie crusts, which are used for all the pies in this section, begin on page 162; the standard cookie crust recipe is on page 172. If you want to prebake the crust, pop it into a preheated 400°F oven for 8 to 10 minutes. Let it cool before adding the filling.

2. Whip the filling

Some fillings for no-bake pies contain heavy cream or other liquid that needs to be whipped to become firm. After whipping, they are sometimes folded with other flavorful ingredients. For whipping instructions, see page 56. For folding instructions, see page 57.)

. . . or cook the filling

Some no-bake pie fillings like custards and puddings are cooked on the stovetop. This usually requires constant stirring or whisking to keep the mixture smooth. If your filling has lumps, either remove them with a spoon or run the filling through a strainer.

Peanut Butter Pie

Is there a better flavor combination than peanut butter and chocolate? Well, this frozen pie has it all—a chocolate cookie crust with a creamy peanut butter filling. It doesn't get any better than this.

Ingredients

4-ounce package cream cheese, softened
$^{1}/_{2}$ cup peanut butter
$^{3}/_{4}$ cup confectioner's sugar
$^{1}/_{2}$ cup milk
1 cup whipped cream
1 recipe chocolate cookie crust (page 172) or commercial variety

Yield: 8 to 10 servings

Stuff You'll Need

1. Place the cream cheese, peanut butter, sugar, and milk in a large bowl and beat with an electric mixer until smooth and uniform in color.

2. Add the whipped cream and gently fold it into the peanut butter mixture until there are no streaks.

3. Spoon the peanut butter filling into the prepared pie crust. Spread it evenly and smoothly with a spoon or rubber spatula. Cover and freeze at least 4 hours.

4. Thaw the pie a few minutes before cutting and serving. Refreeze any unused portions.

Chocolate Cream Pie

Here's a no-bake pie that's loaded with chocolate and topped with whipped cream, so you know it's a guaranteed crowd pleaser.

Ingredients

1 recipe graham cracker crust (page 172) or commercial variety

2 tablespoons butter

3½ ounces semi-sweet baking chocolate (3½ squares)

2 cups milk

½ cup granulated sugar

¼ cup all-purpose flour

3 beaten egg yolks*

1 teaspoon vanilla extract

Topping

½ cup heavy cream

1 teaspoon confectioner's sugar

Grated chocolate for garnish

* For egg separating instructions, see page 51.

Yield: 8 to 10 servings

Important Tip

Heat up the chocolate mixture slowly and stir it quickly and constantly to avoid lumps. If any lumps form, remove them with a spoon or run the mixture through a strainer.

Stuff You'll Need

1. Place the butter and chocolate in a medium pot and melt over medium-low heat. Add the milk, sugar, and flour, and stir until smooth.

2. Remove the pot from the heat and let the mixture cool for at least 5 minutes. Add the vanilla and egg yolks, and stir until well blended.

3. Pour the filling into the prepared pie crust. Cover and refrigerate at least 2 hours or until well chilled.

4. Before serving, whip the heavy cream and confectioner's sugar with an electric mixer until stiff peaks form.

5. Spread the whipped cream on top of the chilled filling, garnish with grated chocolate, and serve.

Key Lime Pie

When I lived in Miami, I had a key lime tree in my backyard—and I perfected the recipe for key lime pie. Key limes are different from the green Persian limes found in most grocery stores. They are smaller, juicier, and have a more distinctive aroma. They are also yellow in color. If you are not able to find key limes for this recipe, you can still use the green limes. This pie is luscious with either.

Ingredients

3 egg yolks*
²⁄₃ cup fresh lime juice
1 tablespoon lime zest
14-ounce can sweetened condensed milk
1 recipe graham cracker crust (page 172) or commercial variety
1¹⁄₂ to 2 cups whipped cream

* For egg separating instructions, see page 51.

Yield: 8 to 10 servings

Stuff You'll Need

1. Place the egg yolks, lime juice, and lime zest in a large bowl and beat with an electric mixer until smooth.

2. Add the condensed milk and continue to beat until the mixture is thoroughly blended.

3. Pour the filling into the prepared pie crust, and bake in a preheated 375°F oven for 12 to 15 minutes, or until the filling is set. Do not let it brown. Remove and let cool.

4. Cover the pie and refrigerate at least 4 hours. Before serving, spread the whipped cream on top of the pie.

5. Serve cold or at room temperature.

Choco-Banana Cream Pie

In case you haven't noticed, I'm a chocolate lover, so I couldn't resist adding some of that good stuff to my banana cream pie. This pie has a chocolate crust, a filling of sliced bananas and rich chocolate ganache, and a topping of luscious pastry cream. It doesn't get any sweeter than this!

Ingredients

1 recipe chocolate graham cracker
   crust (page 172)
1 cup semi-sweet chocolate morsels
$^1/_2$ cup heavy cream
2 large ripe bananas

Pastry Cream Topping

$1^1/_4$ cups whole milk
3 large egg yolks*
$^1/_4$ cup granulated sugar
2 tablespoons flour
2 tablespoons cornstarch
2 teaspoons Grand Marnier (optional)
* For egg separating instructions, see page 51.

Yield: 8 to 10 servings

Important Tip

Make sure the heavy cream is boiling hot when pouring it over the chocolate. Don't let it cool at all.

Stuff You'll Need

1. Place the chocolate morsels in a medium heatproof bowl and set aside. Bring the cream to a boil in a small saucepan, then pour it over the morsels.

2. Whisk together the morsels and boiling cream until the chocolate has melted. Set aside.

3. Slice the bananas.

4. Pour the chocolate mixture into the prepared crust and spread it evenly over the bottom.

5. While the chocolate is still warm, arrange the banana slices on top in two layers. Set aside.

6. Place all the pastry cream ingredients except the Grand Marnier in a medium pot and whisk until well blended. Set the pot over medium heat and continue whisking until the mixture starts to boil and thicken. Cook another minute, remove from the stove, and stir in the Grand Marnier (if using).

7. Allow the pastry cream to cool about 5 minutes, then spread it evenly over the bananas. Refrigerate at least 1 hour or until the cream is firm. Serve at room temperature.

Simple Simon met a pie man.

On the following pages, you will find easy-to-prepare recipes for many of the classic baked pies that we all know and love. There are fruit-filled favorites like Mom's Apple Pie, Georgia Peach Pie, and a Triple Berry Pie that's bursting with berries. And if you like pecans, check out my Nuts 4 Pecan Pie. Just thinking about them makes my mouth water. Although you can use premade pastry crusts, don't be afraid to make your own.

Basic Steps for Making Baked Pies

1. Prepare the crust

After making the dough (page 173), form the crust. Instructions for forming single and double pie crusts, including decorative lattice tops, begin on page 164. If prebaking the bottom crust, pop it into a 425°F oven 12 to 15 minutes or until light golden brown. Cool before filling.

2. Coat the filling

Many baked pies are filled with fruit, which contain juice. This juice is released from the fruit as the pie bakes and needs to be thickened (or the filling will be too runny). Coating the raw fruit with flour or cornstarch helps bind and thicken the juicy filling.

. . . or cook the filling

Some pies, like lemon meringue, contain filling ingredients that are cooked on a stovetop before the pie is baked. This usually requires constant stirring to keep the mixture smooth and lump free. If your filling has lumps, remove them with a spoon or run the filling through a strainer.

Nuts 4
Pecan Pie

This down-home holiday favorite is sweet and nutty and easy to make.

Ingredients

Half recipe Flaky Pastry Pie Crust (page 173) or commercial 9-inch single crust

$1/2$ cup butter (1 stick)

$1^1/2$ cups pecan halves

3 eggs

$3/4$ cup maple syrup

$1/2$ cup granulated sugar

1 teaspoon vanilla extract

$1/2$ teaspoon salt

Yield: 8 to 10 servings

Stuff You'll Need

1. Melt the butter in a medium pot over medium-low heat. Transfer to a large mixing bowl, leaving 1 tablespoon in the pot. Add the pecans to the pot, reduce the heat to low, and warm the nuts for 2 to 3 minutes while stirring often. Remove the pot from the heat and let cool.

2. Add the eggs, maple syrup, sugar, vanilla, and salt to the bowl with the melted butter, and stir until well blended. Add the cooled pecans and stir until well coated.

3. Pour the pecan mixture into the prepared pie crust. Place on a foil-lined cookie sheet (to catch any drippings) and bake in a preheated 350°F oven for 45 minutes or until the crust is golden brown and the filling is firm.

4. Cool at least 30 minutes before cutting. Serve warm or at room temperature.

Mom's Apple Pie

No baking book would be complete without a recipe for that all-time favorite—apple pie

Ingredients

1 recipe Flaky Pastry Pie Crust (page 173) or commercial 9-inch double crust

4 cups sliced McIntosh or Granny Smith apples (about 1½ pounds)

½ cup firmly packed brown sugar

2 tablespoons flour

1 tablespoon fresh lemon juice

2 tablespoons cold butter, cut into chunks

2 tablespoons butter, melted

1 tablespoon granulated sugar (optional)

Yield: 8 to 10 servings

Important Tip

This recipe calls for a double crust. If you are using store-bought commercial crusts, which come frozen and only as bottom crusts, be aware that you can use a bottom crust as a top. Just let it thaw out until the dough becomes workable, then place it over the filling as a top crust or cut it into strips to create a lattice top.

Stuff You'll Need

1. Place the apple slices, brown sugar, flour, and lemon juice in a medium bowl. Stir until the apples are fully coated.

2. Spoon the apple mixture into the prepared bottom pie crust. Dot with chunks of cold butter.

3. Place the top crust over the filling. Trim away the excess, crimp the edges, and vent the top. (See page 166 for detailed steps.)

4. Using a pastry brush, coat the top crust with melted butter. Sprinkle with granulated sugar (if using).

5. Place on a foil-lined cookie sheet (to catch any drippings) and bake in a preheated 325°F oven for 55 to 60 minutes or until the crust is golden brown. Cool at least 30 minutes before cutting. Serve warm or at room temperature.

Lemon Meringue Pie

This pie is just the ticket if you're a fan of sweet and tart. The filling is a little tart, and the meringue is light and sweet—it's also soft and fluffy.

Ingredients

Half recipe Flaky Pastry Pie Crust (page 173) or commercial 9-inch single crust, prebaked

4 egg yolks*

1/2 cup fresh lemon juice

1 cup granulated sugar

5 tablespoons butter

1 tablespoon lemon zest

Meringue

4 egg whites*

1/4 cup granulated sugar

1/4 teaspoon cream of tartar

* For egg separating instructions, see page 51.

Yield: 8 to 10 servings

Important Tips

▶ For best results, use fresh lemon juice for the filling.

▶ Spread the meringue over the filling while the filling is still hot—otherwise the meringue won't become firm properly.

Stuff You'll Need

1. Place the egg yolks, lemon juice, sugar, butter, and zest in a medium pot. Bring to a boil while whisking. Remove from heat and whisk another minute.

2. Pour the hot lemon filling into the prebaked pie crust. Set aside.

3. Place all of the meringue ingredients in a medium bowl and beat with an electric mixer until stiff peaks form.

4. Immediately spoon the meringue over the hot filling. Create some peaks in the meringue with a spoon or rubber spatula.

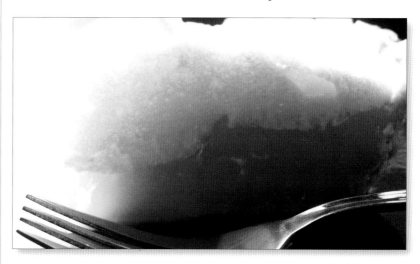

5. Place the pie on a foil-lined cookie sheet (to catch any drippings) and bake in a preheated 350°F oven for 25 to 30 minutes or until the peaks of the meringue are browned. Cool at least 30 minutes before cutting. Serve at room temperature or slightly chilled.

Triple Berry Pie

Feel free to try any combination of berries for this pie—just keep the total amount to four cups.

Ingredients

1 recipe Flaky Pastry Pie Crust (page 173) or commercial 9-inch double crust

2 cups blueberries, fresh or frozen

1 cup raspberries, fresh or frozen

1 cup sliced strawberries, fresh or frozen

1/4 cup granulated sugar

2 tablespoons cornstarch

2 tablespoons flour

2 tablespoons cold butter, cut into chunks

2 tablespoons milk or cream

Yield: 8 to 10 servings

Important Tip

This recipe calls for a double crust. If you are using store-bought commercial crusts, which come frozen and only as bottom crusts, be aware that you can use a bottom crust as a top. Just let it thaw out until the dough becomes workable, then place it over the filling as a top crust or cut it into strips to create a lattice top.

Stuff You'll Need

1. Place the blueberries, raspberries, strawberries, sugar, cornstarch, and flour in a large bowl. Stir until the berries are fully coated.

2. Spoon the berry mixture into the prepared bottom pie crust. Dot with chunks of cold butter.

3. Place the top crust over the filling. Trim the excess, crimp the edges, and vent the top. (See page 166 for detailed steps.)

4. Using a pastry brush, coat the top crust with milk.

5. Place on a foil-lined cookie sheet (to catch any drippings), and bake in a preheated 350°F oven for 40 to 45 minutes or until the crust is a light golden brown. Cool at least 30 minutes before cutting. Serve warm or at room temperature.

Georgia Peach Pie

I try to take advantage of peaches when they are in season, and often find myself turning those ripe luscious peaches into pies . . . several pies as a matter of fact. One to enjoy fresh from the oven, others to freeze for later.

Ingredients

1 recipe Flaky Pastry Pie Crust
   (page 173) or commercial 9-inch
   double crust
4 cups sliced peaches
1 cup loosely packed brown sugar
1/2 cup flour
1/2 teaspoon ground cinnamon
1 tablespoon fresh lemon juice
2 tablespoons butter, melted
1 tablespoon granulated sugar

Yield: 8 to 10 servings

Important Tip

This recipe calls for a double crust. If you are using store-bought commercial crusts, which come frozen and only as bottom crusts, be aware that you can use a bottom crust as a top. Just let it thaw out until the dough becomes workable, then place it over the filling as a top crust or cut it into strips to create a lattice top.

Stuff You'll Need

1. Place the peach slices in a large bowl.

2. Add the brown sugar, flour, cinnamon, and lemon juice. Stir until the peaches are fully coated.

3. Spoon the peach mixture into the prepared bottom pie crust.

4. Place the top crust over the filling, or add a decorative lattice top, like the basket weave crust shown here. (See page 169 for detailed instructions.) Using a pastry brush, coat the top crust with melted butter.

5. Sprinkle the top with sugar. Place on a foil-lined cookie sheet (to catch any drippings), and bake in a preheated 350°F oven 50 to 60 minutes or until the crust is light golden brown. Cool at least 30 minutes before cutting. Serve warm or at room temperature.

A pie by any other name.

The recipes in this section are not exactly pies, but they come close. As I mentioned earlier in this chapter, I consider them "upside-down" pies because their sweet crunchy crusts are on top of their fruit fillings. (For detailed descriptions, see page 161.) Along with being heartwarming, delicious, and easy to make, cobblers, crisps, and crumbles are very versatile—you can make them with just about any fruit, so feel free to substitute.

Basic Steps for Making Cobblers, Crisps & Crumbles

1. Prepare the filling

All the fillings in this section contain fresh seasonal fruits, which contain juice. This juice is released during baking and needs to be thickened (or the filling will be runny). Coating the raw fruit with flour or cornstarch helps bind and thicken the juicy filling.

2. Prepare the topping

Toppings for crumbles and crisps often include a simple combination of ingredients like brown sugar, flour, chopped nuts, and oat. If butter is used, it may be cut into the other ingredients with a pastry blender. Cobblers are topped with a batter, which is spooned over the filling.

3. Add the topping

For crisps and crumbles, simply sprinkle the toppings over the fillings as indicated in the recipe. When making a cobbler, top the filling with spoonfuls of batter, which will bake into a biscuit-like crust.

Peachy Blue Cobbler

Peaches and blueberries are my all-time favorite fruit combination for cobblers. You can make this an all-peach or an all-blueberry cobbler if you prefer—just make sure the fruit measures three cups.

Ingredients

2 cups peaches, cut into bite-sized
    pieces
2 rounded tablespoons brown sugar
1 cup fresh blueberries
2 tablespoons cold butter, cut
    into chunks

Topping

1 cup all-purpose flour
$1/2$ cup granulated sugar
$1/2$ cup milk
1 egg
1 teaspoon baking powder
1 teaspoon vanilla extract
$1/2$ teaspoon salt

Yield: 6 to 8 servings

Stuff You'll Need

1. Place the peaches and brown sugar in a large bowl, and stir until the peaches are coated.

2. Place all the topping ingredients in a medium bowl, and whisk to form a smooth batter.

3. Spoon the peaches into a greased 2-quart casserole dish, and sprinkle the blueberries on top. Dot with chunks of cold butter.

4. Spoon the batter over the filling and smooth with a rubber spatula.

5. Bake in a preheated 350°F oven for 30 to 35 minutes, or until the top is golden brown. Break up the top crust a bit. Spoon portions of the filling and crust into serving bowls. Enjoy warm.

Apple Crispy

Served warm with a scoop of vanilla ice cream, dis stuff is really "da bomb." My mom used to make it often when I was a kid. The brown sugary-oat topping for this dessert goes under the filling as well as on top—for twice the crispy crunch!

Ingredients

3 cups apples, cut into bite-sized
   chunks
$^{1}/_{4}$ cup loosely packed brown sugar
1 teaspoon ground cinnamon
1 teaspoon ground nutmeg
1 teaspoon lemon juice
2 tablespoons cold butter, cut
   into chunks

Topping

$^{1}/_{2}$ cup butter (1 stick)
1 cup all-purpose flour
$^{3}/_{4}$ cup loosely packed brown sugar
1 cup old-fashioned rolled oats

Yield: 6 to 8 servings

Stuff You'll Need

1. Place the apples, brown sugar, cinnamon, nutmeg, and lemon juice in a large bowl. Stir until the apples are well coated. Set aside.

2. To make the topping, melt the butter. Remove from the heat.

3. Place the remaining topping ingredients in a large bowl, add the melted butter, then stir until well combined.

4. Spoon half the topping mixture over the bottom of a greased 2-quart casserole dish. Top with the apple mixture.

5. Sprinkle the remaining topping over the apple mixture. Dot with chunks of cold butter.

6. Bake in a preheated 325°F oven for 45 to 50 minutes or until the topping is lightly browned and the filling is hot and bubbly. Serve hot or warm.

Try These Variations!

You can crisp just about any fruit. Try these suggestions:

▶ Blackberry Crispy

▶ Peach Crispy

▶ Raspberry-Apple Crispy

Nutty Blueberry Crispy

Substitute

3 cups blueberries

Add

$1/2$ cup coarsely chopped walnuts

Follow the directions for Apple Crispy, but substitute blueberries for the apples and add the walnuts in Step 1.

Cherry-Apple Crumbly

I couldn't have a pie chapter without a recipe for cherry pie, even if it's an "upside down" pie (and it also contains apples!). Although you can make this with fresh cherries, having to pit them is both labor intensive and messy. I find it a lot easier to use canned pie filling, but the choice is yours.

Ingredients

1$\frac{1}{2}$ cups McInstosh or Granny Smith
    apples, cut into bite-sized chunks
$\frac{1}{3}$ cup loosely packed brown sugar
1 tablespoon cornstarch
21-ounce can cherry pie filling
    (about 2$\frac{1}{3}$ cups)

Topping

1$\frac{1}{2}$ cups all-purpose flour
$\frac{1}{3}$ cup granulated sugar
$\frac{1}{2}$ cup cold butter, cut into chunks
1 teaspoon baking powder
$\frac{1}{4}$ teaspoon almond extract
$\frac{1}{3}$ cup slivered almonds

Yield: 6 to 8 servings

Stuff You'll Need

1. Place the apple chunks, brown sugar, and cornstarch in a large bowl. Sir until the apples are well coated.

2. Add the cherry filling and stir until well combined.

3. Spoon the apple-cherry mixture into a greased 8-inch square baking pan. Set aside.

4. To make the topping, combine the flour, sugar, baking powder, almond extract, and salt in a medium bowl. Cut the cold butter into the dry ingredients until it resembles a crumbly meal.

5. Add the topping in an even layer over the fruit.

6. Sprinkle almonds over the topping. Place on a foil-lined cookie sheet (to catch any drippings), and bake in a preheated 325°F oven for 25 to 30 minutes, or until the filling is hot and bubbly and the topping is a light golden brown. Cool 15 minutes before serving.

More crust, less filling!

Very common in Europe, the tart is an open-faced, bottom-crusted pie. If you're a crust lover, you'll flip over their sweet cookie-like crusts, which are typically filled with heavenly ingredients like creamy custards and then topped with luscious fresh fruit. Tarts can be as appealing to the eye as they are to the palate.

Basic Steps for Making Tarts

1. Prepare the crust

After making the dough (page 174), form the crust. Instructions for forming tart and tartlet crusts begin on page 170. Most need to be prebaked before adding a prepared filling. To prebake, pop it into a preheated 350°F oven 12 to 15 minutes or until light golden brown.

2. Make the filling

Most tarts contain custards or other fillings that are prepared on the stovetop. This usually requires constant stirring or whisking to keep the mixture smooth and lump free. If your filling has lumps, either remove them with a spoon or run the filling through a strainer.

3. Add a topping

Tarts are often topped with fruit that is artistically arranged over the filling. (Here's a good opportunity to be creative.) The fruit is typically brushed with a thin coat of glaze—often made from jelly. This adds a beautiful shine and preserves the color and freshness of the fruit.

Strawberry Chocolate Tart

I love strawberries dipped in chocolate, so I thought this would be a great combination for a tart. The almond-flavored crust elevates the taste to even greater heights.

Ingredients

1 recipe Sweet Tart Crust (page 174)
2 cups semi-sweet chocolate morsels
1 cup heavy cream
1 pound fresh strawberries, sliced
Fruit Glaze (page 101), optional

Yield: 8 to 12 servings

Stuff You'll Need

1. Prepare the crust in a 12-inch standard tart pan and prebake. (For detailed steps on forming the crust, see page 170.) Let cool.

2. Place the chocolate morsels in a medium bowl. Add the cream to a small saucepan and bring to a boil. Pour the boiling cream over the morsels and whisk until the chocolate has melted. Pour into the prepared crust. Let cool until semi-solid.

3. Starting at the outside edge of the tart, arrange the strawberry slices in a circular pattern, letting them overlap slightly. Continue until the tart is covered. If not serving within a few hours, brush the berries with Fruit Glaze and refrigerate. Serve within a day or so.

Fabulous Fruit Tart

This tart is almost too beautiful to eat, but you've got to try it! With so many flavor and textures, it's a real treat for the senses.

Ingredients

1 recipe Sweet Tart Crust (page 174)
1 recipe Pastry Cream (page 93)
1 kiwi, peeled and sliced
1 cup fresh raspberries
1 cup fresh blueberries
Fruit Glaze (page 101), optional

Yield: 10 to 12 servings

Stuff You'll Need

1. Prepare the crust in a 12-inch standard tart pan and prebake. (For detailed steps on forming the crust, see page 170.) Let cool.

2. Prepare the Pastry Cream filling.

3. Pour the filling into the prepared crust. Spread it in an even layer with a rubber spatula. Let cool at least 5 minutes.

4. Arrange the kiwi slices in the center of the tart as shown. Surround the kiwi with a circle of raspberries. Place another circle of raspberries along the edge of the tart.

5. Arrange the blueberries in the space between the raspberries. If you are not serving the tart within a few hours, brush the fruit with Fruit Glaze and refrigerate. Serve within a day or so.

Triple Nutty Tartlets

These bite-sized tartlets have just the right blend of sweetness and nutty crunch. They're one of my most requested desserts.

Ingredients

1 recipe Sweet Tart Crust (page 174)
1 tablespoon butter
2 cups nuts, preferably a mixture
  of pecans, hazelnuts, walnuts,
  and/or almonds
1 cup loosely packed brown sugar
1/4 cup water
2 tablespoons light corn syrup
1/2 cup heavy cream

Yield: 24 mini (2-inch) tartlets

Important Tip

Tartlet crusts are very fragile so be extremely careful when removing them.

Stuff You'll Need

1. Prepare the dough for the crust.

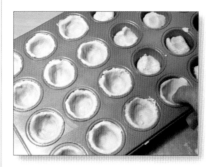

2. Divide the dough into 24 equal-sized balls.

3. Place the balls in the cups of a 24-cup mini muffin pan. Shape the dough according to the instructions in the inset on page 171. Bake in a preheated 350°F oven for 10 to 15 minutes or light golden brown. Let cool.

4. Place the nuts in food processor and pulse until coarsely chopped.

5. Melt the butter in a medium pot over medium heat. Add the nuts, brown sugar, water, and corn syrup. Cook, stirring often, for 2 to 3 minutes or until the mixture thickens. Reduce the heat to low, add the cream, and stir for about a minute.

6. Fill the baked crusts with the nut filling. Let sit until the filling cools and has set. Serve at room temperature.

Try These Variations!

You can fill tartlet crusts with just about anything. Here are two more of my favorite fillings.

Chocolate Ganache Tartlets

Substitute

Chocolate Ganache (page 92)

Substitute the Triple Nutty Tartlet filling with chocolate ganache.

Lemon Tartlets

Substitute

Lemon Custard filling (page 91)

Substitute the Triple Nutty Tartlet filling with lemon custard.

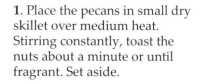

Canadian Butter Tartlets

Our hockey (pronounced HAY-key) playing brothers to the north created this delicious treat that is a Canadian holiday favorite. Dose hosers up der' came up with something really good this time, EH?

Ingredients

1 recipe Sweet Tart Crust (page 174)
$1/2$ cup coarsely chopped pecans
$1/3$ cup melted butter
1 cup firmly packed brown sugar
2 eggs
1 teaspoon vanilla extract
$1/4$ cup light cream

Yield: 12 medium (3-inch) tartlets

Important Tip

Tartlet crusts are very fragile so be extremely careful when removing them.

Stuff You'll Need

1. Place the pecans in small dry skillet over medium heat. Stirring constantly, toast the nuts about a minute or until fragrant. Set aside.

2. Place the butter, sugar, eggs, vanilla, and cream in a medium bowl and beat with an electric mixer until smooth.

3. Divide the dough into 12 equal-sized balls. Place the balls in the cups of a 12-cup standard muffin pan. Shape the dough according to the instructions in the inset on page 171.

4. Distribute the toasted pecans equally on the bottoms of the tart crusts.

5. Spoon the butter mixture over the pecans, filling each cup nearly to the top. Bake in a 350°F oven for 25 to 30 minutes or until the tops are bubbly and the shells are golden brown.

An Eye for Pye

Although pie is often considered an all-American dish, its origins can be traced back to ancient Egypt. By the fourteenth century, pies were popular throughout Europe. It is the English settlers who are responsible for bringing the "pye" – a filling surrounded by a crust – to America.

Crust or a Coffyn?

Initially, pies crusts – known in England as *coffyns* – were not meant to be eaten. They were hard and thick and served as bowls that were designed to hold or preserve fillings, which were generally savory, not sweet. Sweet pies and edible crusts began to appear in America around the mid-1700s, the same time that sugar became more readily available.

And the Most Popular Pie Is . . .

Can you guess which pie is the country's most popular? According to the American Pie Council, the most popular pies are as follows: (1) apple, (2) pumpkin, (3) sweet potato, (4) anything chocolate, (5) lemon meringue, (6) cherry.

Moon Pies and RC

If you are from the country's Deep South or have ever spent time there, you'll know that one of the area's traditional snack combos is a moon pie and an RC (Royal Crown) cola. Moon pies are made of marshmallow fluff that is sandwiched between two round graham crackers and then covered in chocolate. They were created in 1917 by the Chattanooga Bakery in Tennessee as snacks for coal miners. Each year, the RC and Moon Pie Festival is held in Bell Buckle, Tennessee. It features country music, lots of Southern food, and, of course, deep-fried moon pies! Ooo-wee, that's some good eatin'!

Key Lime Pie

Sweetened condensed milk, which was first produced in the 1850s, came as a true blessing to the natives of Key West, where the lack of cows made dairy products like milk and cream hard to come by. The canned milk was used to create pie fillings that were flavored with the limes that grew in abundance on the island. The first key lime pies were made with a pastry crust, but later evolved to a graham cracker crust. They are served plain or topped with whipped cream or meringue. The key lime pie is the official state pie of Florida.

Pie-Eating Contests

Pie-eating contests have been popular for over 100 years. From their humble beginnings as friendly events at local county fairs, these contests have become popular international eating competitions. In sanctioned events, the goal of competitors, who refer to themselves as "gurgitators," is to consume the largest amount of pie within a set amount of time. In March of 2006, Patrick "Deep Dish" Bertoletti ate a record 10.8 pounds of key lime pie in eight minutes. In July of that same year, he held the record for eating Strawberry Rhubarb Pie – 7.9 pounds in eight minutes.

No-Bake Cheesecake 206
White Chocolate Cheesecake
with Fruit Topping, 208
Vanilla Cheesecake with
Caramel Sauce, 210
Lemon Chiffon
Cheesecake, 212

Cheesecake Bake 214
Italian Cheesecake, 216
Pumpkin Chiffon
Cheesecake, 217
New York Strawberry
Cheesecake, 218
Chocolate Swirl
Cheesecake, 220
White Chocolate-Raspberry
Swirl Cheesecake, 222

8. Cheesecake Shots

I love cheese and I love cake, so this has gotta be good . . .

The first cheesecake is believed to have made its debut in Greece during the first Olympic Games, where it was served to the participating athletes. Its origins may date back to ancient Greece, but it took an American to invent cream cheese—the essential ingredient in modern cheesecake. If you have never made a cheesecake before, you are going to be surprised at the impressive results you can achieve with minimal effort.

In this chapter, I will be sharing some of my favorite cheesecake recipes with you, starting with a variety of incredibly easy-to-prepare no-bake choices that are all made on cookie crusts. Instead of popping them in the oven to bake, simply place them in the refrigerator to chill until the filling sets. (Pretty cool, huh?) Next come recipes for some spectacular baked cheesecakes, which are a little more difficult to make, but not much. You will find recipes for classic Italian and New York-style cheesecakes, as well as a few simple varieties that are brightened with swirls of delicious melted chocolate or flavorful fruit sauces.

One of the biggest problems with baked cheesecakes is that they are prone to cracking on the surface. But don't worry – I'll show you some simple things you can do to reduce or even eliminate this problem.

After all, you sure as heck don't want people cracking up while they're making cheesy wisecracks about your cracked cheesecake!

No-Bake Cheesecake

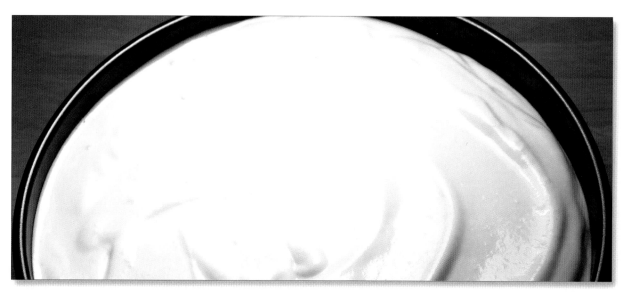

No bake? For goodness sake!

Preparing these recipes is about as easy as it gets. All you need is a bowl, a spoon, an electric mixer—and you're good to go. You can't burn or undercook these cheesecakes, and they don't crack. Instead of popping them in the oven to bake, you do the opposite and chill them in the refrigerator.

Basic Steps for Making No-Bake Cheesecakes

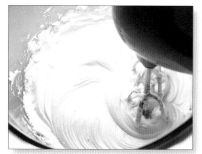

1. Prepare the crust
Instructions for forming cookie crusts, which are used for the no-bake cheesecakes in this chapter, begin on page 162; the standard cookie crust recipe is found on page 172. Some of the cheesecakes are made in 9-inch pie pans; others are made in springform pans (see page 215).

2. Beat the filling
To prepare the filling, beat softened cream cheese (or other soft fresh cheese) with the other ingredients as instructed in the recipe. Use an electric mixer and beat until the mixture is smooth.

3. Whip the cream
Whipped cream is usually added to the cream cheese base for no-bake cheesecakes. Beat the heavy cream with an electric mixer until it is light and airy—typically until stiff peaks form. (For whipping instructions, see page 56.)

Cream Cheese
A Delicious Mistake

There are dozens of cheesecake varieties that, depending on their ingredients, range in texture from light and airy to dense and rich to soft and creamy. The one ingredient that all cheesecakes have in common is cheese – with cream cheese, ricotta, and cottage cheese among the most popular.

Cream cheese, which arguably ranks as the *most* popular cheesecake choice, was created by accident. In 1872, while trying to reproduce an unripened French cheese called Neufchâtel, William Lawrence of Chester, New York, accidentally developed a method for producing cream cheese. Although the two cheeses look alike and are somewhat similar in taste, cream cheese is higher in fat than Neufchâtel. It is also richer and creamier – the perfect cheesecake choice.

4. Fold
Spoon the whipped cream over the heavier cream cheese filling mixture (Step 2 at left). Using a spatula and a circular motion, bring up the mixture from the bottom of the bowl and gently fold it over the lighter whipped cream until blended. (For folding instructions, see page 57.)

Helpful Tips

▶ Although it isn't necessary to prebake cookie crusts for no-bake cheesecakes, I recommend it. Baking the crust will make it firmer, crispier, and hold together better. To prebake the crust, pop it in a preheated 400°F oven for eight to ten minutes. Let it cool before filling.

▶ Do not underestimate the amount of time you need to let a cheesecake set. No-bake types should chill from six to eight hours in the refrigerator to set properly. Baked cheesecakes also need to chill from four to eight hours, depending on the filling ingredients.

▶ Before refrigerating a baked cheesecake, it needs to cool completely for at least one hour—preferably on a wire rack and away from drafts. Some recipes instruct letting the cake cool right in the oven with the heat turned off and the oven door opened slightly.

▶ For the smoothest batters, make sure all of the ingredients are at room temperature.

▶ Do not use low-fat or fat-free cream cheese, which tend to produce cheesecakes with a rubbery or crumbly texture.

▶ Bake cheesecakes on the middle rack of a preheated oven.

▶ When properly assembled, springform pans should not leak. If, however, you want to be extra careful, wrap the bottom in foil or place it on a cookie sheet during baking.

▶ Do not open the oven door during the first thirty minutes of baking. Drafts can cause cheesecakes to fall.

▶ A baked cheesecake will shrink as it cools. Once you have removed it from the oven, carefully run a knife around the inside edge of the pan so the cake can easily pull away from the sides.

▶ Whipped cream, fresh fruit, and flavorful sauces are just a few favorite toppers for cheesecakes. When adding a topping to any cheesecake, whether it's baked or not, it is best to do so right before serving. Either cover the entire cheesecake or individual slices.

▶ After removing the outer ring of a springform pan, the sides of the cheesecake may be a bit crumbly or uneven. To get a seamless look, smooth the sides with a hot wet knife.

Storage Tips

▶ It is best to eat cheesecake soon after it is made. No-bake cheesecake crusts become soggy within a few days, and baked cheesecakes tend to dry out. For short-term storage, cover with foil or plastic wrap and store in the refrigerator.

▶ Most baked cheesecakes freeze well because of their high-fat content. Cool them completely and wrap securely in heavy-duty foil or plastic wrap. Place in a freezer storage bag and label the contents and date. Don't freeze longer than a month.

▶ Do not freeze cheesecakes with garnishes or toppings.

▶ Thaw wrapped frozen cheesecake in the refrigerator about eight hours. Once thawed, remove the wrapping to prevent water droplets from forming on top of the cake.

White Chocolate Cheesecake with Fruit Topping

Creamy, flavorful, and simple to make!

Ingredients

1 recipe graham cracker crust
  (page 172) or commercial variety
3/4 cup white chocolate morsels
2 packages (8 ounces each) cream
  cheese, softened
1/3 cup granulated sugar
1 teaspoon vanilla extract
3/4 cup heavy cream
1 tablespoon confectioner's sugar
20-ounce can blueberry pie filling

Yield: 10 to 12 servings

Stuff You'll Need

1. Prepare the graham cracker crust.

2. If desired, prebake the crust in a preheated 400°F oven for 8 to 10 minutes. Let cool before filling.

3. Place the white chocolate morsels in the top of a double boiler over medium-low heat or in a small saucepan over *very low* heat. Stir until fully melted, then transfer to a large mixing bowl.

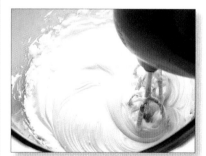

4. Add the cream cheese, sugar, and vanilla to the melted chocolate. Beat with an electric mixer on medium speed until smooth and well blended.

5. Place the heavy cream and confectioner's sugar in a separate mixing bowl. Beat with an electric mixer on high speed until thick, airy, and able to form stiff peaks.

6. Spoon one-third of the whipped cream on top of the cream cheese mixture, and fold together until nearly combined. Add the remaining whipped cream and continue folding until well blended and uniform in color. (For folding instructions, see page 57.)

7. Spoon the filling into the pie crust and smooth with a rubber spatula. Cover and refrigerate at least 6 hours.

8. Before serving, spoon the blueberry pie filling on top of the entire pie or on individual slices.

Vanilla Cheesecake with Caramel Sauce

I love vanilla, which is this cheesecake's featured flavor. Although this dessert is fabulous plain, it reaches heavenly heights when topped with the buttery-rich caramel sauce.

Ingredients

1 recipe vanilla wafer cookie crust (page 172) or commercial variety
12 ounces cream cheese, softened
14-ounce can sweetened condensed milk
2 teaspoons vanilla extract
1 cup prepared whipped cream

Caramel Sauce

$1/2$ cup granulated sugar
$1/2$ cup firmly packed brown sugar
$1/2$ cup heavy cream
$1/4$ cup butter ($1/2$ stick)
1 teaspoon vanilla extract

Yield: 8 to 10 servings

Stuff You'll Need

1. Prepare the cookie crust.

2. If desired, prebake the crust in a preheated 400°F oven for 8 to 10 minutes. Let cool before filling.

3. Place the cream cheese, condensed milk, and vanilla in a large mixing bowl. Beat with an electric mixer on medium speed until smooth and well blended.

4. Spoon the whipped cream on top of the cream cheese mixture, and fold until well blended. (For folding instructions, see page 57.)

5. Spoon the filling into the pie crust and smooth with a rubber spatula. Cover and refrigerate at least 6 hours.

Important Tip
Do not overcook the caramel sauce or it will harden.

6. Shortly before serving, prepare the caramel sauce. Place all the sauce ingredients except the vanilla in a medium pot over medium heat. Stirring briskly, bring to a gentle boil. Continue stirring for another minute.

7. Remove the pot from the heat, allow the sauce to cool for a minute, then add the vanilla. Stir well. Let cool a few minutes or until warm.

8. Spoon the warm caramel sauce over individual servings of the cheesecake.

Lemon Chiffon Cheesecake

There's something about the tart flavor of lemon in this sweet creamy dessert that really tickles my taste buds. Unlike the other no-bake cheesecakes in this chapter, this one is prepared in a springform pan rather than a pie pan. For information on these pans, see the inset on page 215.

Ingredients

1 cup boiling water
3-ounce package lemon gelatin
$\frac{1}{4}$ cup fresh lemon juice
8-ounce package cream cheese, softened
1 cup granulated sugar
12-ounce can evaporated milk, cold

Crust

1 cup graham cracker crumbs
$\frac{1}{4}$ cup butter ($\frac{1}{2}$ stick), melted
1 tablespoon granulated sugar

Yield: 12 to 16 servings

1. Place all of the crust ingredients in a medium mixing bowl, and stir until the crumbs have absorbed the butter. Spoon the moistened crumbs into a 9-inch springform pan and press them evenly on the bottom either with your hand or a flat-bottomed drinking glass. Set aside.

2. Pour the boiling water into a large mixing bowl. Add the gelatin and lemon juice, and stir until the gelatin is dissolved. Set aside for 5 minutes to cool.

3. Add the cream cheese and sugar to the cooled gelatin mixture. Beat with an electric mixer on medium speed until smooth and well blended. Set aside.

4. Place the cold evaporated milk in another large mixing bowl and beat with the electric mixer on high speed for about 5 minutes, or until soft peaks form.

5. Fold the whipped evaporated milk with the lemon mixture until well blended and uniform in color. (For folding instructions, see page 57.)

6. Pour the filling over the crust in the springform pan and smooth with a rubber spatula. Cover and refrigerate at least 6 hours.

Important Tips

▶ In order to whip the evaporated milk properly, it must be very cold.

▶ When folding the lemon mixture with the whipped evaporated milk, be sure to really scrape the bottom of the bowl with the rubber spatula. The heavier lemon mixture will tend to stay on the bottom of the bowl.

7. When ready to serve, remove the outer ring from the springform pan, but leave the cake on the pan's base. Cut into wedges and serve as is or with a garnish of lemon wedges.

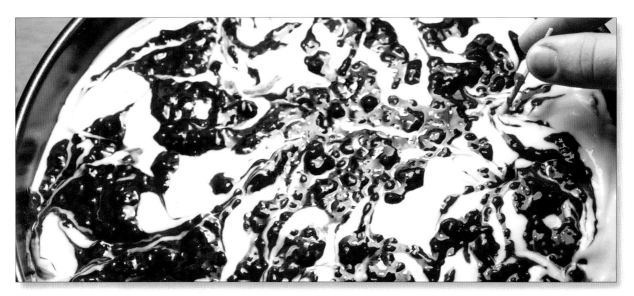

The wonderful world of baked cheesecakes.

There is nothing more decadent than a slice of creamy cheesecake. It doesn't matter if it's made from a no-frills cream cheese recipe and served in a simple unadorned state, or if it contains fruit or chocolate and is covered under a blanket of whipped cream. Coming up are my "5-star" cheesecakes that are guaranteed to help you reach nirvana. Time to pick up a fork and get started!

Basic Steps for Making Baked Cheesecakes

How to Swirl

1. Prepare the crust

Instructions for forming cookie crusts, which are used for the baked cheesecakes in this chapter, begin on page 162; the standard cookie crust recipe is found on page 172. Most of these cheesecakes are made in springform pans (see page 215).

2. Make the filling

To prepare the filling, beat softened cream cheese (or other soft fresh cheese) with other ingredients as instructed in the recipe. Use an electric mixer and beat until the mixture is smooth. Add eggs to the batter one at a time, stirring after each until just incorporated.

Adding a swirl of your favorite fruit jam or some melted chocolate to a basic cheesecake is a great way to liven it up.

Simply drizzle the mixture on top of the batter. Then use a toothpick, skewer, or knife to gently swirl it into the batter. Just don't overdo it or you will ruin the effect.

Keep your cheesecake from "cracking up"

Surface cracks are one of the most common complaints when it comes to cheesecakes. Fortunately, there are a number of things you can do to minimize the chance of this happening. But in spite of your best efforts, if your cheesecake still "cracks up," don't worry. It's not the end of the world. You can always cover it up with fruit, whipped cream, or some other topping.

▶ Don't overbeat the batter. This incorporates additional air, which expands during baking and causes cracks.

▶ Because eggs will hold air in the batter, add them last. Stir them gently and as little as possible after each addition. It is best to do this with a wooden spoon. If using an electric mixer, use the lowest speed.

▶ Spray the sides of the pan with nonstick cooking spray before adding the batter. This will help prevent the cake from sticking to the pan as it bakes.

▶ Bake cheesecakes slowly at a low temperature—usually at 325°F. If the temperature is too high, the cake won't bake evenly and will tend to crack.

▶ The slowest way to bake cheesecake is in a water bath. This keeps the oven moisture high and the heat gentle. Wrap the bottom and sides of the springform pan in foil, then place it in a larger pan that is few inches deep. Place in the preheated oven and fill the outer pan with enough hot water (I use a teapot to do this) to reach halfway up the pan. Bake as instructed.

▶ Do not open the oven door during the first thirty minutes of baking. Drafts can cause cracks.

▶ Cool a freshly baked cheesecake for at least one hour before refrigerating. Either cool it on a wire rack on the counter or let it cool right in the oven after baking. Just turn the heat off and leave the door open slightly.

▶ Cheesecake shrinks as it cools. After removing it from the oven, run a knife around the inside edge of the pan so the cake can easily pull away from the sides as it cools and lessen the chance of cracking.

▶ Before placing the pan in the oven, gently tap it on the countertop to eliminate any trapped air bubbles.

Springform – The Ultimate Cheesecake Pan

The springform is the preferred baking pan for most cheesecakes. Its removable outer ring lets you remove the pan from the cheesecake rather than the cheesecake from the pan! This helps minimize damage to your luscious dessert!

One pan, two pieces

A springform pan has two parts – a solid round base and an expandable outer ring. The ring attaches to the base and clasps shut, forming the deep sides of the pan. After the baked cake has cooled, the outer ring is unclasped and easily lifted off. The cake can remain on the base and be served from it.

Getting the clasp of it

It is essential to get a complete seal when clamping the pan's outer ring to the base. Make sure the ring fits securely in the groove that runs along the edge of the base. The clasp should be shut, and the base unable to move. If you don't get it right the first time, unclasp the ring and try again.

Ready to bake cake

Once the pan is assembled, you can prepare the crust. But before adding the filling, I recommend spraying the sides of the pan with cooking spray. This will help keep the cake from sticking to it during baking. Once the cake has been properly cooled, unclasp and remove the ring.

Italian Cheesecake

Since the Romans are credited with "promoting" cheesecake around the world, it is appropriate to start off this baked cheesecake section with a recipe for traditional Italian cheesecake. Instead of cream cheese, this cake is made with ricotta cheese, which is lighter in texture and flavor. I guarantee you're gonna love it.

Ingredients

4 cups ricotta cheese
1¼ cups granulated sugar
¼ cup all-purpose flour
½ cup heavy cream
2 teaspoons vanilla extract
1 tablespoon fresh lemon juice
4 eggs

Crust

1 cup graham cracker crumbs
¼ cup butter (½ stick), melted
1 tablespoon granulated sugar

Yield: 12 to 16 servings

Stuff You'll Need

1. Place all the crust ingredients in a medium mixing bowl, and stir until the crumbs have absorbed the butter. Spoon the moistened crumbs into a 9-inch springform pan and press them evenly on the bottom either with your hand or a flat-bottomed drinking glass. Set aside.

2. Place the ricotta, sugar, flour, cream, vanilla, and lemon juice in a large mixing bowl. Beat with an electric mixer on medium speed until smooth and well blended. Add the eggs one at a time, stirring after each until just incorporated into the batter.

3. Pour the batter over the crust and smooth with a rubber spatula. Bake in a preheated 325°F oven for 1 hour, or until the center of the cheesecake has set (it doesn't jiggle when you *gently* shake it). Remove from the oven and let cool completely—at least 1 hour.

4. Once the cake has cooled, cover the pan and refrigerate at least 4 hours. When ready to serve, remove the outer ring from the pan, but leave the cake on the pan's base. Cut into wedges and serve.

Pumpkin Chiffon Cheesecake

At times I find cheesecake too rich and pumpkin pie too "pumpkiny," but this dessert offers the perfect combination of both.

Ingredients

1 recipe graham cracker crust (page 172) or commercial variety

8-ounce package cream cheese, softened

10-ounce can pumpkin purée

$3/4$ cup firmly packed brown sugar

$1/2$ cup heavy cream

1 teaspoon cinnamon

$1/2$ teaspoon salt

3 eggs

Yield: 8 to 10 servings

1. Prepare the graham cracker crust. Set aside.

2. Place the cream cheese, pumpkin purée, brown sugar, cream, cinnamon, and salt in a large mixing bowl. Beat with an electric mixer on medium speed until smooth and well blended. Add the eggs one at a time, stirring after each until just incorporated into the batter.

3. Pour the batter into the pie crust and smooth with a rubber spatula. Bake in a preheated 325°F oven for 1 hour, or until the center of the cheesecake has set (it doesn't jiggle when you *gently* shake it). Remove from the oven and cool completely— at least 1 hour.

4. Once the cake has cooled, cover and refrigerate at least 4 hours. Cut the chilled cake into wedges and serve as is or topped with a generous helping of whipped cream.

Stuff You'll Need

New York Strawberry Cheesecake

This, in my opinion, is the all-time classic "bad boy" cheesecake. It's loaded with creamy richness and makes my heart pound just thinking about it.

Ingredients

4 packages (8 ounces each) cream cheese, softened
1 1/2 cups granulated sugar
1 cup sour cream
3/4 cup milk
1/4 cup all-purpose flour
1 tablespoon vanilla extract
4 eggs
16-ounce container fresh strawberries (about 16 to 20 medium)
2 tablespoons strawberry jam

Crust

1/4 cup butter (1/2 stick)
1 cup graham cracker crumbs
1 tablespoon granulated sugar

Yield: 12 to 16 servings

Stuff You'll Need

1. To make the crust, melt the butter and pour it into a medium mixing bowl.

2. Add the graham cracker crumbs and sugar to the bowl and stir until the crumbs have absorbed the butter.

3. Spoon the moistened crumbs into a 9-inch springform pan and press them evenly on the bottom either with your hand or a flat-bottomed drinking glass. Set aside.

4. Place the cream cheese, sugar, sour cream, milk, flour, and vanilla in a large mixing bowl. Beat with an electric mixer on medium speed until smooth and well blended.

5. Add the eggs one at a time, stirring after each until just incorporated into the batter.

6. Pour the batter over the crust and smooth with a rubber spatula. Bake in a preheated 325°F oven for 1 hour or until the center of the cheesecake has set. Turn off the heat, open the oven door slightly, and let the cheesecake cool in the oven for 2 hours.

7. Once the cake has cooled, cover and refrigerate at least 8 hours. Before serving, remove the outer ring from the pan, but leave the cake on the pan's base. Slice the strawberries, arrange them on top, and brush with strawberry jam. Cut into wedges and serve.

Chocolate Swirl Cheesecake

Swirls of rich dark chocolate complement the creamy goodness of this luscious cheesecake.

Ingredients

2 packages (8 ounces each) cream cheese, softened
1 cup granulated sugar
1 cup sour cream
$1/3$ cup all-purpose flour
2 teaspoons vanilla extract
2 eggs
6-ounces semi-sweet chocolate morsels

Crust

1 cup graham cracker crumbs
$1/4$ cup butter ($1/2$ stick)
1 tablespoon granulated sugar

Yield: 12 to 16 servings

Stuff You'll Need

1. To make the crust, melt the butter and pour it into a medium mixing bowl.

2. Add the graham cracker crumbs and sugar to the bowl and stir until the crumbs have absorbed the butter.

3. Spoon the moistened crumbs into a 9-inch springform pan and press them evenly on the bottom either with your hand or a flat-bottomed drinking glass. Set aside.

4. Place the cream cheese, sugar, sour cream, flour, and vanilla in a large bowl and beat with an electric mixer on medium speed until smooth and well blended. Add the eggs one at a time, stirring after each until just incorporated into the batter. Set aside.

5. Place the chocolate morsels in the top of a double boiler over medium-low heat or in a medium saucepan over *very low* heat. Stir until melted, then remove from the heat and let cool for 1 minute.

Important Tip

When cooling the melted chocolate, don't let it get too cool or it will start to harden and be difficult to swirl into the batter. If this happens, just heat it up again.

6. Pour the batter over the crust and smooth with a rubber spatula. Drizzle the melted chocolate over the top.

7. Gently swirl the chocolate into the batter with a toothpick or skewer. Do not overswirl. Bake in a preheated 325°F oven for 1 hour or until the center of the cheesecake has set (it doesn't jiggle when you *gently* shake it). Remove from the oven and let cool completely— at least 1 hour.

8. Once the cake has cooled, cover the pan and refrigerate at least 6 hours. Before serving, remove the outer ring from the pan, but leave the cake on the pan's base. Cut into wedges and serve.

White Chocolate Raspberry Swirl Cheesecake

Okay, this is absolutely without a doubt my favorite cheesecake. I like this version with raspberries best, but it is also great with blackberries or blueberries. For me, the secret ingredient is the white chocolate which adds extra flavor!

Ingredients

2 cups white chocolate morsels
1/2 cup heavy cream
3 packages (8 ounces each) cream
   cheese, softened
1/2 cup granulated sugar
1 teaspoon vanilla extract
3 eggs

Raspberry Sauce

2 cups frozen raspberries
2 tablespoons granulated sugar
2 teaspoons cornstarch
1/2 cup water

Crust

1 cup graham cracker crumbs
1/4 cup butter (1/2 stick), melted
1 tablespoon granulated sugar

Yield: 12 to 16 servings

Stuff You'll Need

1. Place all the crust ingredients in a medium mixing bowl, and stir until the crumbs have absorbed the butter. Spoon the moistened crumbs into a 9-inch springform pan and press them evenly on the bottom either with your hand or a flat-bottomed drinking glass. Set aside.

2. Place all of the raspberry sauce ingredients in a medium pot over medium-low heat. Stirring frequently, simmer for 5 minutes. Remove from the heat and set aside to cool.

3. Heat the white chocolate and cream in small saucepan over *very low* heat. Stir until smooth, then remove from the heat and set aside to cool for a few minutes.

4. Place the cream cheese, sugar, and vanilla in a large mixing bowl. Beat with an electric mixer on medium speed until smooth and well blended. Add the eggs one at a time, stirring after each until just incorporated into the batter.

5. Pour the melted white chocolate over the batter and fold together until well blended. (For folding instructions, see page 57.)

6. Spoon half the batter over the crust and smooth with a rubber spatula. Drizzle half the raspberry sauce over the top. Add the remaining batter and drizzle with the remaining sauce.

7. Gently swirl the sauce into the batter with a toothpick or skewer. Do not overswirl. Bake in a preheated 325°F oven for 1 hour or until the center of the cheesecake has set (it doesn't jiggle when you *gently* shake it). Remove from the oven and let cool completely—at least 1 hour.

8. Once the cake has cooled, cover the pan and refrigerate at least 6 hours. Before serving, remove the outer ring from the pan, but leave the cake on the pan's base. Cut into wedges and serve.

The Wonderful World of Cheesecake

*Not many desserts can compare in creamy richness to the heavenly cheesecake.
Like many baked desserts, it originated in Greece. Over time, just about every
country developed its own special version of this universally loved treat.*

International Delights

The standard American cheesecake has a cream cheese-based filling and a graham cracker crust. Here are some of the ways other countries make their cheesecakes:

▶ A number of Asian countries flavor their cheesecakes with green tea and add lychee and mango to the filling.

▶ Brazilians like to top their cheesecakes with guava marmalade.

▶ The French use Neufchâtel cheese as a base for their cheesecakes and add gelatin to bind it. The cakes are very light and only about an inch high.

▶ For their traditional cheesecake filling, the Greeks use mizithra cheese made from goat or sheep milk.

▶ The Dutch and Belgians use melted dark chocolate to flavor their cheesecakes. They also use a *speculaas* crust made from biscuit dough.

▶ Italian cheesecakes are made with ricotta or mascarpone cheese and often decorated with candied fruit.

▶ For their cheesecake fillings, Germans use uncooked quark cheese, which is soft and similar in fat content to yogurt.

▶ The Swedes use the enzyme rennet to curdle cream for their cheesecakes, which are usually served warm and topped with ice cream or whipped cream.

Basement Beginnings

In 1949, Evelyn Overton baked a dense, creamy New York-style cheesecake for her husband's boss, who loved it so much, he requested several more to give as gifts. Evelyn suddenly became interested selling her cakes. Eventually she renovated the basement kitchen of her Detroit home and used it to bake her cheesecakes, which she supplied to a number of local restaurants. By 1970, the Overtons moved to Los Angeles where they opened a bakery called The Cheesecake Factory. In 1978, their son David opened the first Cheesecake Factory restaurant in Beverly Hills. Today, there are nearly 150 throughout the United States.

Garlic Cheesecake

In Stockholm, Sweden, there is an all-garlic restaurant that serves a special garlic cheesecake. Hold the whipped cream, please!

Cheesecake Muy Grande!

In 2009, a team of fifty-five pastry chefs in Mexico City worked sixty hours straight to set a Guinness World Record for the World's Biggest Cheesecake. The two-ton calorie-laden bomb used nearly a ton of cream and yogurt, 551 pounds of sugar, 331 pounds of butter, and 772 pounds of pastry. As a finishing touch, the monster cake was topped with fresh strawberries. Organizers cut it into 20,000 slices, which were given out to people in the area.

Biscuits 'n Scones 226
  Cranberry Butter Biscuits, 228
  Blueberry Corn Biscuits, 230
  Mom's Buttermilk Biscuits, 232
  Blueberry Scones, 234

Muffins, Man! 236
  Choc-Choc Muffins, 238
  Almond Poppyseed Muffins, 239
  Raisin Bran Muffins, 240
  Blueberry Buttermilk Muffins, 242
  Lemon Poppyseed Muffins, 244
  Cornberry Muffins, 246

Drop Dead Bread 248
  Pumpkin Bread, 249
  Banana Berry Bread, 250
  Date-Nut Bread, 252
  Zucchini Bread, 254

How much bread do you want for that muffin?

Yeasted dough makes delicious breads and other baked goods. But if you've ever tried to make it (without the benefit of an automatic bread-making machine), you know that it isn't easy. It's a time-consuming, multi-step process that – if not followed carefully – can produce disappointing results. One of the biggest culprits for failure lies with the yeast itself, which can easily lose its leavening ability for any number of reasons.

Thankfully, there are easy-to-make "quick" breads that rely on baking powder and/or baking soda as leavening agents – and are better suited for the novice baker. Included among these baked goods are beautiful biscuits, scrumptious scones, marvelous muffins, and delicious dessert breads. All are found in this chapter . . . and all are easy to make and practically foolproof.

Starting off, you'll find melt-in-your-mouth down-home biscuits and their denser English cousins – the scones. Next comes a nice variety of muffins, followed by some sweet, delicious quick breads. For the most part, the recipes for muffins and quick breads are interchangeable (it's just a question of whether you're using a muffin pan or a loaf pan). But no matter how you bake 'em, you're gonna love 'em all!

"Y'all want some biscuits?" *or* "Give us a scone, Love!"

Biscuits and scones are very similar. Biscuits tend to be lighter and fluffier than scones because they have a higher volume of liquid and a lower saturation of butter. You can usually tell how light or dense these baked goods will be by the consistency of the dough. As a general rule of thumb, the wetter the dough, the lighter the results.

Basic Steps for Making Biscuits and Scones

1. Combine
When making the biscuits and scones on the following pages, combining the flour and other dry ingredients is the first step. Make sure the ingredients are well mixed – especially the leavening agents (baking powder and/or soda) – to ensure even distribution throughout the mixture.

2. Cut
The next step involves cutting cold butter (or other fat) into the flour mixture until it resembles a crumbly meal and sticks together when pressed with your hands. This is done with a pastry blender, two knives in a criss-cross motion, or a wooden spoon with a stabbing motion. (For cutting instructions, see page 55.)

3. Stir
Gently stirring the liquid ingredients (like eggs and cream) and any add-ins (like raisins or berries) into the crumbly flour mixture is the final step when preparing the dough, which can range from wet and sticky to stiff and somewhat dry.

Basic Techniques for Shaping Biscuits and Scones

Drop

For dough that is wet and sticky (and unsuitable for shaping), dropping it in spoonfuls onto a parchment-lined or well-greased baking sheet is a very popular technique. If it is extremely sticky, you can use a second spoon or your finger to remove it from the spoon.

Roll

Another way to shape wet dough is to roll it in flour. Simply spoon portions of the dough onto a floured surface and gently roll them into balls. For a classic biscuit shape, flatten the flour-coated balls slightly into rounded discs.

Flatten and cut

Dough that is firm and stiff is perfect for shaping and cutting. Place the dough on a floured surface and flatten it with a rolling pin to a thickness between $1/2$ and $3/4$ inch. Then cut the dough into squares or triangles with a sharp knife, or use a biscuit cutter for round biscuits.

Helpful Tips

▶ Do not overmix or overwork the dough. Stir the ingredients until moist and just combined. A few lumps in the batter are fine, even preferred. Do not knead the dough.

▶ If you are flattening the dough with a rolling pin, keep some flour handy. You may need some to rub on the rolling pin to prevent the dough from sticking to it. Avoid adding flour directly to the dough as it will make the biscuits heavy.

▶ When using fresh berries like blueberries and raspberries, be aware that they tend to break apart and bleed when mixed into the dough. You can firm them up by putting them in the freezer for about forty-five minutes before using. If you use frozen berries from the grocery store, be aware that they may be coated with juice, which will also discolor the dough. It is advisable to rinse the frozen berries with cold water to remove any frozen juice.

▶ Lining your baking pans with parchment paper or greased aluminum foil is suggested for biscuit and scone recipes that contain berries, which can burst during baking and bleed onto the pan. The baked-on mess is very difficult to remove and will probably discolor the pan

▶ Use a very sharp knife when cutting biscuit dough. And be sure to cut all the way through the dough to the bottom.

▶ If you use a biscuit cutter, make the cuts as close together as possible. Unlike scraps of cookie dough, which can be gathered up and rolled out again to make more cookies, biscuit dough scraps should not be reworked. Overworked dough results in tough biscuits.

Storing Biscuits and Scones

▶ Biscuits dry out and harden more quickly than most baked goods. For this reason, it's best to eat them shortly after they are made – within a day or two at most. Scones generally last a little longer than biscuits, but only another day or so.

▶ Be sure to cool biscuits completely before wrapping them in plastic wrap or foil. If they are still warm, moisture will form and cause them to get soggy.

▶ It is best to freeze biscuits while they are still fresh. Wrap each one tightly in foil, place in a freezer bag, and freeze (do not refrigerate) up to a month. When ready to serve, pop them foil and all into a 300°F oven. Heat about ten minutes if thawed and twenty minutes if frozen.

Cranberry Butter Biscuits

This recipe is the result of a very fortunate accident. While trying to make scones, I accidentally doubled the amount of cream, which made the dough too sticky to shape. So I dropped it in spoonfuls onto a cookie sheet. What I got were these super light, buttery biscuits!

Ingredients

1¼ cups all-purpose flour
2 tablespoons granulated sugar
2 teaspoons baking powder
6 tablespoons cold butter, cut into small pieces
1 cup heavy cream, cold
1 egg
½ cup dried cranberries (Craisins)

Yield: 8 to 10 biscuits

1. Combine the flour, sugar, and baking powder in a medium mixing bowl.

2. Add the butter to the bowl and cut it into the dry mixture until it resembles a crumbly meal.

3. Add the cream, egg, and cranberries to the flour mixture. Gently stir to form a wet, sticky dough.

4. Drop rounded tablespoons of dough on a parchment-lined (or well greased) cookie sheet, leaving about an inch of space between them. Bake in a preheated 400°F oven for 12 to 15 minutes, or until the edges are slightly browned. Serve warm.

Stuff You'll Need

Blueberry Corn Biscuits

These biscuits are similar to scones in the way they're shaped and cut. They are also are heavy like scones. You can use any type of frozen berries for this recipe.

Ingredients

1 ³/₄ cups all-purpose flour

¹/₄ cup cornmeal

2 teaspoons baking powder

2 tablespoons granulated sugar

1 cup cold butter (2 sticks), cut into
   small pieces

³/₄ cup buttermilk, cold

1 egg

1 cup fresh blueberries

Yield: 16 biscuits

Important Tip

Fresh blueberries tend to break apart and bleed when mixed into the dough. To make them firm, place in the freezer for forty-five minutes before using.

Stuff You'll Need

1. Combine the flour, cornmeal, baking powder, and sugar in a large mixing bowl.

2. Add the butter to the bowl and cut it into the dry mixture until it resembles a crumbly meal.

3. Add the buttermilk, egg, and blueberries to the flour mixture. Gently stir to form a stiff, sticky dough. (You can use your hands to complete the mixing if necessary.)

4. Place the dough on a lightly floured surface. Rub a little flour on a rolling pin, and roll out the dough into a 12-inch square about ³/₄ inch thick.

5. Cut the dough into 16 squares with a very sharp knife. Make sure to cut all the way through the dough.

6. Place the squares on a cookie sheet lined with parchment paper (or foil that has been greased), leaving a little over an inch of space between them.

7. Bake in a preheated 400°F oven for 15 to 18 minutes, or until the biscuits are light golden brown and crisp on the outside. Serve warm.

Mom's Buttermilk Biscuits

My mother used to make these delicious and easy-to-make biscuits for Sunday brunch. They're light as well as rich.

Ingredients

1 cup all-purpose flour
1 teaspoon granulated sugar
2 teaspoons baking powder
$1/4$ teaspoon salt
1 tablespoon shortening
1 tablespoon butter, cold
$1/2$ cup buttermilk
1 tablespoon vegetable oil

Yield: 8 biscuits

Important Tip

For the lightest biscuits, don't work this dough too much. To shape the biscuits, roll each piece of dough just once in the flour.

Stuff You'll Need

1. Combine the flour, sugar, baking powder, and salt in a medium mixing bowl.

2. Add the shortening and butter to the bowl, and cut them into the dry mixture until it resembles a crumbly meal.

3. Add the buttermilk to the flour mixture and gently stir to form a soft sticky dough.

4. Lightly flour a smooth flat surface. Divide the dough into 8 equal pieces, shape into balls, and roll in the flour. Flatten the balls a little into round discs.

5. Coat the bottom of 13-x-9-inch baking pan with the vegetable oil. Add the biscuits, leaving about 2 inches of space between them. Bake in a preheated 400°F oven for 12 to 15 minutes, or until light golden brown. Serve warm.

Blueberry Scones

'Ow about a nice 'ot buttered scone, Gub'ner?

Ingredients

2 cups all-purpose flour
$1/3$ cup granulated sugar
2 teaspoons baking powder
6 tablespoons cold butter, cut into
   small pieces
$1/2$ cup cream
1 egg
1 teaspoon vanilla extract
1 cup frozen blueberries
$1/4$ cup milk

Yield: About 24 scones

Important Tip

Fresh blueberries tend to break apart and bleed when mixed into the dough. To make them firm, place in the freezer for forty-five minutes before using.

Stuff You'll Need

1. Combine the flour, sugar, and baking powder in a medium mixing bowl.

2. Add the butter to the bowl and cut it into the dry mixture until it resembles a crumbly meal.

3. Add the cream, egg, and vanilla to the flour mixture, and stir to form a stiff, sticky dough. (You can use your hands to finish mixing if necessary.)

4. Gently fold the frozen blueberries into the dough.

5. Place the dough on a lightly floured surface, and sprinkle a little flour on top.

6. Rub a little flour on a rolling pin, and roll out the dough into a 12-inch square about $1/2$ inch thick.

7. Cut the dough into 12 squares with a very sharp knife. Make sure to cut all the way through the dough. Next cut each square diagonally in half to form triangles.

8. Place the scones on a cookie sheet lined with parchment paper (or foil that has been greased), leaving about an inch of space between them. Brush the tops with milk.

9. Bake in a preheated 400°F oven for 20 to 25 minutes, or until the scones are light golden brown and crisp on the outside. Serve warm.

All Hail the Muffin Man!

Although muffins and cupcakes have the same basic shape, they're pretty different. Cupcakes are basically miniature cakes. They are light and airy, sweet, and often topped with icing or frosting. Muffins are denser and heavier in weight than cupcakes. They can also contain bran, fruit, nuts, and other add-ins, which isn't common in cupcakes. And muffins are never frosted, nor are they especially sweet.

Basic Steps for Making Muffins

1. Blend
The first step when making the muffins in this section is blending together the eggs, butter or oil, and any liquid ingredients. You can blend the ingredients with a whisk, a wooden spoon, or an electric mixer.

2. Combine
Combining the flour and other dry ingredients in a separate bowl is the next step. Mix the ingredients together well – especially the leavening agents (baking powder and/or soda) – to ensure even distribution throughout the mixture.

3. Stir
Gently stirring together the blended liquid ingredients (and any add-ins) with the dry flour mixture is the final step when preparing the muffin batter. It is important not to overstir the batter. Stir the ingredients just until mixed.

Helpful Tips

▶ It is very important not to overstir muffin batter. This is because the flour contains gluten, which, when mixed with a liquid, causes the mixture to become sticky and elastic. The more you mix, the more gluten develops. And although this may be fine for some baked goods, it is not good for muffins or quick breads, which will become tough and dense. To avoid this, stir the batter as little as possible.

▶ When filling muffin cups, use a ladle or large spoon for thin muffin batters. Drop thicker batters into the cups with a tablespoon. If necessary, use your finger or a rubber spatula to remove the batter from the spoon.

▶ If using fresh berries like blueberries and raspberries, be aware that they tend to break apart and bleed when mixed into the batter. You can firm them up by putting them in the freezer for about forty-five minutes before using. If you use frozen berries from the grocery store, be aware that they may be coated with juice, which will also discolor the batter. It is advisable to rinse the frozen berries with cold water to remove any frozen juice.

▶ Allow the muffins to cool at least ten minutes before removing them from the tin. If you remove them too soon, the hot muffins may break apart.

▶ After the muffins have cooled, if they don't fall out of their baking cups easily, gently cut around the edge of the cup with a dull knife to release them.

How Many Minis Can I Make?

Most of the recipes in this section are for standard-size muffins, but you can use the batter to make jumbo or mini muffins as well.

A recipe that yields

12 standard
($2\,^3/_4$ inch) muffins

Also Makes

6 jumbo (3 inch) or
32 mini ($1^1/_2$ inch) muffins

▶ Although you can use baking cups to line the muffin tin, I find that the muffins (especially when they're warm) tend to stick to the paper. Instead, I prefer using nonstick cooking spray to coat the cups.

Storing Muffins

▶ To store leftover muffins, wrap them individually in plastic wrap or foil, or place them in an airtight container up to five days. Refrigerated, they will keep about two weeks.

▶ Be sure to cool the muffins completely before wrapping them in plastic wrap or foil. If they are still warm, moisture form and the muffins will become soggy.

▶ If you want to freeze muffins, it is best to do so shortly after they are made, when they are freshest. After wrapping them individually in foil, place them in a plastic freezer bag and store in the freezer for up to three months. Once frozen, most muffins look alike, so it's a good idea to label them. To reheat, simply place them foil and all in a 300°F oven. Heat standard-size muffins twelve to fifteen minutes; heat jumbo muffins twenty-five to thirty minutes.

Add-Ins

Muffins are good. Muffins with add-ins are better.

▶ **Seeds**

Poppyseeds
Sunflower seeds
Pumpkin seeds

▶ **Nuts**

Almonds, Cashews,
Hazelnuts, Macadamias,
Peanuts, Pecans,
Pistachios, Walnuts

▶ **Fruit**

Blackberries, Blueberries,
Dates, Raisins,
Raspberries, Strawberries

▶ **Morsels/Chips/Chunks**

Milk chocolate
Semi-sweet chocolate
White chocolate

Choc-Choc Muffins

Ricotta cheese makes these muffins extra rich. And if you're a lover of chocolate, this recipe will give you a double whammy – it has both cocoa and chocolate chips!

Ingredients

1 cup ricotta cheese

1 1/2 cups milk

2 eggs

4 tablespoons butter (1/2 stick), softened

1 cup granulated sugar

1 tablespoon vanilla extract

2 cups all-purpose flour

2/3 cup cocoa powder

2 teaspoons baking powder

1/2 teaspoon salt

1 cup semi-sweet chocolate morsels

Yield: 16 standard muffins

Stuff You'll Need

1. Place the ricotta cheese, milk, eggs, butter, sugar, and vanilla in a large mixing bowl. Beat with an electric mixer on low speed for 1 to 2 minutes or until well blended. Set aside.

2. Combine the flour, cocoa powder, baking powder, and salt in a medium mixing bowl.

3. Add the chocolate morsels and ricotta mixture to the flour mixture and stir just until mixed. Do not overstir.

4. Spoon the batter into a greased standard muffin tin. Fill each cup nearly to the top.

5. Bake in a preheated 350°F oven for 18 to 20 minutes or until a toothpick inserted into the center of a muffin comes out clean. Cool at least 10 minutes before removing the muffins from the tin.

Almond Poppyseed Muffins

Whoa! I love these muffins. The crunchy almond crust that forms on top makes me go bananas!

Ingredients

2 cups all-purpose flour
1 teaspoon baking powder
$1/2$ teaspoon salt
2 cups granulated sugar
$1/2$ cup butter (1 stick), softened
1 cup milk
2 eggs
4 teaspoons poppyseeds
2 teaspoons almond extract
$1/2$ cup sliced almonds

Yield: 12 standard muffins

Stuff You'll Need

1. Combine the flour, baking powder, and salt in a medium mixing bowl. Set aside.

2. Place the sugar, butter, milk, eggs, almond extract, and poppyseeds in a large mixing bowl, and stir until well blended. Add the flour mixture and stir just until mixed. Do not overstir.

3. Spoon the batter into a greased standard muffin tin. Fill each cup about three-quarters full. Sprinkle with sliced almonds.

4. Bake in a preheated 350°F oven for 18 to 20 minutes, or until a toothpick inserted into the center of a muffin comes out clean. Cool at least 10 minutes before removing the muffins from the tin.

Raisin Bran Muffins

These hearty fiber-rich muffins have just the right touch of sweetness. I often bake them into mini muffins!

Ingredients

2 cups bran flakes cereal
1 cup buttermilk
$2/3$ cup firmly packed brown sugar
$1/3$ cup vegetable oil
1 egg
1 teaspoon vanilla extract
1 cup whole wheat flour
1 teaspoon baking soda
1 teaspoon baking powder
$1/2$ teaspoon salt
$1/2$ cup raisins

Yield: 32 mini muffins or 12 standard muffins

Stuff You'll Need

1. Place the bran flakes in a zippered plastic storage bag, then crush with a rolling pin. You can also crush the flakes in a food processor.

2. Place the crushed flakes in a small bowl, add the buttermilk, and stir. Let the mixture stand for 10 minutes.

3. Place the brown sugar, oil, egg, and vanilla in a large mixing bowl, and stir until well blended.

4. Combine the flour, baking soda, baking powder, and salt in a medium mixing bowl. Add this mixture, the soaked bran, and raisins to the liquid mixture and stir just until combined. Do not overstir.

5. Spoon the batter into a greased mini muffin tin. Fill each cup nearly to the top. Bake in a preheated 350°F oven for 15 to 18 minutes, or until a toothpick inserted into the center of a muffin comes out clean. Cool at least 10 minutes before removing the muffins from the tin.

Blueberry Buttermilk Muffins

Blueberries are my favorite muffin add-ins. And they're especially great in buttermilk muffins. Oooo doggie, you're gonna luv 'em!

Ingredients

2 1/2 cups all-purpose flour
1 teaspoon baking powder
1 teaspoon baking soda
1/4 teaspoon salt
3/4 cup granulated sugar
3/4 cup buttermilk
2/3 cup vegetable oil
1 egg
1 teaspoon vanilla extract
2 cups fresh blueberries

Yield: 12 standard muffins

Important Tip

Fresh blueberries tend to break apart and bleed when mixed into the batter. To make them firm, place in the freezer for forty-five minutes before using.

1. Combine the flour, baking powder, baking soda, and salt in a medium mixing bowl. Set aside.

2. Place the sugar, buttermilk, oil, egg, and vanilla in a large mixing bowl and stir until well blended.

3. Add the flour mixture and blueberries to the blended buttermilk mixture and stir just until mixed. Do not overstir.

4. Spoon the batter into a greased standard muffin tin. Fill each cup nearly to the top.

Stuff You'll Need

5. Bake in a preheated 350°F oven for 18 to 20 minutes or until a toothpick inserted into the center of a muffin comes out clean. Cool at least 10 minutes before removing the muffins from the tin.

Try This Variation!

This recipe works with just about any type of berry. Try it with blackberries, gooseberries, and even huckleberries!

Raspberry-Chocolate Buttermilk Muffins

Add

▶ ¹/₂ cup semi-sweet chocolate morsels

Substitute

▶ 2 cups frozen raspberries

Use raspberries instead of blueberries. Add them along with the chocolate morsels in Step 3 of the recipe.

Lemon Poppyseed Muffins

I love lemons and I love poppyseeds – and with these muffins I get both! The lemon glaze that's drizzled on top adds just the right spark of tangy sweetness!

Ingredients

3/4 cup granulated sugar

1/2 cup butter (1 stick), softened

2 eggs

1 cup plain yogurt (do not use nonfat)

3 tablespoons fresh lemon juice

1 teaspoon lemon zest

1 teaspoon vanilla extract

2 cups all-purpose flour

2 tablespoons poppyseeds

1 teaspoon baking powder

1 teaspoon baking soda

1/2 teaspoon salt

Glaze

2 tablespoons fresh lemon juice

1/2 cup confectioner's sugar

Yield: 12 standard muffins

Stuff You'll Need

1. Place the sugar, butter, eggs, yogurt, lemon juice, lemon zest, and vanilla in large mixing bowl. Beat with an electric mixer on low speed for 1 to 2 minutes or until well blended. Set aside.

2. Combine the flour, poppyseeds, baking powder, baking soda, and salt in a medium mixing bowl. Add this flour mixture to the blended lemon-yogurt mixture and stir just until mixed. Do not overstir.

3. Spoon the batter into a greased standard muffin tin. Fill each cup nearly to the top. Bake in a preheated 350°F oven for 18 to 20 minutes, or until a toothpick inserted into the center of a muffin comes out clean. Cool at least 10 minutes before removing from the tin.

4. When the muffins have cooled, prepare the glaze. Stir the lemon juice and confectioner's sugar until well blended and smooth.

5. Drizzle the glaze over the cooled muffins.

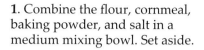

Cornberry Muffins

These muffins are real corny – and that's just the way I like 'em. You can use just about any berry or combination of berries in this recipe; but if you use strawberries, coarsely chop them first.

Ingredients

1¹/₂ cups all-purpose flour
³/₄ cup cornmeal
1 tablespoon baking powder
¹/₂ teaspoon salt
1 cup milk
1 egg
¹/₂ cup granulated sugar
¹/₃ cup vegetable oil
1 teaspoon vanilla extract
1 cup fresh raspberries

Yield: 16 standard muffins

Important Tip

Fresh raspberries are delicate and tend to break apart and bleed when mixed into the batter. To make them firm, place in the freezer for forty-five minutes before using.

Stuff You'll Need

1. Combine the flour, cornmeal, baking powder, and salt in a medium mixing bowl. Set aside.

2. Place the milk, egg, sugar, oil, and vanilla in a large mixing bowl. Stir until well blended.

3. Add the flour-cornmeal mixture and the raspberries to the milk mixture and stir until just mixed. Do not overstir.

4. Spoon the batter into a greased standard muffin tin. Fill each cup nearly to the top.

5. Bake in a preheated 350°F oven for 18 to 20 minutes or until a toothpick inserted into the center of a muffin comes out clean. Cool at least 10 minutes before removing the muffins from the tin.

Try This Variation!

Blueberry corn muffins are really popular. This one has a touch of maple flavor. I sometimes use the batter to make pancakes!

Blueberry-Maple Corn Muffins

Add

▶ 1 teaspoon maple extract

Substitute

▶ 1 cup fresh blueberries

Add the maple extract in Step 2 of the recipe, and use blueberries instead of raspberries in Step 3.

These bread recipes are a piece of cake!

Quick breads are leavened with baking powder and/or baking soda, so they don't have to be kneaded and they don't need time to rise. That's what makes 'em so quick! Serve slices of these luscious breads for dessert or enjoy them as snacks or even side dishes. Since the batter and the techniques for making muffins and quick breads are the same, so are most of the Helpful Tips on page 237.

Basic Steps for Making Quick Breads

1. Blend
The first step for making the quick breads in this section is blending together the eggs, butter or oil, and any liquid ingredients. You can blend these ingredients with a whisk, a wooden spoon, or an electric mixer.

2. Combine
Combining the flour and other dry ingredients in a separate bowl is the next step. Mix the ingredients together well – especially the leavening agents (baking powder and/or soda) – to ensure even distribution throughout the mixture.

3. Stir
Gently stirring together the blended liquid ingredients (and any add-ins) with the dry flour mixture is the final step when preparing quick bread batter. It is important not to overstir the batter. Stir the ingredients just until mixed.

Pumpkin Bread

This easy-to-make holiday quick bread is delicious plain or topped with a little butter.

Ingredients

2 cups all-purpose flour
1 teaspoon baking soda
$\frac{1}{2}$ teaspoon ground nutmeg
$\frac{1}{2}$ teaspoon ground cinnamon
$\frac{1}{2}$ teaspoon salt
$1\frac{1}{2}$ cups sugar
$\frac{1}{2}$ cup vegetable oil
2 eggs
1 cup pumpkin purée
$\frac{1}{3}$ cup water
$\frac{1}{4}$ cup coarsely chopped walnuts
$\frac{1}{4}$ cup raisins (optional)

Yield: 9-inch loaf

Stuff You'll Need

1. Combine the flour, baking soda, nutmeg, cinnamon, and salt in a medium mixing bowl. Set aside.

2. Place the sugar, oil, eggs, pumpkin purée, and water in a large mixing bowl. Beat with an electric mixer, whisk, or wooden spoon until smooth and well blended. Add the flour mixture, walnuts, and raisins (if using), and stir just until mixed. Do not overstir.

3. Spoon the batter into a greased and floured 9-x-5-inch loaf pan. Bake in a preheated 350°F oven for 50 to 60 minutes, or until a toothpick inserted into the center of the loaf comes out clean.

4. Cool for 15 minutes before removing the bread from the pan.

Banana Berry Bread

Adding blueberries to banana bread makes it a little moister and more flavorful. For traditional banana bread, just eliminate the berries.

Ingredients

2 very ripe large bananas
$1/2$ cup butter (1 stick), softened
$1/2$ cup granulated sugar
2 eggs
1 teaspoon vanilla extract
$1^1/2$ cups all-purpose flour
1 tablespoon baking powder
$1/2$ teaspoon salt
1 cup fresh blueberries

Yield: 9-inch loaf

Important Tip

Fresh blueberries tend to break apart and bleed when mixed into the batter. To make them firm, place in the freezer for forty-five minutes before using.

1. Place the bananas in a large mixing bowl and mash well. Add the butter, sugar, eggs, and vanilla, and beat with an electric mixer, whisk, or wooden spoon until smooth and well blended.

2. Combine the flour, baking powder, and salt in a medium mixing bowl.

3. Add the flour mixture and blueberries to the blended banana mixture and stir just until mixed. Do not overstir.

4. Spoon the batter into a greased and floured 9-x-5-inch loaf pan.

Stuff You'll Need

5. Bake in a preheated 350°F oven for 50 to 60 minutes, or until a toothpick inserted into the center of the loaf comes out clean. Cool for 15 minutes before removing the bread from the pan.

Try This Variation!

If you like a more traditional banana bread, try this "nutty" variation.

Banana Nut Bread

Substitute

1 cup pecan or walnut halves

Instead of blueberries, add the nuts in Step 3 of the recipe.

Date-Nut Bread

I normally don't eat dates, but I love them in baked goods like this quick bread. I coarsely chop them (as well as the walnuts) so there's a tasty surprise in every bite.

Ingredients

8 ounces pitted dates
3 tablespoons butter
1 cup boiling water
$1/2$ cup granulated sugar
$1/2$ cup firmly packed brown sugar
1 egg
1 teaspoon vanilla extract
$2 1/2$ cups all-purpose flour
1 tablespoon baking powder
$1/2$ teaspoon salt
$1/2$ cup coarsely chopped walnuts
   or pecans

Yield: 9-inch loaf

Stuff You'll Need

1. Coarsely chop the dates and place in a small bowl.

2. Cut up the butter, add to the bowl with the dates, and cover with the boiling water. Set aside.

3. Place the sugars, egg, and vanilla in a large mixing bowl. Beat with an electric mixer, whisk, or wooden spoon until smooth and well blended.

4. Add the date-butter mixture to the egg mixture and stir well.

5. Combine the flour, baking powder, and salt in a medium mixing bowl. Add this flour mixture and the walnuts to the date mixture and stir just until mixed. Do not overstir.

6. Spoon the batter into a greased and floured 9-x-5-inch loaf pan. Bake in a preheated 350°F oven for 50 to 60 minutes, or until a toothpick inserted into the center of the loaf comes out clean.

7. Cool for 15 minutes before removing the bread from the pan.

Try This Variation!

I know this is restated several times in this chapter, but quick bread recipes are also great for muffins. Try 'em both!

Chocolate-Date Muffins

Add

1/2 cup semi-sweet chocolate morsels

Instead of walnuts, add the chocolate morsels in Step 5 of the recipe, and use a greased standard muffin tin instead of a loaf pan. Bake for about 30 minutes instead of an hour.

Yield: 12 standard muffins

Zucchini Bread

The first time I had this bread was in a restaurant. The idea of zucchini as an ingredient in a dessert bread seemed a little odd to me, but it was surprisingly good. It's also a delicious way to sneak a vegetable into your diet!

Ingredients

1$^1/_2$ cups shredded zucchini
  (2 medium zucchini)
1$^1/_2$ cups firmly packed brown sugar
$^3/_4$ cup vegetable oil
2 eggs
1 teaspoon vanilla extract
2 cups all-purpose flour
2 teaspoons ground cinnamon
1 teaspoon baking powder
1 teaspoon baking soda
$^1/_2$ teaspoon salt
$^1/_2$ cup chopped walnuts

Yield: 9-inch loaf

Stuff You'll Need

1. Shred the zucchini.

2. Place the brown sugar, oil, eggs, and vanilla in a large mixing bowl. Beat with an electric mixer, whisk, or wooden spoon until smooth and well blended. Add the zucchini and stir well.

3. Combine the flour, cinnamon, baking powder, baking soda, salt, and walnuts in a medium mixing bowl.

4. Add the flour mixture to the blended zucchini mixture and stir just until mixed. Do not overstir.

5. Spoon the batter into a greased and floured 9-x-5-inch loaf pan. Bake in a preheated 350°F oven for 50 to 60 minutes or until a toothpick inserted into the center of the loaf comes out clean. Cool for 15 minutes before removing the bread from the pan.

Muffin Madness

Baked goods like muffins, biscuits, and quick breads are suitable to enjoy at just about any time of the day. As an added bonus, because they get their "lift" from baking powder or baking soda, they can be ready in no time. Here are some interesting bits of info about them.

A "Wale" of a Muffin

The first muffins were made during the tenth century in Wales and came to be known as English muffins. They were cooked in hooplike rings that were placed directly on the stove or in a skillet. Unlike America's cake-like muffins, English muffins are yeast-based and famous for their "nooks and crannies."

The Muffin Man

> *"Do you know the muffin man,*
> *the muffin man, the muffin man?*
> *Do you know the muffin man,*
> *who lives on Drury Lane?"*

In this abbreviated version of a nineteenth-century English nursery rhyme, Drury Lane refers to a famous street in London where muffin men would deliver their wares to Victorian households.

Official Muffins

I have heard of state birds, state trees, and state flowers; but official state muffins? To date, four US states have chosen the following:

- ▶ Massachusetts – the corn muffin
- ▶ Minnesota – the blueberry muffin
- ▶ New York – the apple muffin
- ▶ Washington – the blueberry muffin

As far as New York's apple muffin, it was a group of elementary school children who were responsible for getting the Governor to sign the bill for this official honor.

In a Jiffy

In 1930, Mabel White Holmes, whose family owned a flour milling company in Chelsea, Michigan, set her sights on packaging a mixture of all the dry ingredients needed to make a batch of biscuits. The goal, in her words, was, "By simply adding liquid, even the father of a motherless brood would be able to make good biscuits." When deciding on a name for her no-brainer product, she remembered when she was a little girl and thought about the family cook, who always promised that the good hot biscuits would be ready "in a jiffy!" Mabel was convinced the name would sell, so Jiffy Mixes were born. Today, there are twenty-two Jiffy Mix varieties, with over a million boxes produced each day.

Boat Anchor, Anyone?

In the 1970s and '80s, muffins were all the rage. Because they were often packed with fiber, people considered them the new "health food." I've eaten muffins that were so heavy they could have made good boat anchors, and loaded with so much fiber, they practically scratched my throat when I swallowed them!

It's Number One!

Can you guess which "fruity" muffin is the most popular? If you picked blueberry, you're right. Apple-cinnamon and banana-nut follow close behind.

Buttery-Nuttery Coffeecakes 258
  Chocolate Chunk Coffeecake, 260
  Butter Pecan Coffeecake, 262
  Cinnamon-Nut Coffeecake, 264

  Butter-Butter Coffeecake, 266
  Choco-Walnut Coffeecake, 268
  Apple-Pecan Coffeecake, 270
  Fresh Strawberry Coffeecake, 272

  Almond-Berry Coffeecake, 274
  Blueberry Buckle, 276

Wake up and smell the coffee(cake)

Do you ever want to eat cake for breakfast? Well then consider this your lucky day, because this chapter is loaded with recipes for the ultimate breakfast treat – the coffeecake. These rich and delicious cakes are a great way to start your day off right because they're made to go perfectly with a cup of coffee (hence the name). They're also a most-excellent choice to serve at brunches, holiday meals, or even as desserts.

Many coffeecake recipes are made with yeasted dough, which can be a little complicated for the novice baker to work with. For this reason, the recipes in this chapter use baking powder and/or baking soda as leavening agents. They take less time and are a lot easier to make than those made with yeast.

On the following pages, you'll find a nice selection of what I call my "nuttery-buttery" coffeecakes. With ingredients like sour cream, yogurt, and lots of butter, these cakes are wonderfully rich and moist, which is the main reason I always share them with friends and family. Otherwise I'd need bigger clothes or have to join a health club.

Most of the coffeecakes in this chapter have fruits and nuts as their star ingredients. Lucky for me, I live in California, also known as "*The Land of Fruits and Nuts*," so I never have a problem finding friends to help me eat coffeecake!

I wish I could be this rich and nutty!

The first coffeecakes came from Germany—a type of sweet bread called "kaffee kuchen." Coffeecakes are typically single-layer cakes that are usually square, round, or in the shape of a ring. Commonly flavored with cinnamon, nuts, and fruits, these cakes often have a crumb or crumbly streusel topping and/or a drizzle of glaze. They're perfect for any occasion!

Basic Steps for Making "Buttery-Nuttery" Coffeecakes

1. Blend
Beat together the liquid and/or semi-solid ingredients with an electric mixer, wooden spoon, or whisk until smooth and well blended.

2. Combine
Combine the flour and other dry ingredients, then stir this into the blended liquid mixture. You can use either a wooden spoon or an electric mixer on the lowest speed to do this. Stir just until the ingredients are mixed to form a batter. Don't overstir.

3. Prepare topping/filling
Many coffeecake recipes have streusel-like toppings and/or fillings—combos of nuts, sugar, flour, butter, and/or cinnamon. In some recipes, you can simply stir these ingredients together. In others, you have to cut butter into the dry ingredients. (For cutting instructions, see page 55.)

Helpful Tips

▶ Coffeecake batters are often very thick and sticky—more like dough. This may make them difficult to pour into the pan. You may find it easier to drop large spoonfuls of batter into the pan, and then spread it out in a even layer with the back of the spoon or a rubber spatula

▶ Allow coffeecakes ample time to cool. Unless the recipe instructs otherwise, let them cool at least fifteen minutes before attempting to cut or remove them from the pan.

▶ As the cake bakes, it may stick to the sides of the pan. To help release the baked cake, run a dull knife around the inside edge of the pan.

▶ Although you can use all-purpose flour for the recipes in this chapter with good results, using cake flour is even better. Cake flour's low-gluten content results in cake that is very light.

▶ When using an electric mixer to stir the dry flour mixture into the blended liquids, run it on the lowest speed. If you are using a wooden spoon, use quick round strokes. And stir the batter as little as possible— just until the ingredients are combined. This is because the flour contains gluten, which, when mixed with a liquid, causes the mixture to become sticky and elastic. The more you mix, the more gluten develops. And although this may be fine for some baked goods, it is not good for coffeecakes, muffins, or quick breads, which will become tough and dense.

▶ Don't be afraid to add variety to your streusel-style toppings. Experiment. Add some flaked coconut to the mixture or toss in a handful of oats, raisins, or chocolate morsels. This will add both flavor and texture to an already delicious topping.

Storing Coffeecake

▶ If you are planning to eat your freshly baked coffeecake within twenty-four hours after it's made, you can leave it in the pan loosely covered with foil.

▶ To store coffeecake in the refrigerator, where it will keep for two or three days, remove it from the pan, and wrap it tightly in foil or plastic wrap. You can also cut the cake into large pieces, and wrap each piece individually.

▶ Make sure the coffeecake is completely cool before wrapping it. Covering it while it's still warm will cause moisture to form and the cake will get soggy.

▶ You can freeze coffeecake up to a month. Remove the cake from the pan, wrap it tightly in foil, and place in a freezer storage bag. You can reheat coffeecake in an oven or toaster oven directly from the freezer while it's still wrapped in foil (it isn't necessary to thaw it out first).

Add-Ins

Coffeecake is good. Coffeecake with add-ins is better.

▶ **Morsels**

    Semi-sweet chocolate
    Milk chocolate
    Chocolate chunks
    Butterscotch

▶ **Nuts**

    Almonds
    Hazelnuts
    Pecans
    Walnuts

▶ **Dried fruit**

    Cranberries (Craisins)
    Dates
    Raisins

▶ **Fruit**

    Apples
    Blackberries
    Blueberries
    Cherries
    Raspberries
    Strawberries

Chocolate Chunk Coffeecake

I was elated when chocolate chunks suddenly appeared on supermarket shelves. These giant morsels are great additions to lots of baked goods. In this recipe, they are combined with pecans and tossed with sugar and cinnamon for a coffeecake topping that is simply "outta dis world."

Ingredients

³/₄ cup butter (1¹/₂ sticks), softened
1 cup granulated sugar
1 cup sour cream
1 teaspoon vanilla extract
3 eggs
2¹/₂ cups cake flour, or
    all-purpose flour
1 teaspoon baking soda
¹/₂ teaspoon baking powder
¹/₂ teaspoon salt

Topping

12-ounce package semi-sweet
    chocolate chunks
³/₄ cup coarsely chopped pecans
¹/₂ cup granulated sugar
1 teaspoon ground cinnamon

Yield: 12 to 15 servings

Stuff You'll Need

1. Place the butter, sugar, sour cream, vanilla, and eggs in a large mixing bowl. Beat with an electric mixer, whisk, or wooden spoon until smooth and well blended.

2. Combine the flour, baking soda, baking powder, and salt in a medium mixing bowl. Gradually add this flour mixture to the butter mixture, and stir just until mixed to form a thick batter. Do not overstir.

3. Spoon the batter into a greased and floured 13-x-9-inch baking pan. Spread it out evenly with a rubber spatula.

4. Place the topping ingredients in a medium bowl and mix until the chocolate and pecans are well coated with the sugar and cinnamon.

5. Sprinkle the topping evenly over the batter. Bake in a preheated 350°F oven for 40 to 45 minutes or until a toothpick inserted into the center of the cake comes out clean. Serve warm or at room temperature.

Butter Pecan Coffeecake

The first time I tried to create this coffeecake I put the nut mixture on top of the batter, but it sank to the bottom during baking. During my next attempt, I used the mixture as a filling, but it sank again. The good news is that each attempt was a delicious disaster and gave me the idea to "go with the flow" and turn the recipe into an upside-down coffeecake. Here is the delicious result!

Ingredients

$^1/_2$ cup pecan pieces
2 cups cake flour, or all-purpose flour
1 teaspoon baking powder
$^1/_2$ teaspoon baking soda
$^1/_2$ teaspoon salt
$1^1/_2$ cups granulated sugar
1 cup butter (2 sticks), softened
2 eggs
1 teaspoon vanilla extract
$1^1/_2$ cups sour cream

Topping

$^1/_4$ cup butter ($^1/_2$ stick)
1 cup coarsely chopped pecans
$^3/_4$ cup firmly packed brown sugar

Yield: 10 to 12 servings

Stuff You'll Need

1. Very finely grind the pecan pieces in a food processor or coffee grinder until they are powdery and somewhat pasty.

2. Transfer the ground pecans to a medium mixing bowl along with the flour, baking powder, baking soda, and salt. Stir until well combined. Set aside.

3. Place the sugar, butter, eggs, sour cream, and vanilla in a large mixing bowl. Beat with an electric mixer on a low speed until smooth and well blended. Gradually add the flour mixture, and continue beating on low speed to form a thick sticky batter. Do not overstir. Set aside.

4. To make the topping, melt the butter in a small pot over medium-low heat. Add the pecans, stir with the melted butter, then add the brown sugar. Continue stirring for a minute or so until the pecans are well coated.

5. Line the bottom of a 9-inch springform pan with parchment paper, coat the sides with cooking spray, then add a little more than half the coated pecans.

Important Tip

Although I use a springform pan for this recipe, you can also use a 9-inch baking pan that is at least 2 inches deep. It must also be fully lined with parchment or you'll have a hard time removing the fragile, sticky cake. (For more information on springform pans, see page 215.)

6. Spoon half the batter over the pecans and spread it out evenly with a rubber spatula. Sprinkle the remaining pecans over the batter.

7. Spread the remaining batter over the filling. Bake in a preheated 350°F oven for 60 to 70 minutes, or until a toothpick inserted into the center of the cake comes out clean.

8. Cool least 30 minutes before removing the cake from the pan. First, run a knife along the inside edge to release any cake that may be stuck. Then carefully remove the sides of the pan. Invert the cake onto a plate, remove the bottom of the pan, and gently peel off the parchment paper. Serve at room temperature.

Cinnamon-Nut Coffeecake

I love the combination of cinnamon and raisins in lots of baked goods. I also enjoy nuts in or on just about anything! Put 'em all together and what do you get? Why, this delicious coffeecake, of course!

Ingredients

1 cup granulated sugar
3/4 cup vegetable oil
1 cup plain yogurt
3 eggs
1 teaspoon vanilla extract
2 cups cake flour, or all-purpose flour
1 teaspoon baking soda
1/4 teaspoon salt
1/2 cup raisins

Topping

1 tablespoon melted butter
1 cup coarsely chopped walnuts
1/2 cup firmly packed brown sugar
1 tablespoon ground cinnamon

Yield: 12 to 15 servings

Stuff You'll Need

1. Place the sugar, oil, yogurt, eggs, and vanilla in a large mixing bowl and beat with an electric mixer, whisk, or wooden spoon until smooth and well blended.

2. Combine the flour, baking soda, salt, and raisins in a medium mixing bowl. Gradually add this flour mixture to the liquid mixture, and stir just until mixed to form a thick batter. Do not overstir.

3. Spoon the batter into a greased and floured 13-x-9-inch baking pan. Spread it out evenly with a rubber spatula.

4. Place all of the topping ingredients in a medium bowl, and stir until the walnuts are well coated with sugar and cinnamon.

5. Sprinkle the topping over the batter. Using the blade of a knife, swirl the topping into the batter. Bake in a preheated 350°F oven for 40 to 45 minutes or until a toothpick inserted into the center of the cake comes out clean. Serve warm or at room temperature.

Butter-Butter Coffeecake

If you like coffeecake that is super buttery, you've just found your favorite recipe. When it's fresh from the oven, this buttery cake is further infused with a rich butter sauce. Nothing like a double buttery blast of the good stuff!

Ingredients

2 cups cake flour, or all-purpose flour
$1/2$ teaspoon baking powder
$1/2$ teaspoon baking soda
$1/2$ teaspoon salt
$2/3$ cup butter (1 stick plus 3 tablespoons), softened
$1^1/4$ cups granulated sugar
$2/3$ cup buttermilk
3 eggs
1 teaspoons vanilla extract

Butter Sauce

$1/2$ cup granulated sugar
$1/4$ cup butter
2 tablespoons water
$1^1/2$ teaspoons vanilla extract

Yield: 10 to 12 servings

Stuff You'll Need

1. Combine the flour, baking powder, baking soda, and salt in a medium mixing bowl. Set aside.

2. Place the butter, sugar, buttermilk, eggs, and vanilla in a large mixing bowl. Beat with an electric mixer, whisk, or wooden spoon until smooth and well blended.

3. Gradually add the dry ingredients to the liquid mixture, and stir just until mixed to form a thick batter. Do not overstir.

4. Spoon the batter into a greased and floured 9-inch Bundt or tube pan, and spread it out evenly with a rubber spatula. Bake in a preheated 325°F oven for 45 to 50 minutes, or until a toothpick inserted into the center of the cake comes out clean.

5. After the cake has cooled about 10 minutes, place all the butter sauce ingredients in a small saucepan over medium heat. Stir until the sugar has fully dissolved. Set aside.

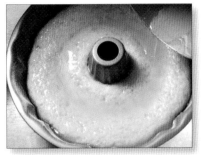

6. Using a toothpick, poke holes into the bottom of the warm cake. (This will help the butter sauce soak into it.)

7. Pour the butter sauce evenly over the cake. Leave the cake in the pan for 1 hour to absorb the sauce.

8. Turn the cake out of the pan and onto a plate. Serve at room temperature.

Choco-Walnut Coffeecake

My mother often served this rich sour cream coffeecake at our family's traditional Sunday brunches.

Ingredients

3 cups cake flour, or all-purpose flour

1 1/2 teaspoons baking soda

1 1/2 teaspoons baking powder

1/2 teaspoon salt

3/4 cup butter (1 1/2 sticks), softened

1 1/2 cups granulated sugar

2 cups sour cream

3 eggs

1 tablespoon vanilla extract

Topping

1 1/2 cups coarsely chopped walnuts

1 cup loosely packed brown sugar

1 tablespoon ground cinnamon

1 tablespoon unsweetened
   cocoa powder

Icing

1 cup confectioner's sugar

1 tablespoon milk

Yield: 12 to 15 servings

Stuff You'll Need

1. Combine the flour, baking soda, baking powder, and salt in a medium mixing bowl. Set aside.

2. Place the butter, sugar, sour cream, eggs, and vanilla in a large mixing bowl. Beat with an electric mixer, wooden spoon, or whisk until smooth and well blended. Gradually add the flour mixture, and stir just until mixed to form a thick batter. Do not overstir.

3. Place all the topping ingredients in a medium bowl and stir until well combined. Set aside.

4. Drop half the batter in large spoonfuls on the bottom of a greased and floured 13-x-9-inch baking pan. Spread it out evenly with the back of the spoon or a rubber spatula. Sprinkle half the topping mixture over the batter.

5. Spoon the remaining batter over the topping, spread it out, then sprinkle with the remaining topping. Bake in a preheated 350°F oven for 50 to 60 minutes, or until a toothpick inserted into the center of the cake comes out clean. Let cool at least 30 minutes.

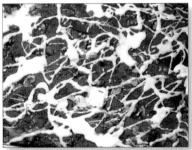

6. To make the icing, place the confectioner's sugar and milk in a small bowl, and stir with a spoon or whisk until smooth.

7. Drizzle the icing over the top of the cooled cake. Serve at room temperature.

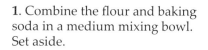

Apple-Pecan Coffeecake

If you love apples and cinnamon, you're gonna love making this coffeecake!

Ingredients

1½ cups cake flour, or all-purpose flour
1 teaspoon baking soda
½ cup butter (1 stick), melted
½ cup firmly packed brown sugar
1 egg
1 teaspoon vanilla extract
2 McIntosh or Granny Smith apples, peeled and cut into small chunks
½ cup coarsely chopped pecans
1 teaspoon cinnamon

Yield: 8 to 10 servings

Stuff You'll Need

1. Combine the flour and baking soda in a medium mixing bowl. Set aside.

2. Place the butter, brown sugar, egg, and vanilla in a large bowl, and beat with an electric mixer on low speed until light and fluffy.

3. Place the apples, pecans, and cinnamon in a medium bowl and mix well.

4. Add the apple mixture to the brown sugar-butter mixture, and stir well. Next, gradually add the flour mixture, and stir just until mixed to form a thick batter. Do not overstir.

5. Spoon the batter into a greased and floured 9-inch bundt pan. Bake in a preheated 350°F oven 40 to 45 minutes, or until a toothpick inserted into the center of the cake comes out clean. Cool 15 minutes before turning the cake out of the pan onto a plate. Serve warm or at room temperature.

Fresh Strawberry Coffeecake

Although you can use frozen strawberries in this recipe, it is much better with fresh, especially when strawberries are in season. I love how the crunchy almonds and juicy strawberries make this coffeecake taste light and fresh.

Ingredients

2 cups sliced fresh or frozen
   strawberries
$1/2$ cup granulated sugar
3 tablespoons butter, melted
$1/2$ cup milk
1 egg
1 teaspoon vanilla extract
1 cup cake flour, or all-purpose flour
1 teaspoon baking powder
$1/4$ teaspoon salt

Topping

$1/2$ cup all-purpose flour
$1/2$ cup granulated sugar
4 tablespoons cold butter ($1/2$ stick),
   cut into small chunks
$1/4$ cup sliced almonds

Yield: About 9 servings

Stuff You'll Need

1. Slice the strawberries.

2. Place the sugar, butter, milk, egg, and vanilla in a large mixing bowl. Beat with an electric mixer, whisk, or wooden spoon until smooth and well blended.

3. Combine the flour, baking powder, and salt in a medium mixing bowl. Gradually add this to the liquid mixture and stir just until mixed to form a thick batter. Do not overstir. Set aside.

4. To make the topping, place the flour and sugar in a medium bowl. Cut the cold butter into the dry ingredients until it resembles a crumbly meal.

5. Spoon the batter into a greased and floured 8-inch square baking pan. Arrange the strawberry slices in an even layer on top.

6. Sprinkle the crumbly flour topping over the strawberries.

7. Scatter the almonds on top. Bake in a preheated 350°F oven for 40 to 45 minutes, or until a toothpick inserted into the center of the cake comes out clean.

8. Cool the cake at least 15 minutes before cutting. Serve warm or at room temperature.

Almond-Berry Coffeecake

Here's a deliciously rich coffeecake that works well with most fruit jams and preserves. Raspberry jam is my personal favorite, although blackberry and boysenberry are also high on my list. This cake's added richness comes from the sour cream batter and the cream cheese topping.

Ingredients

3 cups cake flour, or all-purpose flour
1 cup granulated sugar
1 cup cold butter (2 sticks), cut into small chunks
1 1/2 cups sour cream
2 eggs
1 1/2 teaspoons baking powder
1 1/2 teaspoons baking soda
1 1/2 teaspoons almond extract
1/2 teaspoon salt

Topping

12-ounce package cream cheese, softened
3/4 cup granulated sugar
1 egg
1 cup raspberry jam, at room temperature
1/2 cup slivered almonds

Yield: 12 to 15 servings

Stuff You'll Need

1. Combine the flour and sugar in a large mixing bowl. Cut the cold butter into the dry ingredients until it resembles a crumbly meal. Remove 1 cup of the mixture and reserve for later use.

2. Add the sour cream, eggs, baking powder, baking soda, almond extract, and salt to the crumbly flour mixture. Beat with an electric mixer, whisk, or wooden spoon until just mixed to form a thick batter. Do not overstir.

3. Spoon the batter into a greased and floured 13-x-19-inch baking pan. Spread it out evenly with a rubber spatula.

4. To make the topping, place the cream cheese, sugar, and egg in a medium mixing bowl. Beat with an electric mixer on medium speed until smooth and well blended.

5. Spread the cream cheese mixture on top of the batter. Top with a layer of jam (if the jam is too thick to spread, first stir it with a spoon). Cover with the reserved flour mixture.

6 Sprinkle the almonds over the top. Bake in a preheated 350°F oven for 40 to 45 minutes, or until a toothpick inserted into the center of the cake comes out clean.

7. Cool the cake at least 15 minutes before cutting. Serve warm or at room temperature.

Blueberry Buckle

I was fixin' to fix a Southern-style coffeecake when this li'l ol' recipe came to mind. I hope y'all like it!

Ingredients

$1/4$ cup butter ($1/2$ stick), softened
$3/4$ cup granulated sugar
1 egg
$1/2$ teaspoon vanilla extract
2 cups cake flour, or all-purpose flour
$1 1/2$ teaspoons baking powder
$1/2$ cup milk
2 cups fresh blueberries

Topping

$1/3$ cup cold butter, cut into
  small chunks
$1/2$ cup all-purpose flour
$2/3$ cup granulated sugar
$1/2$ teaspoon ground cinnamon

Yield: 8 to 12 servings

1. Place the butter, sugar, egg, and vanilla in a large mixing bowl. Beat with an electric mixer on low speed until smooth and fluffy.

2. Combine the flour and baking powder in a medium mixing bowl. Add this to the butter mixture along with the milk, and continue to beat until a thick batter forms.

3. Spoon the batter into a greased and floured 9-inch round (or 8-inch square) cake pan. Spread it out evenly with a rubber spatula.

4. Place all the topping ingredients in a medium mixing bowl. Cut the cold butter into the dry ingredients until it resembles a crumbly meal. Set aside.

Stuff You'll Need

5. Arrange the fresh blueberries over the batter in a single layer.

6. Sprinkle the topping over the blueberries. Place in a preheated 350°F oven for 40 to 45 minutes, or until a toothpick inserted into the center of the cake comes out clean.

7. Cool the cake at least 15 minutes before cutting. Serve warm or at room temperature.

Coffee + Coffeecake = Good

Pairing sweet cake with coffee is natural . . . a match made in heaven.
The word coffeecake comes from the Dutch word kaffeeklatcsh,
which means "coffee chat."

It Should Be a Holiday!

Did you know that April 7 is National Coffeecake Day? When I discovered this bit of info, I also found out that there is a "day" for just about every type of food. Here are a few more national days dedicated to some of our favorite baked goods.

▶ January 27 – *Chocolate Cake Day*

▶ February 22 – *Cherry Pie Day*

▶ March 4 – *Pound Cake Day*

▶ April 13 – *Peach Cobbler Day*

▶ May 26 – *Blueberry Cheesecake Day*

▶ June 5 – *Gingerbread Day*

▶ July 12 – *Pecan Pie Day*

▶ August 23 – *Sponge Cake Day*

▶ September 21 – *Pecan Cookie Day*

▶ October 23 – *Boston Cream Pie Day*

▶ November 10 – *Vanilla Cupcake Day*

▶ December 8 – *Chocolate Brownie Day*

I Love C-C-C-Coffee

Even though Americans consume over 400 billion cups of coffee a day – more than any other nation in the world – they rank only twenty-second on consumption per capita. Finland takes the number one spot with its people consuming an average of twenty-four pounds per person, per year. (Americans average nine pounds.)

Nobody Doesn't Like Sara Lee

In 1935, Charles Lubin and his brother-in-law bought three neighborhood Chicago bakeries called Community Bake Shops. Lubin named one of the cakes he sold after his eight-year-old daughter, Sara Lee. He also changed the name of his business to Kitchens of Sara Lee, which eventually expanded to seven bakeries. In 1956, the Consolidated Foods Corporation bought Kitchens of Sara Lee, and in 1985, the corporate name became Sara Lee Corporation. The company became well known for its long-time advertising jingle, "Everybody doesn't like something, but nobody doesn't like Sara Lee," which was often incorrectly sung as "Nobody does it like Sara Lee."

Bundt or Hit?

In 1950, David Dahlquist, owner of the Minneapolis-based kitchenware company Nordic Ware, invented the Bundt pan. He did so at the request of two Jewish women who wanted a special pan – one with a hole in the middle – to make the rich dense cakes of their European childhood. Dahlquist based his design on the ring-shaped pans called *bundkuchens,* which were used in Germany and Austria to make coffeecakes. It wasn't until 1966, when a pound cake baked in a Bundt pan was the winning entry of the Pillsbury Bake-Off that the pan became popular. Today, over a million Bundt pans are sold each year.

Easy as Cake (and Cupcakes) . . . 280
  Buttery Yellow Cupcakes, 282
  Chocolate Cupcakes, 283
  Coconut Cupcakes, 284
  Pumpkin Cupcakes, 286
  Chocolate Bomb Cupcakes, 287

Gimme Some Cake! 288
  Buttermilk Pound Cake, 290
  Coconut-Coconut Cake, 291
  Rich 'n Delicious
    Chocolate Cake, 292
  Debbie's White Cake, 294
  Greek Honeycake, 296
  Pineapple-Carrot Cake, 298
  German Chocolate Cake, 300
  Devil's Food Cake, 302
  Chocolate Heart Attack Cake, 304
  Chocolate-Almond Torte, 306

Celebrate with cake!

Cake is probably the most important dessert on the planet. The love of this food crosses cultures, borders, and religions, and is the original "feel good treat" of the ages. Cake is served at just about every major event in life – an anticipated highlight at birthdays, graduations, weddings, anniversaries, and each and every important occasion in between.

If you have never made a cake from scratch before, you're going to be happy to discover that it's pretty darn easy. And as far as taste . . . well, let's just say that once you have tasted a homemade cake, you'll never prefer one made from a boxed mix again.

In the first part of this chapter, I share recipes for some of my most requested cupcakes, which you can enjoy either plain or topped with your favorite frosting. Next comes an assortment of delicious and easy-to-make cakes that will knock-your-socks-off! You'll find a double-layer Pineapple-Carrot Cake complete with cream cheese frosting, and a Chocolate Heart Attack Cake that is so rich and dense it has been compared to a chocolate bar you can eat with a fork! There's even a Devil's Food Cake that is so light, you'll swear it was made by angels.

So blow out the candles already – and let's have some cake!

First big, then little.

Americans – who are always on the go, go, go – created the first cupcakes at the beginning of the nineteenth century. They baked their cake batters in muffin cups, which is believed to be how they got their name. Portable and easy to carry around, these miniature cakes also baked more quickly than larger cakes. Cupcakes can be as simple or as elaborate as you want. Be sure to check out Chapter 14 for lots of ways to decorate them.

Basic Steps for Making Cupcakes

1. Combine

Combining the flour and other dry ingredients is usually the first step when preparing cupcake batter. Make sure the ingredients are well mixed – especially the leavening agents (baking powder and/or baking soda) – to ensure that they are evenly distributed throughout the mixture.

2. Blend

The next step usually involves beating sugar with the liquid and/or semi-solid ingredients, such as butter, eggs, and flavored extracts. This is best done with an electric mixer until the ingredients are smooth and well blended.

3. Stir

Stirring the dry mixture into the blended liquids is often the next and final step in preparing the batter. This can be done with an electric mixer on low speed or by hand with a wooden spoon. Typically, the ingredients should be stirred until they are mixed thoroughly and form a smooth batter.

Helpful Tips

Whether you are making cakes or cupcakes, you will find the following guidelines helpful.

▶ Unless otherwise specified, all ingredients—butter, eggs, liquids—should be at room temperature for best results.

▶ Before starting, have all the ingredients measured, the pans prepared, and the oven heated.

▶ When using an electric mixer to stir the dry flour mixture into the blended liquid mixture, run it on the lowest speed. If you are using a wooden spoon, use quick round strokes.

▶ Although you can use all-purpose flour for the recipes in this chapter with good results, using cake flour is even better. Cake flour's low-gluten content results in cake that is very light and tender.

▶ Allow freshly baked cakes ample time to cool—at least fifteen minutes—before you attempt to cut or remove them from the pan. If you remove the cake while it's still hot, there is a good chance it will break apart.

▶ Make sure the cake is completely cool before you add frosting. Otherwise the frosting will become runny or melt into the cake.

▶ When making cupcakes, although you can grease and flour the cups of a muffin tin before adding batter, I prefer to use paper liners. Most cupcakes are delicate and the liners help keep them from falling apart.

▶ When preparing cupcakes, don't fill the cups too high. During baking, the batter is likely to rise up too high and spill onto the top of the muffin pan where it will burn.

▶ To determine when most cakes and cupcakes are done, simply insert a wooden toothpick into the center. If the toothpick comes out clean, the cake is done; if it comes out with batter, more baking time is needed.

▶ For frosting and decorating ideas, check out Chapter 14.

Storing Cupcakes

▶ Cupcakes are best stored in an airtight container at room temperature for three to five days.

▶ Be sure your cupcakes are completely cool before storing. Covering them while they're still warm will cause moisture to form and make them soggy.

▶ To freeze cupcakes, wrap them individually in foil or plastic wrap and store in a plastic freezer bag or airtight container. You can also refrigerate cupcakes for several days, although I don't recommend this because the cake tends to dry out.

Garnishes, Garnishes, Garnishes . . .

The easiest way to add flavor, texture, and visual appeal to frosted cakes and cupcakes is by sprinkling on a garnish. Here are some of my favorites.

▶ **Candy Sprinkles**

Chocolate
Multicolored

▶ **Chocolate**

Candy-coated chocolate
Cocoa powder
Grated chocolate
Mini chocolate morsels
Shaved chocolate

▶ **Chopped Nuts**

Almonds
Hazelnuts
Peanuts
Pecans
Walnuts

▶ **Fun Stuff**

Mini butterscotch morsels
Shredded coconut
Toffee pieces

Buttery Yellow Cupcakes

These cupcakes are rich and buttery—and perfect with just about any frosting. I usually choose Choc-Choc Frosting (page 77) or Pineapple Frosting (page 78), but feel free to experiment with any of the others in Chapter 4.

Ingredients

2 1/2 cups cake flour, or
   all-purpose flour
1 tablespoon baking powder
1/2 teaspoon salt
1 cup butter (2 sticks), softened
1 1/2 cups granulated sugar
1 cup milk
2 teaspoons vanilla extract
4 eggs

Yield: 24 cupcakes

Stuff You'll Need

1. Combine the flour, baking powder, and salt in a medium mixing bowl. Set aside.

2. In a large bowl, beat the butter, sugar, milk, and vanilla on medium speed until smooth. Add the eggs and beat until well blended.

3. Gradually add the flour mixture to the blended liquid, stirring with the mixer on low speed to form a smooth batter.

4. Spoon the batter into a paper-lined muffin tin. Fill each cup about two-thirds full.

5. Bake in a preheated 350°F oven for 20 to 25 minutes or until a toothpick inserted into the center of a cupcake comes out clean. Cool the cupcakes at least 15 minutes before removing from the tin. Allow to cool completely before frosting.

Chocolate Cupcakes

I especially love chocolate cupcakes, because they're made with my favorite ingredient – chocolate! Try these with the one of the frostings in Chapter 4, and then sprinkle on a garnish or two!

Ingredients

2 1/2 cups cake flour, or
   all-purpose flour
1/2 cup unsweetened cocoa powder
1 teaspoon baking powder
1/2 teaspoon baking soda
1/2 teaspoon salt
1 1/4 cups butter (2 1/2 sticks), softened
1 1/2 cups granulated sugar
3/4 cup sour cream
2 teaspoons vanilla extract
3 eggs
1/2 cup hot water

Yield: 24 cupcakes

Stuff You'll Need

1. Combine the flour, cocoa, baking powder, baking soda, and salt in a medium bowl. Set aside.

2. In a large bowl, beat the butter, sugar, sour cream, and vanilla on medium speed until smooth. Add the eggs and beat until well blended.

3. Add the hot water and flour mixture to the blended liquid, stirring with the mixer on low speed to form a smooth batter.

4. Spoon the batter into a paper-lined muffin tin. Fill each cup about two-thirds full.

5. Bake in a preheated 350°F oven for 20 to 25 minutes or until a toothpick inserted into the center of a cupcake comes out clean. Cool the cupcakes at least 15 minutes before removing from the tin. Allow to cool completely before frosting.

Coconut Cupcakes

These cupcakes are amazingly light, so light that you have to be careful when peeling off the liners (or the cake will peel off along with them). Try them covered with the Coconut Frosting on page 79.

Ingredients

1 1/3 cups cake flour, or all-purpose flour
1 teaspoon baking powder
1/4 teaspoon salt
1/2 cup butter (1 stick), softened
1 cup granulated sugar
1/2 cup milk
1 teaspoon vanilla extract
1/4 teaspoon coconut extract
2 eggs, separated*

* For egg separating instructions, see page 51.

Yield: 12 cupcakes

Important Tip

Don't fill the cups too high or the batter will spill over the top and stick to the muffin pan.

Stuff You'll Need

1. Combine the flour, baking powder, and salt in a medium mixing bowl. Set aside.

2. Place the butter, sugar, milk, and coconut and vanilla extracts in a large bowl. Beat with an electric mixer on medium speed until smooth. Add the eggs yolks and beat until well blended. Gradually add the flour mixture, stirring with the mixer on low speed to form a smooth batter.

3. Place the egg whites in a medium mixing bowl. Whip with the mixer on high speed until stiff peaks form. (For whipping instructions, see page 56.)

4. Fold the whipped egg whites into the batter until well blended and uniform in color. (For folding instructions, see page 57.)

5. Spoon the batter into a paper-lined muffin tin. Fill each cup about two-thirds full. Bake in a preheated 350°F oven 20 to 25 minutes or until a toothpick inserted into the center of a cupcake comes out clean. Cool 15 minutes before removing from the tin. Cool completely before frosting.

Pumpkin Cupcakes

These cupcakes will remind you of pumpkin pie, especially if you cover them with the Whipped Cream Frosting on page 80. Make a batch of these and you'll swear it's Thanksgiving, even if it's the middle of summer!

Ingredients

2 1/4 cups cake flour, or
   all-purpose flour
1 tablespoon baking powder
1/2 teaspoon baking soda
1 teaspoon ground cinnamon
1/2 teaspoon ground nutmeg
1/4 teaspoon salt
1/2 cup butter (1 stick), softened
1 1/3 cups granulated sugar
1 cup canned pumpkin purée
3/4 cup milk
2 eggs

Yield: 24 cupcakes

Stuff You'll Need

1. Combine the flour, baking powder, baking soda, cinnamon, nutmeg, and salt in a medium mixing bowl. Set aside.

2. Place the butter, sugar, pumpkin, and milk in a large bowl. Beat with an electric mixer on medium speed until smooth. Add the eggs and beat until well blended.

3. Gradually add the flour mixture to the blended liquid, stirring with the mixer on low speed to form a smooth batter.

4. Spoon the batter into a paper-lined muffin tin. Fill each cup about two-thirds full.

5. Bake in a preheated 350°F oven for 20 to 25 minutes or until a toothpick inserted into the center of a cupcake comes out clean. Cool the cupcakes at least 15 minutes before removing from the tin. Allow to cool completely before frosting.

Chocolate Bomb Cupcakes

The combination of chocolate cake and cream cheese filling makes these cupcakes "da bomb!" They are so rich and chocolaty, I usually skip the frosting.

Ingredients

2 cups cake flour, or all-purpose flour
1/4 cup unsweetened cocoa
1 teaspoon baking soda
1/2 teaspoon baking powder
1 cup granulated sugar
1/3 cup vegetable oil
2 eggs
2 teaspoons vanilla extract
1 cup hot water

Filling

8 ounces cream cheese, softened
1/3 cup granulated sugar
1 egg
1 cup miniature semi-sweet
   chocolate morsels

Yield: 24 cupcakes

1. Combine the flour, cocoa, baking soda, and baking powder in a medium mixing bowl. Set aside.

2. In a large bowl, beat the sugar, oil, eggs, and vanilla with an electric mixer on medium speed until smooth. Add the hot water and flour mixture, stirring on low speed to form a smooth batter.

3. Place all of the filling ingredients in a medium bowl and stir until well combined.

4. Spoon the batter into a paper-lined muffin tin. Fill each cup about half full. Drop a tablespoon of filling in the middle of each.

5. Bake in a preheated 350°F oven for 20 to 25 minutes or until a toothpick comes out clean when inserted into the center of a cupcake. Cool the cupcakes at least 15 minutes before removing from the tin.

Stuff You'll Need

Who wants cake?!

Homemade cakes made from scratch are great for so many reasons. You don't have to rely on a bakery every time need or want cake. You can use your own fresh pure ingredients and not have to worry about the preservatives, artificial colors, and artificial flavorings that are contained in commercial cake mixes. And finally, homemade cakes are the best because they're made with your own loving hands.

Basic Steps for Making Cakes

1. Combine
Combining the flour and other dry ingredients is usually the first step when preparing cake batter. Make sure all of the ingredients are well mixed – especially the leavening agents (baking powder and/or baking soda) – to ensure that they are evenly distributed throughout the mixture.

2. Blend
The next step usually involves beating sugar with the liquid and/or semi-solid ingredients, such as butter, eggs, and flavored extracts. This is best done with an electric mixer until the ingredients are smooth and well blended.

3. Stir
Stirring the dry mixture into the blended liquids is often the next and final step in preparing the batter. This can be done with an electric mixer on low speed or by hand with a wooden spoon. Typically, the ingredients should be stirred until they are mixed thoroughly and form a smooth batter.

Basic Steps for Assembling a Two-Layer Cake

1. Loosen the cake from the pan
Even if you have greased and floured the pans properly, your freshly baked cake may be stuck to the sides. To loosen it, first let the cake cool about fifteen minutes, then run a dull knife around the inside edge of the pan. This will allow the cake to be released from the pan easily.

2. Flip the bottom layer
After loosening the cake, place a serving plate over the top of the pan. Holding the plate and pan together, flip them over to release the cake onto the plate. The flat bottom side of the cake will be on top—the perfect surface to spread a layer of frosting and then cover with the top cake layer.

3. Add the top layer
When removing the cake from the second pan, release it onto a wire rack to cool. When both cakes are completely cool, spread frosting on the bottom layer. Carefully flip the top layer from the cooling rack onto your hand. Then with both hands, place it flat-side down on the bottom layer.

Storing Cakes

▶ Both frosted and unfrosted cakes store best at room temperature. Unless they have a perishable frosting or filling, do not store cakes in the refrigerator as this will dry them out.

▶ Wrap unfrosted cakes in plastic wrap or store in an airtight container.

▶ Cake plates with dome-shaped lids are perfect for storing frosted cakes, but you can also turn a large bowl upside down and place it over the cake. You can also "tent" plastic wrap over the cake as shown in the inset at right.

▶ To freeze a frosted cake, first place it uncovered in the freezer for two hours to harden the frosting. Wrap the cake in plastic wrap or foil, then place it in an airtight container. Most cakes freeze well for about two months.

How to Wrap a Frosted Cake ... Without Destroying It

A handful of toothpicks and some plastic wrap are all you need to create your own dome for covering a cake without destroying the frosting. Although the example below is for a two-layer cake, this "tenting" method can be used for frosted cakes of any shape and size.

1. Position the wrap and toothpicks
Stick a few toothpicks into the top of the cake. Around the edges, insert the toothpicks on angles as shown in the photo above.

2. Make the tent
Drape a long sheet of plastic wrap over the cake, making sure it is supported by the toothpicks and doesn't touch the frosting. Place both ends of the wrap under the plate to seal. Repeat with another piece of plastic to completely cover the cake.

Buttermilk Pound Cake

Not too sweet, this buttery pound cake is perfect topped with a simple sprinkling of confectioner's sugar or a drizzle of icing. It's also good for strawberry shortcake.

Ingredients

3 cups cake flour, or all-purpose flour
1/2 teaspoon salt
1/4 teaspoon baking soda
1 cup butter (2 sticks), softened
3 cups granulated sugar
1 cup buttermilk
1 tablespoon fresh lemon juice
1 teaspoon vanilla extract
6 eggs

Yield: 10 to 12 servings

Important Tip

This cake will collapse in the center if you open the oven door too early. Wait at least 60 minutes before first inspecting it . . . or face the consequences!

Stuff You'll Need

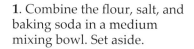

1. Combine the flour, salt, and baking soda in a medium mixing bowl. Set aside.

2. Place the butter, sugar, buttermilk, lemon juice, and vanilla in a large bowl. Beat with an electric mixer on medium speed until smooth. Add the eggs and beat until well blended. Gradually add the flour mixture, stirring with the mixer on low speed to form a smooth batter.

3. Pour the batter into a greased and floured 9-inch bundt or tube pan. Bake in a preheated 325°F oven for 90 minutes or until a toothpick inserted into the center of the cake comes out clean.

4. Cool at least 30 minutes before turning the cake out of the pan. Enjoy warm or at room temperature.

Coconut - Coconut Cake

I'm a big fan of coconut, which is why this cake is one of my favorites. It's made with both coconut milk and shredded coconut—and once it's frosted, I cover it with even more luscious coconut. Talk about coco-nutty!

Ingredients

2¼ cups cake flour, or all purpose flour
2 teaspoons baking powder
½ teaspoon salt
½ cup sweetened shredded coconut
¾ cup butter (1½ sticks), softened
1¼ cups granulated sugar
1 cup canned coconut milk
1 teaspoon vanilla extract
3 eggs
1 recipe Vanilla Buttercream
    (page 76)
Coconut for garnish

Yield: 8 to 12 servings

Important Tip

For even more coconut flavor, stir ½ teaspoon coconut extract into the buttercream frosting.

Stuff You'll Need

1. Combine the flour, baking powder, salt, and coconut in a medium mixing bowl. Set aside.

2. Place the butter, sugar, coconut milk, and vanilla in a large bowl. Beat with an electric mixer on medium speed until smooth. Add the eggs and beat until well blended. Gradually add the flour mixture, stirring with the mixer on low speed to form a smooth batter.

3. Pour an equal amount of batter into two greased and floured 9-inch round cake pans. Bake in a preheated 350°F oven for 25 to 30 minutes or until a toothpick inserted into the center of each cake comes out clean.

4. Cool at least 15 minutes before removing the cakes from the pans. Allow to cool completely before frosting and garnishing with coconut. (Steps for frosting a double-layer cake are on page 366.)

Rich 'n Delicious Chocolate Cake

If you've only eaten chocolate cake made from a box mix, you're in for a real treat with this one. There is simply no comparison.

Ingredients

2 cups cake flour, or all-purpose flour
3/4 cup unsweetened cocoa
1 1/2 teaspoons baking powder
1 1/2 teaspoons baking soda
1 teaspoon salt
2 cups granulated sugar
1 cup milk
1 cup hot water
1/2 cup vegetable oil
1 teaspoon vanilla extract
2 eggs
1 recipe Choc-Choc Frosting (page 77)
   or Chocolate Buttercream (page 76)

Yield: 8 to 12 servings

1. Combine the flour, cocoa, baking powder, baking soda, and salt in a medium mixing bowl. Set aside.

2. Place the sugar, milk, water, oil, and vanilla in a large mixing bowl. Beat with an electric mixer on medium speed until smooth. Add the eggs and beat until well blended.

3. Gradually add the flour mixture, stirring with the mixer on low speed to form a smooth batter.

4. Pour an equal amount of batter into two greased and floured 9-inch round cake pans. Bake in a preheated 350°F oven for 30 to 35 minutes or until a toothpick inserted into the center of each cake comes out clean.

5. Cool at least 15 minutes before removing the cakes from the pans. Allow to cool completely before frosting. (Steps for frosting a double-layer cake are on page 366.)

Stuff You'll Need

Debbie's White Cake

My friend Debbie—who isn't a fan of super-sweet baked goods—asked me to make her a simple white cake for her birthday. I made this one, which has a simple spread of raspberry jam between the layers and a luscious cream cheese frosting.

Ingredients

2¼ cups cake flour, or all purpose flour
2 teaspoons baking powder
½ teaspoon salt
½ cup butter (1 stick), softened
1¼ cups granulated sugar
1 teaspoon vanilla extract
1 cup milk
4 eggs, separated*
1 cup raspberry jam, or your favorite jam or preserves
1 recipe Cream Cheese Frosting (page 81)

*For egg separating instructions, see page 51.

Yield: 8 to 12 servings

Stuff You'll Need

1. Combine the flour, baking powder, and salt in a medium mixing bowl, and set aside. Place the butter, sugar, and vanilla in a large mixing bowl. Cream with an electric mixer on medium speed until smooth and fluffy.

2. Add half the flour mixture and half the milk to the creamed mixture, stirring with the mixer on low speed until nearly blended. Add the remaining flour, milk, and the egg yolks, and continue stirring to form a smooth batter.

3. Place the egg whites in a medium mixing bowl. Whip with the mixer on high speed until stiff peaks form. (For whipping instructions, see page 56.)

4. Fold the whipped egg whites into the batter until well blended and uniform in color. (For folding instructions, see page 57.)

5. Pour an equal amount of batter into two greased and floured 9-inch round cake pans. Bake in a preheated 350°F oven for 25 to 30 minutes or until a toothpick inserted into the center of each cake comes out clean.

6. Cool at least 15 minutes before removing the cakes from the pans. Allow to cool completely, then spread the jam over the bottom cake layer.

7. Place the second layer on top and frost. (Steps for frosting a double-layer cake are on page 366.)

8. Cut into wedges and serve.

Greek Honeycake

Celebrating the holidays with honey-sweetened cake is a tradition among many cultures. This version is sweet and crunchy, and tastes similar to the famous Greek pastry called baklava. Opah!

Ingredients

1⅓ cups all-purpose flour
1½ teaspoons baking powder
¾ teaspoon ground cinnamon
1 cup coarsely chopped walnuts
1 cup butter (1 stick), softened
1 cup granulated sugar
⅓ cup milk
3 eggs

Syrup

¾ cup honey
½ cup granulated sugar
½ cup water
1 teaspoon lemon juice

Yield: 15 to 20 servings

Stuff You'll Need

1. Combine the flour, baking powder, cinnamon, and walnuts in a medium mixing bowl. Set aside.

2. Place the butter and sugar in a large bowl and beat until fluffy.

3. Gradually add the flour mixture to the butter mixture and stir just until mixed to form a sticky batter. Do not overstir.

4. Grease and flour the sides of a 13-x-9-inch baking pan and line the bottom with parchment paper. Spoon the batter into the pan and bake in a preheated 350°F oven for 25 to 30 minutes or until a toothpick inserted into the center of the cake comes out clean.

5. Let cool about 10 minutes. While the cake is warm and still in the pan, cut it diagonally into diamond shapes. Set aside.

6. Place all the syrup ingredients in a small saucepan over low heat. Stir until the sugar has fully dissolved.

7. Pour the hot syrup over the warm cake.

8. Let the cake absorb the syrup and cool at least 30 minutes before serving.

Pineapple-Carrot Cake

The pineapple in this recipe makes cake that is so moist you might decide to eat it without frosting!

Ingredients

2 cups shredded carrots (2 to 3 large carrots)
2¹/₂ cups all-purpose flour
2 teaspoons baking soda
2 teaspoons salt
1 cup coarsely chopped walnuts
2 cups granulated sugar
1 cup vegetable oil
1 teaspoon vanilla extract
8-ounce can crushed pineapple, drained
4 eggs
1 recipe Cream Cheese Frosting (page 81)

Yield: 8 to 12 servings

Stuff You'll Need

1. Shred the carrots and place in a large mixing bowl. Set aside.

2. Combine the flour, baking soda, salt, and walnuts in a medium mixing bowl. Set aside.

3. Place the sugar, oil, vanilla, and pineapple in the bowl with the shredded carrots. Beat with an electric mixer on medium speed until well mixed. Add the eggs and beat until well blended.

4. Gradually add the flour mixture to the blended pineapple-carrot mixture and stir just until mixed to form a dense batter. Do not overstir.

5. Pour equal amounts of batter in two greased and floured 9-inch round cake pans. Bake in a preheated 350°F oven 45 to 50 minutes or until a toothpick inserted into the center of each cake comes out clean. Cool 15 minutes before removing the cakes from the pans. Cool completely before frosting.

German Chocolate Cake

By ancestry I'm half German, so this cake hits my German roots and makes me want to put on some lederhosen and dance to some ooom-pah music. Ja, der kuchen ist gut! (Yes, this cake is good!)

Ingredients

¹/₂ cup water

4 squares (1 ounce each) German sweet baking chocolate

2 cups cake flour, or all-purpose flour

¹/₂ teaspoon baking soda

¹/₂ teaspoon baking powder

¹/₄ teaspoon salt

1 cup butter (2 sticks), softened

2 cups granulated sugar

1 cup buttermilk

1 teaspoon vanilla extract

4 eggs, separated*

1 recipe German Chocolate Frosting (page 80)

* For egg separating instructions, see page 51.

Yield: 8 to 12 servings

Stuff You'll Need

1. Place the water in a small saucepan over medium heat until near boiling. Add the chocolate and stir until melted and smooth. Set aside to cool slightly.

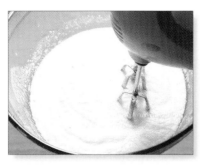

2. Combine the flour, baking soda, baking powder, and salt in a medium bowl and set aside. Place the butter, sugar, buttermilk, and vanilla in a large mixing bowl. Beat with an electric mixer on medium speed until smooth. Add the egg yolks and beat until well blended.

3. Gradually add the dry ingredients to the egg mixture, stirring with the mixer on low speed to form a smooth batter. Add the cooled melted chocolate and continue to stir until well blended.

4. Place the egg whites in a medium mixing bowl. Whip with the mixer on high speed until stiff peaks form. (For whipping instructions, see page 56.)

5. Fold the whipped egg whites into the batter until well blended and uniform in color. (For folding instructions, see page 57.) Grease and flour the sides of two 9-inch round cake pans, and line the bottoms with parchment paper.

6. Pour an equal amount of batter into each pan. Bake in a preheated 350°F oven for 25 to 30 minutes or until a toothpick inserted into the center of each cake comes out clean.

7. Cool at least 15 minutes before removing the cakes from the pans. Allow to cool completely before frosting. (Steps for frosting a double-layer cake are on page 366.)

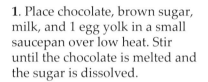

Devil's Food Cake

This cake will really bring out the devil in ya. The whipped egg whites folded into the batter result in a cake that's light and soft. Perfect for your favorite frosting! I chose the Banana-Nut Frosting (page 78) this time.

Ingredients

3 squares (1 ounce each) semi-sweet
   baking chocolate
1 cup firmly packed light brown sugar
1/2 cup milk
3 eggs, separated*†
2 cups cake flour, or all-purpose flour
1 teaspoon baking soda
1/2 cup butter (1 stick), softened
1 cup granulated sugar
1 teaspoon vanilla
3/4 cup hot water

* For egg separating instructions, see page 51.

† This recipe uses 3 egg yolks and 2 whites. After
   separating the 3 eggs, reserve one of the
   whites for later use.

Yield: 8 to 12 servings

Stuff You'll Need

1. Place chocolate, brown sugar, milk, and 1 egg yolk in a small saucepan over low heat. Stir until the chocolate is melted and the sugar is dissolved.

2. Combine the flour and baking soda in a medium mixing bowl. Set aside.

3. Place the butter, sugar, and vanilla in a bowl and cream with an electric mixer on medium speed until light and fluffy. Add the remaining 2 egg yolks and beat until well blended.

4. Add the hot water and flour mixture to the creamed butter mixture, stirring with the mixer on low speed to form a smooth batter. Add the chocolate mixture and continue to stir until fully blended.

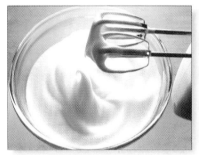

5. Place the 2 egg whites in a medium bowl. Whip with the mixer on high speed until stiff peaks form. (For whipping instructions, see page 56.)

6. Fold the whipped egg whites into the batter until well blended and uniform in color. (For folding instructions, see page 57.)

7. Pour an equal amount of batter into two greased and floured 9-inch round cake pans. Bake in a preheated 350°F oven for 30 to 35 minutes or until a toothpick inserted into the center of each cake comes out clean.

8. Cool for at least 15 minutes before removing the cakes from the pans. Allow to cool completely before frosting. (Steps for frosting a double-layer cake are on page 366.)

Chocolate Heart Attack Cake

This is the richest, densest cake in this chapter. One of my friends compared it to eating a chocolate bar with a fork. When I asked her if she minded, she replied, "Not at all."

Ingredients

1 cup butter (1 stick)

8 squares (1 ounce each) semi-sweet baking chocolate

1/2 cup cake flour, or all purpose flour

1/3 cup unsweetened cocoa powder

1 teaspoon baking powder

1 1/3 cups granulated sugar

1/2 cup sour cream

1 teaspoon vanilla extract

5 eggs

1 recipe Chocolate Ganache (page 92)

Yield: 8 to 12 servings

Stuff You'll Need

1. Cut up the butter, break up the chocolate, and place in the top of a double boiler over medium-low heat or in a medium saucepan over *very low* heat. Stir until melted, then remove from the heat and let cool slightly.

2. Combine the flour, cocoa powder, and baking powder in a medium mixing bowl. Set aside.

3. Place the sugar, sour cream, vanilla, and eggs in a large mixing bowl. Beat with an electric mixer on medium speed until smooth and well blended. Gradually add the flour mixture, stirring with the mixer on low speed to form a smooth batter.

4. Stir the melted chocolate mixture into the batter until well blended and uniform in color. Set aside. Grease and flour the sides of two 9-inch round cake pans and line the bottoms with parchment paper.

5. Pour half the batter into each pan. Bake in a preheated 350°F oven for 25 to 30 minutes or until a toothpick inserted into the center of each cake comes out clean. Cool 30 minutes before removing the cakes from the pans. Cool completely before frosting (see steps on page 366).

Chocolate-Almond Torte

This torte is like three cakes in one. On the outside, it's like a light and luscious brownie; moving towards the center, it becomes a dense chocolate cake; and in the middle, it's like a rich chocolate mousse. It doesn't get much better than this!

Ingredients

1¹/₂ cups whole almonds

¹/₂ cup butter (1 stick)

8 squares (1 ounce each) semi-sweet baking chocolate

7 eggs, separated*

1 cup granulated sugar

¹/₃ cup all-purpose flour

¹/₂ teaspoon salt

* For egg separating instructions, see page 51.

Yield: 9 to 12 servings

Important Tip

Although I use a springform pan for this, you can also use a 9-inch square cake pan. (For more information on springform pans, see page 215.)

Stuff You'll Need

1. Finely grind the almonds in a food processor. Transfer to a large mixing bowl.

2. Cut up the butter, break up the chocolate, and place in the top of a double boiler over medium-low heat or in a medium saucepan over *very low* heat. Stir until melted, then remove from the heat and let cool slightly.

3. Place the melted chocolate in the bowl with the almonds. Add the egg yolks, sugar, flour, and salt, and stir to form a well-blended batter. Set aside.

4. Place the egg whites in a large mixing bowl. Whip with an electric mixer on high speed until stiff peaks form. (For whipping instructions, see page 56.)

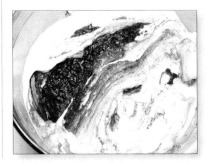

5. Fold the whipped egg whites into the batter until well blended and uniform in color. (For folding instructions, see page 57.) Grease and flour the sides of a 9-inch-springform pan and line the bottom with parchment paper.

6. Spoon the batter into the prepared pan. Bake in a preheated 350°F oven for 40 minutes or until a toothpick inserted into the center of the cake comes out clean. Remove from the oven and let cool about 30 minutes.

7. Run a knife along the inside edge of the pan to release any cake that may be stuck, then carefully remove the sides of the pan. Serve as is or topped with a generous sprinkling of confectioner's sugar.

Classic Cake

Cake has been around since the days of the early Egyptians. Sweetened with honey, the first cakes were more like bread and often contained nuts or dried fruits. In other words, they were basically heavy fruitcakes (ewww). It wasn't until the advent of refined flour and baking powder in the nineteenth century that cakes as we know them today came into being.

Fairy Cakes

Cupcakes, also called *fairy cakes* in some cultures, didn't become popular until muffin tins were created. Prior to that, both cupcakes and muffins were baked in cups or tiny bowls.

Sprinkles of Beverly Hills

All over the United States, there are bakeries dedicated solely to making cupcakes. Two of the most famous are Sprinkles Cupcakes of Beverly Hills and Crumbs Bake Shop of Manhattan. Both have shops throughout the country that offer high-quality gourmet-style cupcakes that look like miniature works of art.

Why Are Cakes Round?

Good question. There are many theories. One is that cakes were originally formed by hand like bread rounds; another is that in the seventeenth century, cake batter was poured into round hoops that were placed on pans and then baked in the oven. Yet another is that cakes were often used in religious ceremonies and the round shape represented the circle of life.

Angel or Devil's Food?

Angel food cake, which first appeared in the early 1900s, was so light in texture, it was considered "food of the angels." Its counterpart, devil's food cake, is closely linked to red velvet cake. Its dark chocolate color has a deep crimson hue – the devil's favorite color. One way that devil's food cake differs from standard chocolate cake is that it is flavored with cocoa rather than chocolate.

A $20 Million Cake

In 2006, a $20 million dollar wedding cake was displayed at the Luxury Brands Bridal Show in Beverly Hills, California. Cake designers from Nahid La Patisserie Artistique teamed up with Mimi So jewelers to create the cake, which was studded with diamonds and other gems. Obviously, it was never meant to be eaten, which is a good thing since no one could even get near it – a team of armed guards surrounded the cake while it was on display!

Drink, I Mean . . . Eat Up!

Infused with enough Scotch to wilt your kilt, the Whisky Dundee Cake from Scotland is a real crowd pleaser. So is the Jack Daniel's-soaked Lynchburg Whiskey Cake. Of course, if you get stopped in your car after eating them, you might have a hard time explaining, "Seriously, officer, (*hic*) I only had just a li'l piece."

You Really "Take the Cake"

During the late 1800s, competitions called *cake walks* were popular in the United States, especially among southern African-American communities. Couples would dress their best and then promenade in a circle to be judged on which pair was the most stylish. The prize was a cake that was on display in the center of the circle. The winning couple would "take the cake," which is the origin of this common expression.

Flaky Pastry Sheets 310
   Apple Strudel, 312
   Apple Turnovers, 314
   Almond Triangle Puffs, 316
   Frangipane Puff Pie, 318
   Golden Palmiers, 320

Puffy Pastry Shells 322
   Mascarpone Puffs, 323
   Cannoli Puffs, 324
   Blueberry Puffs, 325
   Chocolate Cream Puffs, 326
   White Chocolate Cream Puffs, 327

12. Puff the Magic Pastry

The wonderful world of puffs

Buttery dough that "puffs up" into light, flaky layers, puff pastry is perfect for strudels, turnovers, cream puffs, and many other delicious desserts. You can even use it as a pie crust! The dough itself—hundreds of micro-thin layers that are separated by butter—is really quite amazing. It doesn't contain any leavening agents, but during baking, the steam created from the water in the dough causes the layers to separate and puff up into crisp, flaky pastry.

The problem with puff pastry dough is that making it from scratch is a precise process that requires a lot of skill. In other words, it's pretty darn hard. The good news is that you can buy premade puff pastry dough, which comes frozen in flat sheets as well as shells, at your local supermarket. It is easy to work with and bakes up beautifully.

And talk about impressive results! The pastries in this chapter, although super easy to make, will look and taste like you've been slaving over them all day. The first recipes are made with puff pastry *sheets*, which are cut and shaped and used for such wonderful sweet treats as Apple Turnovers, Almond Triangle Puffs, and classic French cookies called palmiers.

Next comes an array of delectable cream puffs made with light, crispy puff pastry *shells*. The fillings, which include such favorites as cannoli, mascarpone, and white chocolate cream—are truly out of this world. Once you've tasted them, if anyone calls you a cream puff in the future, you won't be offended – *because you'll know it means that you are delicious and sweet!*

Don't flake out on me yet!

The way puff pastry dough bakes up into individual melt-in-your-mouth layers is awesome! And working with the premade sheets couldn't be easier. For all the recipes in this section (with the exception of the Golden Palmiers on page 320) the dough is cut and/or shaped and then wrapped around a filling. For this type of filled pastry, the steps below are standard.

Basic Steps for Using Puff Pastry Sheets

1. Cut and fill
Carefully unfold the thawed pastry sheet and place it on a clean flat cutting surface. Using a sharp knife, cut or shape the dough as instructed in the recipe, making sure to cut all the way through the dough. Add the filling as instructed.

2. Crimp the edges
Whether you are using the dough to make turnovers, strudels, or as a crust for pies, you'll have to seal the edges to enclose the filling. Do this by crimping the edges of the dough with your fingers or the tines of a fork.

3. Vent and brush
Cut vents in the top layer of dough to release steam during baking. Brushing egg wash (beaten mixture of egg and water) over the vented dough before baking is an optional step that gives the pastry a beautiful shine and golden glow.

Helpful Tips

Whether you are working with puff pastry sheets or shells, you will find the following guidelines helpful.

▶ It's very important to preheat the oven before baking puff pastry. For some baked goods, you might be able to cheat a tiny bit with the preheating, but *never* with puff pastry!

▶ Frozen puff pastry shells do not require thawing. Place them frozen on an ungreased cookie sheet and bake.

▶ Frozen puff pastry sheets need to be thawed before using. This takes about twenty or thirty minutes at room temperature.

▶ Don't allow pastry sheets to thaw for too long or they will become soft, sticky, and difficult to handle. If this happens, return the sheets to the refrigerator for a few minutes.

▶ When preparing filled pastry, make sure the filling is either cold or at room temperature. If it's too warm, it will melt the dough's buttery layers, and the pastry won't puff up properly during baking.

▶ Most frozen sheets are prefolded. Use care when unfolding them, so that they don't break apart. If they do, simply press the torn pieces together with your fingers.

▶ When working with pastry dough, work quickly and handle it as little as possible to avoid stretching and tearing.

▶ If brushing egg wash on frozen puff pastry shells before baking, be careful to brush only the tops, not the edges. If the edges are brushed, they will stick together and the shells won't rise properly.

▶ I recommend baking most puff pastries, especially those with fillings, on a parchment-lined cookie sheet. The fillings can boil out from the vented dough or seep through its crimped edges. Using parchment will avoid a burnt-on mess.

▶ Puff pastries tend to bake very quickly. Due to differences in oven temperatures, be sure to check on them periodically as they bake.

▶ Fill baked puff pastry shells just before serving.

Storing Puff Pastry

▶ "The fresher the better" is the rule for puff pastry, which is best enjoyed the same day it's baked. The longer it is exposed to the air and humidity, the less crisp and flaky it will become.

▶ If you plan to serve your pastry within a day, you can store it in a cool dry place or inside a brown paper bag.

▶ Filled or not, puff pastries do not refrigerate very well. The moisture causes them to become soft and soggy. You can, however, store them in an airtight container and freeze up to two months.

▶ Baked unfilled shells may be stored in airtight containers and frozen up to six weeks.

▶ Once the baked shells are filled, they should be eaten as soon as possible. The longer they sit, the soggier they will become.

▶ You can freeze unbaked turnovers or other filled puff pastries up to one month. First freeze them on a cookie sheet, then transfer them to an airtight container or freezer storage bag.

Pâte Feuilletée
Qu'est-ce que C'est?

Puff pastry is believed to have been created in 1645 by Claudius Gele. Claudius wanted to bake a loaf of bread for his sick father, who had been prescribed a diet consisting of water, flour, and butter (*I want his doctor*). To make a long story short, Claudius prepared some dough, packed it with butter, and then folded it over and over until he had shaped it into a loaf. And *voila!* Puff pastry was born.

Thank you, Claudius!

Apple Strudel

"You liken der apple strudel, ya?"
This is one of my favorite breakfast
treats. I often serve it for brunch
and on special occasions. Enjoy it
warm for the best flavor.

Ingredients

1 sheet (9-inch square) frozen puff
    pastry dough, thawed
2 large Granny Smith apples, peeled
    and cut into small chunks
1/2 cup raisins
1/4 cup coarsely chopped walnuts
1/4 cup firmly packed brown sugar
1 tablespoon all-purpose flour
1 teaspoon fresh lemon juice
1/4 teaspoon ground cinnamon

Egg wash

1 egg plus 1 teaspoon water, beaten

Yield: 5 to 7 servings

1. Place the apples, raisins, and
walnuts in a medium mixing
bowl. Add the brown sugar,
flour, lemon juice, and
cinnamon, and stir to coat.

2. Lay out the sheet of pastry
dough on a parchment-lined
baking sheet. Spoon the apple
mixture over the dough, leaving
a 1-inch border on the top and
sides and about 1/2 inch on the
bottom.

3. Starting at the bottom, roll
up the dough as if making a
jelly roll.

4. Seal the roll by pinching the
top edge of the dough to create
a seam. Place it seam-side down
on the parchment, and crimp
both ends to seal.

Stuff You'll Need

 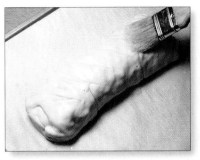

5. With a sharp knife, make several diagonal cuts through the top of the dough about $1^1/_2$ inches apart.

6. Brush the roll with egg wash. Bake in a preheated 375°F oven for 35 to 40 minutes or until the pastry is light golden brown.

7. Serve warm as is or dusted with confectioner's sugar.

Apple Turnovers

Like many recipes in this book, these turnovers can be made with lots of different fillings. Instead of apples, try it with blueberries or chopped peaches.

Ingredients

2 sheets (9-inch squares) frozen puff
    pastry dough, thawed
2 medium Granny Smith apples (about
    2 cups), peeled and thinly sliced
1/3 cup granulated sugar
2 teaspoons cornstarch
1 teaspoon fresh lemon juice
1/8 teaspoon ground cinnamon
Granulated sugar for sprinkling on top

Egg wash

1 egg plus 1 teaspoon water, beaten

Yield: 8 turnovers

Stuff You'll Need

1. Place the apple slices in a medium pot over medium-low heat. Add the sugar, cornstarch, lemon juice, and cinnamon, and stir well.

2. Cook the apples, stirring occasionally, for 8 to 10 minutes or until they become soft. Remove from the heat and set aside to cool.

3. Place the pastry sheets on a clean flat surface. With a sharp knife, cut each sheet into quarters.

4. Spoon some filling on one side of each square (as shown in the photo). Lift up the dough on the unfilled side and fold it over the filling to form a triangle. To seal, crimp the edges together with your fingers or the tines of a fork.

5. Make diagonal cuts through the top of each filled triangle, and place on a parchment-lined cookie sheet. Leave about an inch of space between them to allow for expansion.

 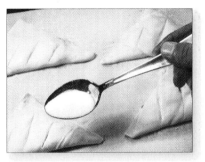

6. Brush the tops with egg wash.

7. Sprinkle with sugar.

8. Bake in a preheated 375°F oven for 25 to 30 minutes or until the turnovers are a light golden brown. Serve warm as is or drizzled with Vanilla Ice (page 82).

Almond Triangle Puffs

A few years ago, I tried making almond croissants with puff pastry dough, but then I realized it wouldn't work because croissant dough contains yeast. These flaky almond pastries, however, are really quite close. When I close my eyes and take a bite, I swear I'm in a French patisserie.

Ingredients

1 sheet (9-inch square) frozen puff
    pastry dough, thawed
7- or 8-ounce tube or can almond paste
1/4 cup sliced almonds
Confectioner's sugar for sprinkling
    on top

Egg wash

1 egg plus 1 teaspoon water, beaten

Yield: 9 puffs

Stuff You'll Need

1. Place the pastry sheet on a clean flat surface. With a sharp knife, cut the dough into 9 squares, then cut each square in half diagonally to form 18 triangles.

2. Divide the almond paste into 9 equal-sized balls. With your fingers, mold one of the balls into a somewhat triangular shape. Place it on the middle of a triangle of dough, leaving about a 1/2-inch border around it.

3. Cover the almond paste with another triangle of dough. To seal, crimp the edges together with your fingers or the tines of a fork. Repeat with the remaining dough and almond paste.

4. Place the filled triangles on a parchment-lined cookie sheet, leaving about an inch of space between them to allow for expansion. Cut 3 diagonal slices through the top of each, then brush with the egg wash.

5. Sprinkle the almonds on top of the triangles. Bake in a preheated 375°F oven for 25 to 30 minutes or until the tops are light golden brown. Serve warm with a sprinkling of confectioner's sugar.

Frangipane Puff Pie

Oh My God! This is good. I mean this is really, really good! And it's so easy to make that nobody will believe you spent about fifteen minutes preparing it!

Ingredients

2 sheets (9-inch squares) frozen puff
  pastry dough, thawed
1 cup whole unblanched almonds
$^{1}/_{2}$ cup granulated sugar
$^{1}/_{4}$ cup all-purpose flour
$^{1}/_{2}$ cup butter (1 stick), softened
3 eggs
1 teaspoon rum extract plus
  2 tablespoons water
  (or 3 tablespoons rum)

Egg wash

1 egg plus 1 teaspoon water, beaten

Yield: 12 to 15 Servings

Stuff You'll Need

1. Finely grind the almonds in a food processor, and transfer to a large mixing bowl.

2. Add the sugar and flour to the almonds, and stir until well mixed.

3. Add the butter, eggs, rum extract, and water to the almond mixture and stir well. Set aside.

4. Place one sheet of the pastry dough in a 9-inch pie pan. Gently pat the dough against the bottom and sides of the pan, and trim the excess. (If there are gaps in the crust, use some of the trimmings to fill them.)

5. Spoon the almond mixture into the crust. Spread it evenly with a rubber spatula.

6. Place the remaining sheet of pastry over the filling, trim off the excess dough, and crimp the edges to seal.

7. Cut a few vents into the top crust, then brush with egg wash. Bake in a preheated 375°F oven for 50 to 60 minutes, or until the top crust is golden brown and a toothpick inserted into a center vent comes out clean.

8. Cool the pie at least 30 minutes before cutting. Serve warm or at room temperature.

Golden Palmiers

Light and crisp with just the right touch of sweetness, these classic French cookies are melt-in-your-mouth good. Perfect to enjoy with a cup of coffee or tea, palmiers are just as popular to serve alongside a dish of ice cream. Because of their shape, they are sometimes called "angel wings" or "elephant ears." For the best taste and crispness, enjoy palmiers within a few hours after making them.

Ingredients

1 sheet (9-inch square) frozen puff
   pastry dough, thawed
$1/2$ cup raw or granulated sugar

Egg wash

1 egg plus 1 teaspoon water, beaten

Yield: 15 to 18 cookies

Important Tip

Be sure to line your cookie sheet with parchment, or these cookies will stick, like, fer sure!

Stuff You'll Need

1. Sprinkle half the sugar on a clean flat surface and place the sheet of pastry dough on top. Roll out the dough so it is about 15 inches long.

2. Sprinkle the remaining sugar evenly over the surface of the dough.

3. Starting with one of the long sides, roll the dough to the center of the sheet. Repeat with the other side, leaving about $1/4$ inch between the two rolls.

4. Using a sharp knife, cut the dough into $1/2$-inch slices.

5. Place the slices on a parchment-lined cookie sheet, leaving at least 2 inches between them to allow for expansion. Lightly brush with egg wash.

6. Bake in a preheated 375°F oven for 7 to 9 minutes or until the edges of the cookies are lightly browned. Cool the cookies about 5 minutes before removing from the parchment.

Try This Variation!
Chocolate Palmiers

If you love chocolate, then you're gonna love these chocolate-dipped palmiers. And you can use any type of chocolate . . . I chose morsels 'cause I always have them on hand.

Add

1/2 cup semi-sweet chocolate morsels, melted and slightly cooled

1. Dip the ends of each cookie into the melted chocolate.

2. Place the cookies on a parchment-lined cookie sheet. Allow the chocolate to set before serving.

You are *such* a cream puff!

Puff pastry shells make the ideal holders for fresh fruit, your favorite ice cream, and all sorts of other delicious fillings (both sweet and savory). I find them perfect to use for cream puffs. A light and luscious creamy filling paired with a buttery flaky pastry shell makes the perfect taste combination. One bite and you'll feel good to be alive—then have fun checking out your cream-filled mustache!

Basic Steps for Using Puff Pastry Shells

1. Bake

Place the frozen shells on an ungreased cookie sheet and bake according to package directions. If you brush the tops with egg wash, be careful not to get any on the sides. Doing so will seal the edges and prevent the shells from rising properly.

2. Remove top

Once the shells are baked and cool enough to handle, run a fork around the circular top and lift it off. Then remove the doughy layers inside the shell to make room for the filling.

3. Fill

Once the shells are baked, the top is removed, and the inner layers of dough are taken out . . . it's time to fill 'er up. In this section, the recipes focus on creamy dessert fillings; but you can use all sorts of tasty treats. Fill the shells right before serving to prevent them from getting soft.

Mascarpone Puffs

Creamy and light . . . it's so right.

Ingredients

6 frozen puff pastry shells
1 cup heavy cream
$^1/_2$ cup mascarpone cheese
3 tablespoons granulated sugar
1 tablespoon Grand Marnier liqueur
Berries for garnish
Confectioner's sugar for garnish

Yield: 6 puffs

1. Place the frozen pastry shells on an ungreased cookie sheet and bake according to package directions. Let cool a bit, then remove the tops and the flaky layers within the shells.

2. Place the cream in a medium mixing bowl. Whip with an electric mixer on high speed until stiff peaks form. (For whipping instructions, see page 56.)

3. Add the mascarpone, sugar, and Grand Marnier to the whipped cream. Stir with the mixer on low speed until the ingredients are well blended and the mixture is thick and creamy.

Stuff You'll Need

4. Spoon the mascarpone cream into the prepared pastry shells. Garnish with fresh berries and a sprinkling of confectioner's sugar. Serve immediately.

Cannoli Puffs

Although puff pastry shells aren't anything like classic cannoli shells, they still make great holders for creamy cannoli filling. You'll see.

Ingredients

6 frozen puff pastry shells
2 cups ricotta cheese
$1/2$ cup granulated sugar
2 teaspoons vanilla extract
$1/2$ cup mini chocolate morsels
Chopped pistachios or sliced almonds for garnish (optional)

Yield: 6 puffs

1. Place the frozen pastry shells on an ungreased cookie sheet and bake according to package directions. Let cool a bit, then remove the tops and the flaky layers within the shells.

2. Place the ricotta cheese, sugar, and vanilla in a large mixing bowl. Beat with an electric mixer on medium speed until smooth.

3. Stir the chocolate morsels into the ricotta mixture until well distributed.

Stuff You'll Need

4. Spoon the cannoli cream into the prepared pastry shells. Serve immediately as is or topped with a garnish of chopped pistachios or sliced almonds.

Blueberry Puffs

Blueberries and cream . . . Oh my!

Ingredients

6 frozen puff pastry shells
1 cup fresh or frozen blueberries
1/4 cup granulated sugar
1 teaspoon cornstarch
1 tablespoon lemon juice or water
1 cup heavy cream
1 tablespoon confectioner's sugar

Yield: 6 puffs

1. Place the frozen pastry shells on an ungreased cookie sheet and bake according to package directions. Let cool a bit, then remove the tops and the flaky layers within the shells.

2. Stir the blueberries, sugar, cornstarch, and lemon juice together in a medium pot. Place over medium heat and bring to a boil. Reduce the heat to low and simmer while stirring for 5 minutes. Remove from the heat and let cool at least 5 minutes.

3. Place the cream and confectioner's sugar in a medium mixing bowl. Whip with an electric mixer on high speed until stiff peaks form. Fold the cooled blueberry mixture into the whipped cream until well combined and uniform in color. (For folding instructions, see page 57.)

Stuff You'll Need

4. Spoon the blueberry cream into the prepared pastry shells and sprinkle with confectioner's sugar. Serve immediately.

Chocolate Cream Puffs

Unlike traditional chocolate mousse (Mousse au Chocolat on page 96), which is made with whipped egg whites, the mousse in this recipe is made with whipped cream. Both are great fillings for puff pastry shells.

Ingredients

6 frozen puff pastry shells
³/₄ cup semi-sweet chocolate morsels
1 cup heavy cream
1 tablespoon confectioner's sugar
Grated chocolate for garnish

Yield: 6 puffs

Stuff You'll Need

1. Place the frozen pastry shells on an ungreased cookie sheet and bake according to package directions. Let cool a bit, then remove the tops and the flaky layers within the shells.

2. Melt the chocolate morsels in the top of a double boiler over medium-low heat or in a medium saucepan over *very low* heat. Remove from the heat and let cool until warm.

3. Place the cream and confectioner's sugar in a medium mixing bowl. Whip with an electric mixer on high speed until stiff peaks form. Fold the whipped cream into the warm melted chocolate until well blended and uniform in color. (For folding instructions, see page 57.)

4. Spoon the chocolate filling into the prepared pastry shells and sprinkle with grated chocolate. Serve immediately.

White Chocolate Cream Puffs

Although white chocolate doesn't contain actual chocolate, it still makes a pretty delicious filling for these puffs. I used fresh blackberries to top them off, but feel free to try other berry varieties!

Ingredients

6 frozen puff pastry shells
3/4 cup white chocolate morsels
1 1/2 cups heavy cream
Fresh berries (optional)

Yield: 6 puffs

Stuff You'll Need

1. Place the frozen pastry shells on an ungreased cookie sheet and bake according to package directions. Let cool a bit, then remove the tops and the flaky layers within the shells.

2. Melt the white chocolate in the top of a double boiler over medium-low heat or in a medium saucepan over *very low* heat. Remove from the heat and let cool a bit until warm.

3. Place the cream in a medium mixing bowl. Whip with an electric mixer on high speed until stiff peaks form. Fold the whipped cream into the warm melted chocolate until well blended and uniform in color. (For folding instructions, see page 57.)

4. Spoon the white chocolate filling into the prepared pastry shells. Garnish with berries and serve immediately.

A Thousand Leaves

*With its multiple buttery layers, puff pastry bakes into a crust that's crisp and light –
perfect for strudels, napoleons, and other flaky pastries.
In France, the term mille-feuilles, which means "a thousand leaves,"
is synonymous with any puff pastry creation – napoleons in particular.*

Who Invented the Puff?

Although the true origin of puff pastry cannot be verified, the French insist that noted pastry chef Claudius Gele invented it in 1645 when he was just an apprentice. As mentioned in the inset on page 311, in an effort to please his sick father (who had been put on a strict diet of flour, water, and butter), Claudius prepared some dough with flour and water, packed it with butter, and then kneaded and folded it over and over into a loaf. The result was a crude version of the multi-layered buttery creation that we have come to know (and love) as puff pastry. This not only made Claudius' father happy, but also delighted the pastry shop owner, whose customers loved the new recipe. While Claudius may (or may not) have invented puff pastry, it was the eighteenth-century French and Italian chefs who perfected it.

Napoleon Didn't Invent Napoleons

The famous French emperor had nothing to do with creating napoleons, but he probably ate his fair share. The pastry's name itself may come from the French word *Napolitain*, which means "from Naples." According to some sources, Naples is where this dessert originated. While this may be true, many believe the napoleon was invented by noted French Chef Marie-Antoine Carême, who was known for his magnificent pastries. He was also a contemporary of Napoleon.

Ahhh . . . Choux!

Choux (pronounced choo) is a light, batter-like pastry dough that is used to make the flaky shells for such heavenly baked goods as cream puffs, éclairs, and brioche. Choux, which is the French word for "cabbages," became popular during the middle of the eighteenth century when it was used primarily to make little cabbage-shaped buns. By the nineteenth century, the recipe was perfected, and is the same one used today.

In a Pig's Ear!

One of the most common puff pastry creations found in French pastry shops are *palmiers* – light, crisp cookies that are sometimes known as *pig ears* or *elephant ears* because of their shape. I have also heard them called *angel wings*. It's almost impossible to find fresh palmiers in the United States. Lucky for you, they are easy to make. (Check out the recipe on page 320.)

Mmm . . . Croissants

Some puff pastry dough is leavened with yeast and used to make baked goods like croissants and Danish. Mmmm, croissants! One of the first recipes for this flaky, multi-layered, buttery roll can be traced back to *Le Cuisinier François* – a book on modern French cuisine by Chef François Pierre de la Varenne that was published in 1651. There are many beliefs regarding the origin of the croissant's crescent moon shape. The most popular is that it evolved from the *kipfel* – an Austrian horn-shaped cookie (or roll) that dates back to the thirteenth century.

Holiday Cookies 330
    Holiday Rum Balls, 330
    Hanukkah Rugelach, 332
    Spanish Polvornes, 334
    Holiday Butter Crisps, 335
    Gingerbread Dudes 'n Pals, 336

Holiday Pies 338
    Pumpkin Pie, 338
    Sweet Po-Tater Pie, 339
    Fiadone Easter Pie, 340

Holiday Breads 342
    Cranberry Bread, 342
    Fruity Christmas Loaf, 343
    Irish Soda Bread, 344

Holiday Puddings 346
    Yuletide Pudding, 346
    Bread Pudding, 347
    Mocha-Banana English Trifle, 348

Holiday Cakes 350
    Southern Red Velvet Cake, 350
    Sponge Cake with Goodies, 352
    Holiday Honey Cake, 354

13. Sweet Holidays

Loosen that belt . . .
It's time for dessert!

Just when you thought you couldn't eat another bite after your second trip to the holiday buffet table, dessert is served. So what do you do? You could go outside and run a few miles and try to make some space in your belly, but it's probably too cold (and you forgot to bring your running shoes). So the only option left is to loosen your belt and maybe undo the top button of your pants. After all, the idea of skipping a holiday dessert is obviously out of the question.

This chapter contains a collection of popular desserts for our favorite *(and sometimes least favorite)* times of the year – the holidays! Representing various religions and cultures, the recipes start with a wonderful assortment of cookies. You'll find everything from no-bake Rum Balls to fun-to-make-and-eat Gingerbread Dudes. Next you can sink your teeth into some delicious pies with such holiday classics as pumpkin and sweet potato.

And 'ow about a luscious dessert inspired by the island 'cross the pond, mate? I've got just the thing for ya—a brilliant English trifle made with bananas and chocolate-mocha cream, and a date pudding topped with rich caramel sauce that is to die for! Finally there is cake, including a lighter-than-air sponge cake, and a velvet cake that's decked out in holiday red.

So go ahead and make those necessary space-making wardrobe adjustments . . . and let's dig into some holiday desserts!

Holiday Rum Balls

I created these delicious no-bake cookies with rum extract, which has the great taste of rum without the actual alcohol "effect." For those who want the "effect," check out the Important Tip below. It gives you the real rum version that's sure to bring out the pirate in you – yo ho ho.

Ingredients

1 cup pecans
2 1/2 cups vanilla wafer crumbs
1 1/2 cups confectioner's sugar, divided
2 tablespoons cocoa
1/3 cup water
3 tablespoons light corn syrup
2 teaspoons rum-flavored extract

Yield: About 3 dozen cookies

Important Tips

▶ Instead of extract, you can use 5 tablespoons dark rum and eliminate the water.

▶ Letting the cookies sit a few days allows them to become dry and firm. They also taste better.

Stuff You'll Need

1. Finely grind the pecans in a food processor.

2. Transfer the ground pecans to a large mixing bowl. Add the cookie crumbs, 1 cup of the confectioner's sugar, the cocoa, corn syrup, water, and rum extract. Stir until well mixed.

3. Roll the mixture into 1 1/4-inch balls, then roll the balls in the remaining confectioner's sugar until well coated.

4. Layer the cookies in an airtight container, and separate each layer with wax paper or parchment. Cover and place in a dry cool area for at least five days before serving.

Hanukkah Rugelach

After the raisins and walnuts are tossed with cinnamon and sugar, they're rolled up in tender cream cheese dough for these cookies. I think of them as miniature Jewish croissants. Delicious!

Ingredients

1 cup all-purpose flour
1/2 cup butter (1 stick), cold
4 ounces cream cheese, cold
3 tablespoons sour cream

Filling

1/2 cup coarsely chopped walnuts
1/4 cup raisins
1/4 cup granulated sugar
1 teaspoon ground cinnamon

Yield: 16 cookies

Stuff You'll Need

1. Place the flour in a large mixing bowl. Cut the cold butter and cream cheese into chunks and add to the bowl along with the sour cream. Using a pastry blender, cut the butter and cream cheese into the mixture until it resembles a crumbly meal.

2. Press the mixture into a ball of dough with your hands. Divide the dough in half and shape each half into a flattened disc. Wrap each disc in plastic wrap and refrigerate at least 4 hours.

3. Place the walnuts, raisins, sugar, and cinnamon in a medium bowl and stir until well combined. Set aside.

4. Unwrap one disc of dough, place on a lightly floured surface, and roll out to 1/8-inch-thick circle. Repeat with the other disc.

5. Sprinkle the filling mixture evenly over each circle of dough. With a sharp knife, cut each circle into eighths to form 16 long triangles.

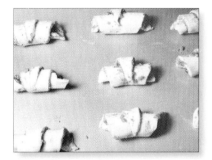

6. Roll up the triangles beginning at the wide end. Place on a lightly greased cookie sheet about 2 inches apart. Bake in a preheated 350°F oven for 12 to 15 minutes or until the cookies are light golden brown. Allow to cool before serving.

Try This Variation!

Here's another way to make rugelach, especially for you chocolate lovers.

Chocolate Chip Hanukkah Rugelach

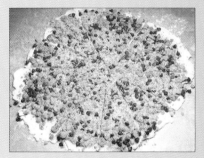

Substitute

$1/4$ cup mini semi-sweet chocolate morsels

Follow the directions for Hanukkah Rugelach, but substitute mini chocolate morsels for the raisins in Step 3.

Spanish Polvornes

Here's a classic Spanish holiday cookie that melts in your mouth!

Ingredients

1 cup butter (2 sticks), softened
1$\frac{1}{2}$ cups confectioner's sugar, divided
1$\frac{1}{2}$ teaspoons ground cinnamon, divided
1 teaspoon vanilla extract
1$\frac{1}{2}$ cups all-purpose flour

Yield: About 2 dozen cookies

Important Tips

▶ These cookies break apart very easily, so be careful when handling and storing them.

▶ For extra sweetness, while the cookies are still warm from the oven, roll them a second time in the cinnamon–sugar.

Stuff You'll Need

1. Place the butter, $\frac{1}{2}$ cup of the confectioner's sugar, and vanilla in a large mixing bowl, and cream with an electric mixer on low speed until light and fluffy. Gradually add the flour and $\frac{1}{2}$ teaspoon of the cinnamon, stirring with a wooden spoon to form a smooth, sticky dough.

2. Combine the remaining confectioner's sugar and cinnamon in a small bowl and set aside. Roll the dough into 1$\frac{1}{4}$-inch balls, then roll the balls in the cinnamon-sugar mixture until well coated.

3. Place the balls on a lightly greased cookie sheet about an inch or so apart. Bake in a preheated 350°F oven for 15 to 20 minutes or until light brown. Cool the cookies a minute before transferring to a wire rack to cool completely.

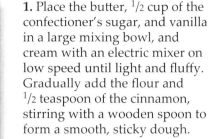

Holiday Butter Crisps

These classic butter cookies are perfect for shaping and decorating. Let your imagination run wild.

Ingredients

1 cup butter (2 sticks), softened
$^2/_3$ cup granulated sugar
1 teaspoon vanilla extract
$2^1/_2$ cups all-purpose flour
$^1/_2$ teaspoon salt

Yield: About 2 dozen cookies

1. Place the butter, sugar, and vanilla in a large mixing bowl, and cream with an electric mixer on low speed until fluffy. Gradually add the flour and salt, stirring with a wooden spoon to form a smooth sticky dough. Form the dough into a ball, cover in plastic wrap, and refrigerate for 3 hours.

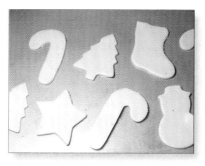

2. Place the dough on a lightly floured surface and roll it out to $^1/_8$-inch thickness.

3. Using cookie cutters, the rim of a glass, or a sharp knife, cut shapes into the dough. Place the shapes on a parchment-lined cookie sheet about 1 inch apart. Gather up the scraps of dough into a ball, roll it out again, and cut more cookies. Continue with the remaining dough.

Stuff You'll Need

4. Bake in a preheated 325°F oven for 6 to 8 minutes, or until the edges are lightly browned. Cool the cookies a few minutes before removing from the sheet. Transfer to a wire rack and allow to cool completely. Enjoy plain or decorated. (For decorating ideas, see Chapter 14.)

Gingerbread Dudes 'n Pals

Is there anything better than having gingerbread dudes and their pals for the holidays? This is a recipe the whole family can enjoy making and decorating.

Ingredients

$^1/_2$ cup butter (1 stick), softened
$^1/_2$ cup firmly packed brown sugar
$^1/_2$ cup dark molasses
1 teaspoon ground ginger
$^1/_2$ teaspoon ground cinnamon
$^1/_2$ teaspoon salt
$^1/_4$ teaspoon ground cloves
$3^1/_2$ cups all-purpose flour
1 teaspoon baking soda

Yield: About 3 dozen cookies

Stuff You'll Need

1. Place the butter, brown sugar, molasses, ginger, cinnamon, salt, and cloves in a large mixing bowl. Beat with an electric mixer on medium speed until smooth and well blended.

2. Combine the flour and baking soda in a medium bowl. Gradually add this flour mixture to the molasses mixture, stirring with a wooden spoon to form a stiff sticky dough. (You may have to use your hands to do the last bit of mixing.)

3. Divide the dough into thirds, and shape each third into a flattened disc. Wrap each disc in plastic wrap and refrigerate at least 2 hours.

4. Unwrap one disc of dough and place on a lightly floured surface. Roll it out to $^1/_4$-inch thickness.

5. Using your favorite holiday cookie cutters, cut shapes into the dough.

6. Place the cut shapes on a parchment-lined cookie sheet about an inch or so apart. Gather up the scraps of dough into a ball, roll it out again, and cut out more shapes. Repeat with the remaining dough.

7. Bake in a preheated 350°F oven for 8 to 10 minutes, or until somewhat crisp but not darkened. (The cookies will spring back a little when you touch them with your finger.) Cool the cookies a few minutes before removing from the sheet. Transfer to a wire rack and cool completely.

8. Enjoy the cookies plain, or decorate them with Vanilla Ice (page 82). For decorating ideas and techniques, see Chapter 14.

Pumpkin Pie

What's Thanksgiving without a classic pumpkin pie? This one is super delicious and super easy to prepare. Top it with some whipped cream. (And don't be skimpy!)

Ingredients

Half recipe Flaky Pastry Pie Crust
   (page 173), or commercial 9-inch
   single crust
3 eggs
15-ounce can pumpkin purée
$1/2$ cup heavy cream
$2/3$ cup firmly packed brown sugar
1 teaspoon ground cinnamon
$1/2$ teaspoon ground nutmeg
$1/2$ teaspoon salt

Yield: 8 to 10 servings

1. Place the eggs in a large mixing bowl and beat well with a whisk or fork.

2. Add the pumpkin purée, cream, brown sugar, cinnamon, nutmeg, and salt. Stir until the mixture is smooth and well blended.

3. Pour the pumpkin mixture into the prepared pie crust.

4. Bake in a preheated 350°F oven for 50 to 60 minutes or until the center has set (it doesn't jiggle when you *gently* shake it). Cool at least 20 minutes before cutting. Serve at room temperature.

Stuff You'll Need

Sweet Po-Tater Pie

Sweet potato pie is similar to pumpkin pie, only lighter. But hey, it's all good!

Ingredients

Half recipe Flaky Pastry Pie Crust
    (page 173), or commercial 9-inch
    single crust
1 large or 2 small sweet potatoes
    (about 1 pound), unpeeled
$1/2$ cup butter (1 stick), softened
1 cup granulated sugar
$1/2$ cup heavy cream
2 eggs
$1/2$ teaspoon ground nutmeg
$1/2$ teaspoon ground cinnamon

Yield: 8 to 10 servings

Stuff You'll Need

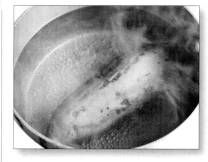

1. Place the sweet potato in a pot of water and bring to a boil. Reduce the heat to low and simmer 45 minutes or until the potato is tender. Drain the water, then cover the potato with ice water. When the potato has cooled, peel off the skin with your fingers.

2. Place the cooked potato in a large mixing bowl and mash with a fork. Add the butter, sugar, cream, eggs, nutmeg, and cinnamon. Beat with an electric mixer on medium speed until smooth and well blended.

3. Pour the potato mixture into the prepared pie crust.

4. Bake in a preheated 350°F oven for 50 to 60 minutes or until the center has set (it doesn't jiggle when you *gently* shake it). Cool at least 20 minutes before cutting. Serve at room temperature.

Fiadone Easter Pie

When warm, this traditional Italian Easter pie tastes like a fruity custard with a crust . . . when cold, it tastes more like cheesecake. Either way, it is totally delicioso!

Ingredients

Half recipe Flaky Pastry Pie Crust (page 173), or commercial 9-inch single crust

2 cups ricotta cheese

1/2 cup granulated sugar

2 teaspoons fresh lemon juice

2 teaspoons fresh orange juice

2 egg yolks*

1/2 cup golden raisins

*For egg separating instructions, see page 51.

Yield: 8 to 10 servings

Important Tip

If the ricotta you are using is fairly solid and doesn't contain much liquid, you can skip Step 1.

Stuff You'll Need

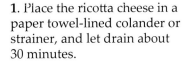

1. Place the ricotta cheese in a paper towel-lined colander or strainer, and let drain about 30 minutes.

2. Transfer the drained ricotta to a large mixing bowl along with the sugar, lemon juice, orange juice, and egg yolks. Stir with a whisk until well blended.

3. Add the raisins to the mixture and stir until well combined.

4. Pour the filling into the prepared pie crust. Bake in a preheated 350°F oven for 50 to 60 minutes or until the top is very lightly browned and the center has set (it doesn't jiggle when you *gently* shake it). Cool 20 minutes before cutting. Serve warm, cold, or at room temperature.

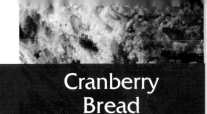

Cranberry Bread

Bursting with cranberries, this easy-to-make holiday bread is delicious plain or topped with butter.

Ingredients

1 cup granulated sugar
2 tablespoons melted butter
³/₄ cup fresh orange juice
1 egg, well beaten
2 cups all-purpose flour
1¹/₂ teaspoons baking powder
¹/₂ teaspoon baking soda
¹/₂ teaspoon salt
2 cups fresh or frozen cranberries, coarsely chopped
1 cup chopped walnuts

Yield: 9-inch loaf

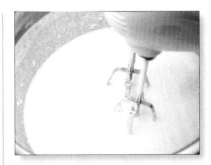

1. Place the sugar, butter, orange juice, and egg in a large mixing bowl. Beat with an electric mixer on medium-low speed until smooth and well blended. Set aside.

2. Combine the flour, baking powder, baking soda, salt, cranberries, and walnuts in a medium mixing bowl. Gradually add this mixture to the blended egg mixture, and stir just until mixed to form a thick batter. Do not overstir.

3. Spoon the batter into a greased and floured 9-x-5-inch loaf pan.

Stuff You'll Need

4. Bake in a preheated 350°F oven for 50 to 60 minutes, or until a toothpick inserted into the center of the loaf comes out clean. Cool for 15 minutes before removing the bread from the pan. Serve warm or at room temperature.

Fruity Christmas Loaf

This quick bread is my version of an "edible" non-alcoholic fruitcake (and it's also easy to make). It is rich, dense, and loaded with butter.

Ingredients

1 cup butter (2 sticks), softened
1 cup granulated sugar
2 eggs
$1/2$ cup orange juice
2 cups all-purpose flour
1 teaspoon baking powder
$1/2$ cup golden raisins
1 cup pitted fresh or canned cherries
$1/2$ cup coarsely chopped pecans

Yield: 9-inch loaf

1. Place the butter and sugar in a large mixing bowl. Cream with an electric mixer on low speed until light and fluffy. Add the eggs and orange juice, and continue to beat until smooth and well blended.

2. Combine the flour, baking powder, raisins, cherries, and pecans in a medium mixing bowl. Gradually add this mixture to the blended egg mixture, and stir just until mixed to form a thick batter. Do not overstir.

3. Spoon the batter into a greased and floured 9-x-5-inch loaf pan. Bake in a preheated 325°F oven for 60 to 90 minutes or until a toothpick inserted into the center of the loaf comes out clean.

4. Cool for 15 minutes before removing the loaf from the pan. Allow to cool completely. Wrap the cooled loaf in plastic wrap or seal in an airtight container. Store in a cool dry place at least two days before serving.

Irish Soda Bread

Top o' the marnin' to ya! It's Saint Patty's day and I'm in the mood for sum celebratin'! So por me a green beer, and will ya also be koind enuf to pass me a wee slice of some of me favorite soda bread?

Ingredients

2 cups all-purpose flour
1 teaspoon baking powder
1/4 teaspoon salt
1 cup raisins
1/2 cup granulated sugar
2/3 cup buttermilk
1/2 cup sour cream
1 egg

Yield: 9-inch loaf

1. Combine the flour, baking powder, salt, and raisins in a medium mixing bowl. Set aside.

2. Place the sugar, buttermilk, sour cream, and egg in a large bowl and beat with a wooden spoon or an electric mixer on low speed until smooth and well blended.

3. Gradually add the flour mixture to the blended egg mixture, and stir just until mixed to form a soft sticky batter. Do not overstir.

4. Spoon the batter into a greased and floured 9-x-5-inch loaf pan. Bake in a preheated 325°F oven for 60 to 70 minutes or until a toothpick inserted into the center of the loaf comes out clean. Cool 15 minutes before removing the bread from the pan. Serve warm or at room temperature.

Stuff You'll Need

Yuletide Pudding

The caramel sauce really makes this holiday pudding sing!

Ingredients

3/4 cup finely chopped pitted dates
1 teaspoon baking powder
1 1/4 cups boiling water
1 cup all-purpose flour
1 teaspoon baking soda
1/4 cup butter (1/2 stick), softened
3/4 cup granulated sugar
1 egg
1 teaspoon vanilla extract
1 recipe Caramel Sauce (page 86)

Yield: 6 to 8 servings

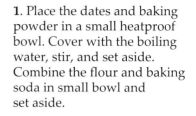

1. Place the dates and baking powder in a small heatproof bowl. Cover with the boiling water, stir, and set aside. Combine the flour and baking soda in small bowl and set aside.

2. Place the butter, sugar, egg, and vanilla in a large mixing bowl. Beat with an electric mixer on medium speed until smooth and well blended. Add the date mixture and stir well, then add the flour mixture, and stir until well combined.

3. Pour the mixture into a greased 2-quart casserole dish. Bake in a preheated 350°F oven for 35 to 40 minutes or until the center of the pudding has set (it doesn't jiggle when you *gently* shake it).

4. Allow the pudding to cool at least 5 minutes. Spoon servings into individual bowls and top with hot caramel sauce (a must!).

Stuff You'll Need

Bread Pudding

This dessert is like a creamy custard with a nice crispy crust. Top it with a few sprinkles of cinnamon and you'll know it's holiday time.

Ingredients

3 cups bread cubes (about ½-inch)*
2 cups whole milk
1 can sweetened condensed milk
¾ cup granulated sugar
6 eggs
1 tablespoon vanilla extract
¼ cup raisins
¼ cup melted butter
1 teaspoon ground cinnamon

* French or Italian bread is recommended.

Yield: 6 to 8 servings

Stuff You'll Need

1. Cut the bread into cubes and place in a greased and floured 9-x-5-inch loaf pan. Set aside.

2. Add the whole milk, condensed milk, sugar, eggs, and vanilla to a blender. Purée for 2 minutes.

3. Pour the puréed mixture over the bread cubes. Bake in a preheated 350°F oven for 50 to 60 minutes or until a toothpick inserted into the center of the pudding comes out clean.

4. Allow to cool at least 15 minutes. Spoon servings into individual bowls. Enjoy warm or cold.

Mocha-Banana English Trifle

My mother used to make an English trifle for Christmas that was loaded with bananas and flavored with chocolate and coffee liqueurs. Sadly, that recipe is just a memory, but I did my best to create my own version. It contains lady fingers and bananas like my mother's did, but mine has coffee and chocolate flavorings instead of liqueur.

Ingredients

4 egg yolks*

$^1/_3$ cup granulated sugar

2 teaspoons instant coffee

2$^1/_4$ cups heavy cream, divided

3 squares (1 ounce each) baking
 chocolate

1 tablespoon confectioner's sugar

16 to 20 lady fingers

3 small ripe bananas, sliced

$^1/_4$ cup sliced blanched almonds

Grated chocolate for garnish

*For egg separating instructions, see page 51.

Yield: 9 to 12 servings

Stuff You'll Need

1. Place the egg yolks and sugar in a medium bowl and stir to form a thick yellow paste. Transfer to a medium saucepan, and set aside.

2. Stir the instant coffee and 1$^1/_4$ cups of the cream in a small bowl until most of the coffee has dissolved. Add to the egg mixture and bring to a boil over high heat. Reduce the heat to medium-low and stir for 3 to 4 minutes or until thickened to a smooth custard. Set aside to cool.

3. Place the remaining cream and confectioner's sugar in a medium mixing bowl. Whip with an electric mixer on high speed until stiff peaks form. Set aside. Melt the chocolate in a double boiler over medium-low heat or in a saucepan over *very low* heat. Transfer to a large bowl and let cool.

4. Gently fold the whipped cream into the cooled chocolate until well combined and uniform in color. Set aside. (For folding instructions, see page 57.)

5. Arrange about 8 ladyfingers on the bottom of a 2$^1/_2$ quart bowl.

6. Cover the lady fingers with half the custard, then top with half the banana slices.

7. Spoon half the chocolate whipped cream over the bananas, then cover with more lady fingers. Repeat the layers.

8. Top with the blanched almonds, and sprinkle with grated chocolate.

9. Refrigerate at least 3 hours before serving.

Southern Red Velvet Cake

The velvety red layers of this Southern specialty are traditionally covered with creamy white frosting . . . the perfect choice for both Christmas and Valentine's Day.

Ingredients

2$^1/_2$ cups cake flour, or all-purpose flour
1 tablespoon unsweetened cocoa
   powder
1 teaspoon baking soda
1 teaspoon salt
1$^1/_4$ cups granulated sugar
1$^1/_2$ cups vegetable oil
1 cup buttermilk
1 tablespoon red food coloring
   ($^1/_2$ ounce)
1 teaspoon white vinegar or
   lemon juice
2 eggs
1 recipe Cream Cheese Frosting
   (page 81)

Yield: 8 to 12 servings

1. Combine the flour, cocoa powder, baking soda, and salt in a medium bowl. Set aside.

2. Place the sugar, oil, buttermilk, food coloring, and vinegar in a large mixing bowl. Beat with an electric mixer on medium speed until smooth. Add the eggs and beat until well blended. Gradually add the flour mixture, stirring with the mixer on low speed to form a smooth batter.

3. Pour an equal amount of batter into two greased and floured 9-inch round cake pans. Bake in a preheated 350°F oven for 25 to 30 minutes or until a toothpick inserted into the center of the cakes comes out clean.

4. Cool at least 15 minutes before removing the cakes from the pans. Allow to cool completely before frosting. (Steps for frosting a double-layer cake are on page 366.)

Stuff You'll Need

Sponge Cake with Goodies

Sponge cake is traditionally served during Passover, when it is permissible to eat only unleavened baked goods. This cake's amazing lightness comes from seven whipped egg whites, which are folded into the batter. Although sponge cake is customarily eaten plain, I couldn't help but add some whipped cream and fresh berries to this one.

Ingredients

7 eggs, separated*
1 teaspoon cream of tartar
1 cup granulated sugar
2 teaspoons vanilla extract
1 cup cake flour, or all-purpose flour
1 tablespoon fresh lemon juice
   (optional)
1 recipe Whippy Cream (page 99)
1 cup fresh raspberries

*For egg separating instructions, see page 51.

Yield: 12 to 16 servings

Stuff You'll Need

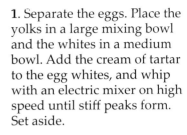

1. Separate the eggs. Place the yolks in a large mixing bowl and the whites in a medium bowl. Add the cream of tartar to the egg whites, and whip with an electric mixer on high speed until stiff peaks form. Set aside.

2. Add the sugar and vanilla to the egg yolks. Beat with the mixer on high speed for 2 minutes.

3. Add the flour to the egg yolk mixture and stir to form a smooth, thick batter.

4. Gently fold the whipped egg whites and lemon juice (if using) into the batter until well combined and uniform in color. (For folding instructions, see page 57.)

5. Grease and flour the sides of a 9-inch springform pan and line the bottom with parchment paper. Spoon the batter into the pan, and bake in a preheated 350°F oven for 45 to 55 minutes or until a toothpick inserted into the center of the cake comes out clean.

6. Cool the cake at least 30 minutes before carefully removing from the pan. Allow to cool completely. Using a long serrated knife, cut the cooled cake in half to form top and bottom layers. Remove the top layer and set aside.

7. Spoon half the whipped cream over the bottom layer, then replace the top layer.

8. Spread the remaining whipped cream on top, decorate with raspberries, and serve.

Holiday Honey Cake

Honey cakes are popular holiday fare for many cultures and religions. This particular version is traditionally served on Rosh Hashanah—the Jewish New Year. It's a dense cake that's a little dry, but sweet and loaded with flavorful spices. Symbolically, it is meant to ensure sweetness for the coming year.

Ingredients

2 cups all-purpose flour
1 teaspoon baking powder
1 teaspoon ground cinnamon
1/2 teaspoon allspice
Pinch salt
2 eggs
2 tablespoons vegetable oil
3/4 cup honey
1/3 cup strong brewed coffee
1/2 cup granulated sugar
1/2 cup finely chopped almonds
1/4 cup sliced almonds for garnish

Syrup

3/4 cup honey
1/2 cup granulated sugar
1/4 cup water
1 tablespoon lemon juice

Yield: 10 to 12 servings

Stuff You'll Need

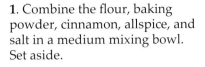

1. Combine the flour, baking powder, cinnamon, allspice, and salt in a medium mixing bowl. Set aside.

2. Place the eggs, oil, honey, coffee, sugar, and chopped almonds in a large mixing bowl. Beat with a whisk until well blended.

3. Gradually add the flour mixture to the honey mixture, and stir to form a well-blended batter.

4. Pour the batter into a greased and floured 9-inch bundt pan. Bake in a preheated 325°F oven for 65 to 75 minutes or until a toothpick inserted into the center of the cake comes out clean. Cool at least 20 minutes before turning the cake out of the pan.

5. Place all the syrup ingredients in a saucepan over low heat. Simmer while stirring until the sugar is dissolved. Remove from the heat and let cool 10 minutes. Pour the warm syrup evenly over the cake, sprinkle with sliced almonds, and serve.

Happy Holidaze

There are many, many traditional holiday desserts from around the world.
Whether it's an English trifle on Christmas, some Chinese bean cakes on New Year's Day,
or Irish soda bread on St. Patrick's Day, one thing is for sure—
it's always a good time for dessert!

A Tasty Log

In Belgium and France, *buche de noel* is a popular holiday cake that is shaped and decorated to look like a yule log. To create this shape, a long rectangular piece of sponge cake is topped with frosting and then rolled up. The outside is then frosted to look like tree bark. Traditionally, it is sprinkled with confectioner's sugar, which is meant to look like snow.

They Love Snowflakes in Iceland

During the Christmas season, the children of Iceland enjoy traditional cakes called *laufabraud*, which actually translates as "leaf bread." Pieces of dough are first flattened into paper-thin circles. Designs are then cut into the dough either by hand or with special rollers – snowflake designs are among the most popular. The dough is then deep-fried in hot oil until crisp and golden brown.

Tomb Cake

In Russia, the traditional Easter cake called *Pashka* is made to resemble Christ's tomb. *Pashka* is the Russian word for Easter.

That's Old Pudding

In England, plum pudding is traditionally prepared a year in advance and left to mellow – it is often soaked in brandy or cognac as it "sets." On Christmas day, the pudding is doused with brandy, decorated with a holly branch, and then lit before serving.

Holy Bread

The Greek Orthodox *Christopsomos*, which literally means "Christ's bread," was originally meant for the Christmas holiday. Now it is served at celebrations of any kind. Before making this holy bread, the baker begins by crossing himself. Only the best, most expensive ingredients are used. Pine nuts, tangerines, and anise are favorite flavorings, and the loaf is decorated with strips of dough that form a cross. Families often engrave their names and important dates in the crust as well.

Spotted Dick or Spotted Dog?

In England, spotted dick (also called spotted dog) is a real holiday favorite – and one of the oldest English desserts. It is a thick steamed pudding made with raisins, apples, brown sugar, lemon, breadcrumbs and shredded suet. Traditionally, this pudding is cut into thick slices and served in warm bowls.

Pan de Muertos

This Mexican "bread of the dead" is traditionally made to celebrate the country's Day of the Dead on November 2 – a holiday similar to Halloween. Yeast bread is shaped into skulls, corpses, and other macabre forms, and then decorated with icing, sprinkled with sugar, or dipped in chocolate.

Sweet Touches. 358

Ice Me Down!. 360

It's Raining Chocolate. 362

Fruity Designs. 363

Dazzling Cupcakes. 364

Frost Me Up!. 366

That's Some Fancy Dec'ratin'. . . .368

Fond of Fondant. 372

The frosting on the cake

If you like to take dessert to the "extreme" (*because that's how you roll . . .*) this chapter will show you ways to "take it to the next level." How? By decorating your sweet creations! From simple and elegant garnishes and accents to more advanced piping and sculpting techniques, there is something in here for every "extreme" baker.

Along with learning fun and easy techniques for drizzling, painting, and drawing with icing, you will discover how the right garnish can add visual beauty and the perfect finishing touch to your delicious baked goods.

There are detailed steps for frosting a two-layer cake, as well as instructions on how to use a pastry bag to pipe frosting onto cakes and cupcakes with professional-looking results. You will learn how to work with fondant, a sugar product that you can sculpt like clay into all sorts of eye-catching shapes for decorating your baked goods. Plus much, much more.

When you start applying the techniques in this chapter, you'll soon become aware of your new-found power. People will start making comments like, "It looks too beautiful to eat." And you'll notice that they are torn between sinking their teeth into your delicious creation and destroying a work of art.

. . . And that is "extremely" satisfying!

It looks good enough to eat!

The presentation of food is important. Two dishes can be made with the exact same ingredients and taste exactly the same, but if they look different, the dish with the most eye appeal is the one people will choose. Sometimes dressing up a dessert is as simple as adding a dollop of whipped cream or placing a cherry on top; but if you use your imagination, the possibilities are endless.

Basic Techniques for Decorating Desserts

Frosting
There are many techniques for adding thick spreadable frosting to cakes and cupcakes—from smoothing it on with a simple butter knife to piping it from a pastry bag into intricate designs to creating beautiful textures with special tools. (See details beginning on page 366.)

Icing
A simple mixture made of confectioner's sugar and milk, icing is a popular topping for cookies, coffeecakes, turnovers, and other pastries. Commonly drizzled, "painted," or drawn onto baked goods, icing hardens when it dries. (See details beginning on page 360.)

Garnishing
You can add a garnish to just about any dessert for added color, flavor, and/or texture. Some popular garnishes, which are usually sprinkled on top of desserts, include items like shredded coconut, shaved or grated chocolate, chopped nuts, and colored sugars or sprinkles.

Basic Techniques for Decorating Desserts

Patterning
Artfully arranging ingredients into eye-catching patterns of color, shape, and texture can turn a ho-hum dessert into a masterful work of art. Fresh fruit is a popular choice for creating patterned designs.

Accenting
You can add the perfect spark of visual interest to a plain-looking dessert by accenting it with a bit of fruit, pieces of chocolate, a colorful fondant flower, or some other type of garnish. A small cluster of berries on top of a simple frosted cake, for instance, can add just the right touch.

Dusting
Dusting a powdered ingredient like cocoa, confectioner's sugar, or ground cinnamon over cakes and pastries is an easy decorating technique. Simply sprinkle it through a sieve, strainer, or sifter onto baked goods, or shake it from a special sugar shaker.

Topping
Along with adding luscious flavor and creamy texture, topping a piece of cake or slice of pie with a scoop of ice cream or dollop of whipped cream can really dress it up. When going "a la mode" (adding ice cream), try to make nice rounded scoops for the best presentation.

Piping
Piping frosting from a pastry bag lends itself to creativity. Use this technique to cover the tops of small items like cupcakes, or to add decorative borders and patterns to larger cakes. You can even pipe messages like "Happy Birthday." (See details beginning on page 370.)

Adding Fondant
An edible sugar product, fondant is soft and pliable and used to cover or to decorate cakes. You can roll it flat and then use it to cover an entire cake (instead of frosting), or you can mold it into flowers or other decorative shapes as accents. (See details beginning on page 372.)

Slight chance of drizzling.

Icing is nothing more than a mixture of confectioner's sugar and milk (or water) . . . and you can add a drop or two of food coloring to make it any color of the rainbow. Unlike frosting, which stays somewhat soft, icing hardens. It's also very versatile. You can drizzle it over a variety of baked goods including coffeecakes, turnovers, and quick breads; spread it over the tops of cookies; or use it to "draw" some sweet designs on your baked creations.

Basic Techniques for Using Icing

Drawing

You can use icing to add a face to your gingerbread dudes or to draw decorative patterns on most baked goods—especially cookies. You can use a toothpick for drawing or dispense the icing from a squeeze bottle or plastic icing bag (see page 361).

Drizzling

Drizzling allows you to create beautiful Jackson Pollack-style freeform patterns with icing. You can drizzle the icing from a spoon, a squeeze bottle, or a plastic icing bag (see page 361). Try to distribute the icing in an even steady stream over the entire surface of the product.

Coating

If you want to completely or partially cover cookies with icing, you can "paint" it on with a spoon. You can also dip the cookies directly into the icing. For some, like the famous black and white cookies, you can use more than one color icing.

Making a Disposable Icing Dispenser

1. Mix the ingredients

To make a dispenser for drizzling icing, begin with a quart-sized plastic freezer bag. If you need a small amount of icing, add a few tablespoons of confectioner's sugar and a few drops of milk (or water) to the bag. Knead until the sugar dissolves and the mixture is smooth and creamy. If it's too thin, add more sugar. If it's too thick, add another drop or so of liquid. For larger amounts, prepare the icing before adding it to the bag.

2. Cut the opening

Once the icing is the right consistency, use a sharp pair of scissors to snip the tip from one corner of the bag. If you want to drizzle the icing in a fine stream, snip off a very tiny piece; for a thicker stream, snip off a little more. Remember, you can always cut off more plastic, but you can't put any back, so snip off a little at a time.

3. Squeeze and drizzle

Work the icing to the cut corner, then squeeze the bag and drizzle the icing over the baked goods. Along with drizzling icing from the bag, you can also draw with it. (I used an icing bag to decorate most of the gingerbread dudes at the top of the previous page.) When drawing, squeeze the bag with one hand while guiding the icing from the tip with the other.

A Condiment Bottle Dispenser

Recycled plastic condiment bottles are perfect to use as icing dispensers. They have ready-made tips and the bottles are made for squeezing. After preparing the icing, spoon it into the bottle, screw on the top, and then squeeze away. You can also store the icing for a few days as long as the bottle is tightly sealed. So if you have any leftover icing, you can save it to use at a later time.

Basic Icing Formula
1 cup confectioner's sugar + 1 tablespoon milk = ½ cup icing

You can never have too much of a good thing.

Shaved chocolate curls, sprinkles of grated chocolate, and dusted cocoa powder can add the perfect finishing touch to many desserts (and as a bonus, they add more chocolate!). Sprinkle these popular garnishes over frosted (and even unfrosted) cakes, whipped cream toppings, and scoops of ice cream. You can never have too much of a good thing, so shave, grate, or dust to your heart's content.

Basic Techniques for Making Chocolate Garnishes

Grating

When grating chocolate, try to use the thickest bar you can find and a grater with fairly small holes. Grate the chocolate directly onto the dessert, and tap the grater occasionally to release any chocolate that's sticking to it.

Shaving or curling

To make chocolate shavings or curls, run a vegetable peeler, a sharp knife, or a cheese slicer along the edge of a bar/block of chocolate. (I prefer the vegetable peeler, which I find the easiest to control.) And as far as size, the larger the block of chocolate, the wider the curls.

Dusting

When dusting with cocoa powder, simply sprinkle it directly onto the dessert through a sieve, strainer, or sifter. You can use either unsweetened or sweetened cocoa, but keep in mind that the unsweetened variety can be a little bitter.

It's so sweet and pretty . . .

I love fruit. It's colorful, flavorful, sweet, and good for you, too! It is also one of my favorite ingredients for creating beautiful designs on tarts, cakes, pies, and lots of other sweet treats. You can use fruit as a simple accent (like a cherry on top of a hot fudge sundae), or to create eye-catching patterns.

Creating Fruity Designs

Before creating a fruit design, try to have a concept of how you want the finished product to look. Next, make fruit selections based on colors and shapes. I chose fresh raspberries, blueberries, and kiwi to decorate the tart above.

First, I arranged some kiwi slices in the center of the tart, then surrounded them with a circle of raspberries. Next, I added another circle of raspberries to create an outside border. As the last step, I filled the space between the two raspberry circles with blueberries, following the same circular pattern.

(For this Fabulous Fruit Tart recipe, see page 198.)

The Fruit Spiral

It's easy to create simple, yet elegant, spiral patterns on pies and tarts with sliced fruits like strawberries and bananas. Starting from the outside border, place the slices next to each other—each one slightly overlapping the next—while working your way to the center. Use a large slice or whole piece of the fruit to crown the center.

Dude, where'd you get that crazy haircut?

Cupcakes are perfect for decorating. Because they're small and baked by the dozen, you can let your imagination run wild and turn each cupcake into a unique work of art. You can use any type of frosting technique and choose from all sorts of wonderful garnishes. Decorating cupcakes are fun – you'll see!

Basic Techniques for Decorating Cupcakes

Spreading

The easiest way to add frosting to a cupcake is by simply spreading it on with a butter knife, a small spatula, or the back of a spoon. I find it easiest to add the frosting with one hand, while holding the bottom of the cupcake and turning it with the other.

Piping

Because cupcakes are small, you can pipe the frosting from a pastry bag to create swirl tops. Choose a wide tip (like a star or a shell), fill the bag with frosting, and pipe the frosting on top. For details on making swirl tops, see the inset on the next page.

Garnishing

Shredded coconut, chopped nuts, candy sprinkles, and colored sugars are just a few of the many garnishes you can sprinkle on frosted cupcakes. Check out the baking aisle in your local supermarket for many more sweet decorative (and tasty) garnishes.

How to Make
Swirly Tops

When making swirly tops with frosting, it's best to pipe it from the pastry bag through a broad tip. A star tip, for instance, is a good choice, as is the shell tip (used in the photo at left). Swirls work best with whipped cream, or soft whipped frostings like buttercream. (For more information on how to pipe frosting from a pastry bag into various shapes and designs, see pages 370 and 371.)

To create a swirly top, start by piping a circle of frosting along the outer edge of the cupcake. Hold the bag with the tip at a 45-degree angle to the top of the cake. Maintaining steady pressure, squeeze out the frosting to create the outer circle while turning the cupcake with your free hand.

Once you have made the outer circle, create the inner swirl. Maintaining the 45-degree angle, pipe the frosting so that it slightly overlaps the outer ring while spiraling inward towards the center of the cake (as shown in the photo). Finish with a small peak in the center.

Swirly tops with fondant bumble bees (page 373)

Sweet and smooth.

Decorating a cake with frosting takes some practice and a delicate touch. But if you've got the desire and a creative flair, you can turn a simple cake into an eye-popping work of art. On this page and the pages that follow, I start with the basic steps for frosting a two-layer cake. Then I show how to add different textures to the frosting with the help of some special tools. Finally, I provide detailed steps for piping the frosting into beautiful borders and designs.

Basic Steps for Frosting a Two-Layer Cake

1. Frost the bottom layer

Place the bottom layer—with the flat bottom-side up—on a serving plate or a revolving cake turntable (see page 367). Spread some frosting on top in a smooth and even ¹/₄-inch thickness with a frosting spatula or a large rubber spatula.

2. Add the top layer and frost

Carefully place the second layer—with the flat bottom-side down—on top of the bottom layer and make sure they are aligned (as shown above). Next, spoon a mound of frosting on top and spread it to a smooth and even ¹/₄-inch thickness.

3. Frost the sides

Spread the frosting on the sides of the cake. If you pick up any crumbs, wipe the spatula with a paper towel before dipping it back in the bowl of frosting. Frosting should cover the entire cake, as it helps shield the cake from the air, which can either dry it out or make it soggy.

Finishing Touches

Smooth it out

It is especially important to smooth out the frosting if you plan to decorate the cake further. A long frosting knife or spreader is recommended. When smoothing out the sides, keep the knife at the same angle (see above). A revolving cake turntable (described below) is helpful for seamless results.

Add texture

Instead of smoothing out the frosting, you can give it texture. Using a butter knife, fork, or spatula, you can create swirls, lines, and other interesting textures in the frosting. Also available are frosting spreaders (described below), including ones with ridged edges for making multiple lines at once.

Garnish

Chopped nuts, shredded coconut, candy sprinkles, and shaved chocolate are just a few of the popular garnishes you can sprinkle on frosted cakes. When covering the sides, you may have to take a handful of the garnish and pat it gently into the frosting.

Advanced Tools for Frosting

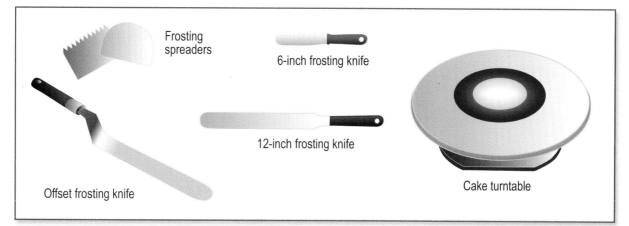

Frosting spreaders

6-inch frosting knife

12-inch frosting knife

Offset frosting knife

Cake turntable

Frosting Spreaders

These wide flat spreaders made of plastic or stainless steel allow you to frost large areas of cake at once. Some varieties have straight edges that are great for smoothing out the frosting, while others have ridged edges for adding texture.

Frosting Knives/Spatulas

Often made of stainless steel, frosting knives or spatulas are made specifically to work with frosting. They are thin, flexible, and come in different lengths. The offset type has a bend in the blade that lets you frost cakes smoothly without dragging your knuckles across the surface.

Cake Turntable

A revolving cake turntable is great for frosting and decorating cakes. Place the cake on top and slowly turn the round turntable as you frost the top and sides. (You stand still while the cake turns.) When buying this item, be sure to get one with a rubber base so it doesn't slip.

This could be your bag, man.

Once upon a time, decorating cakes, cookies, and other baked goods with piped frosting was primarily the job of professional bakers and pastry chefs. Not any more. Today, anyone with a little patience, the right equipment, and a few basic skills can decorate cakes like the pros. This section is designed to show you how, starting with some information on pastry bags—how to assemble, fill, and use them.

Basic Steps for Assembling a Pastry Bag

An assembled pastry bag, whether disposable or reusable, typically has four parts: the bag, a two-piece coupler (a holding screw and a screw-on collar), and a decorator tip.

1. Insert the holding screw
After snipping the tip from the bag (if disposable), slide the base of the coupler (the holding screw) down through the hole so the threads are just inside the opening of the bag. Make sure the bag is tight around the coupler to prevent leakage.

2. Place the tip
After choosing the tip you want to use, place it over the coupler. It should fit snugly over both the bag the coupler's first few threads.

3. Secure the tip
Once the tip is in place, slide the screw-on collar over the tip and screw it to the base of the coupler. Tighten the collar securely to anchor the tip to the bag. Be careful not to over tighten, as this can cause the collar to break.

Basic Steps for Using a Pastry Bag

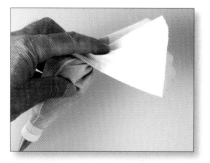

1. Fill with frosting

Before filling the pastry bag, fold the open end halfway down. Add frosting to the bag with a tablespoon, but do not fill it more than halfway. (Soft thick frostings like buttercream that can hold a shape are best for piping. If your frosting isn't thick enough, try beating in some confectioner's sugar to get it to the right consistency.)

2. Make a twist

After adding the frosting to bag, it's important to seal it inside. If you don't, the frosting will ooze from the top of the bag as you're piping. To seal, simply twist the bag just above the spot where it is filled. Although you can start piping at this point, you'll have to maintain a good grip on the top to keep it from untwisting. I recommend securing the bag further by following Step 3.

3. Fold the bag

To make doubly sure that your frosting doesn't ooze from the top of the bag, after twisting it (Step 2), fold the top down to one side and keep it in place by cupping it with the palm of your hand. This step not only prevents the frosting from escaping, but also allows you to maintain a comfortable grip while piping, as shown in the photo below.

Get a Grip! Then Give a Squeeze . . .

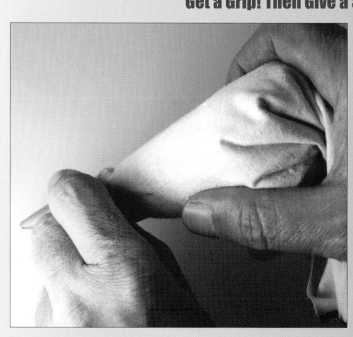

Now that your pastry bag is filled with frosting and securely sealed, all you have to do is give it a squeeze, right? Well yes and no. There are a few basic guidelines to keep in mind for the best results.

- ▶ While holding the bag, squeeze from the top.
- ▶ To pipe the frosting from the bag evenly and consistently, try to maintain constant pressure while squeezing.
- ▶ Always practice the piping technique on a sheet of wax paper before trying it on the cake. Practicing will help you determine the right amount of pressure to apply.
- ▶ While squeezing the bag with one hand, control the tip by guiding it with your free hand.
- ▶ As you work, continue twisting and folding the bag to keep the frosting flowing evenly through the tip.

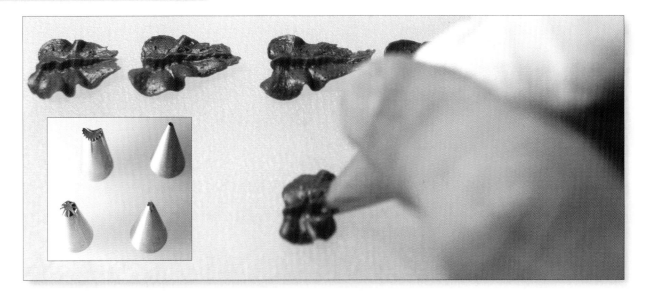

Tried and true tips about tips.

Although there are many dozens of tips for piping frosting into all sorts of different shapes and thicknesses, I have chosen four basic tips to get you started—the star, the shell, the leaf, and the simple hole for drawing lines and writing letters. As mentioned on the previous page, before piping on the actual cake, it's a good idea to first practice the techniques on a sheet of wax paper. Then you can scrape up the frosting and reuse it.

Basic Piping Techniques

Dappling

When creating stars and other designs that are dappled onto cookies or cakes, position the bag at a 90-degree angle with the tip slightly above the surface. Gently squeeze the bag to create the shape, then lift the bag straight up for a clean break. The squeezing and lifting are done almost at the same time.

Edging

To create beautiful decorative edges on cakes, cupcakes, and cookies, position the filled bag at a 45-degree angle to the surface. Apply even, constant pressure while piping the frosting into straight or wavy lines. (I prefer wavy lines, which I think are much more attractive.)

Writing

When writing messages or drawing on cakes and cookies, hold the filled pastry bag at the same angle you use when writing with a pen—or at whatever angle you are the most comfortable. You may (or may not) find it helpful to guide the tip with your free hand. Use the tip with a single hole for this.

Star tip

Star tip

You can use a variety of different star tips to make shapes like stars and flowers as well as beautiful borders. To create a star, hold the bag at a 90-degree angle with the tip slightly off the surface. Squeeze the bag gently to create the star, then pull the bag straight up. To create the border shown in the photo, hold the bag at a 45-degree angle with the tip on the surface, and move the bag gently back and forth while squeezing with constant pressure.

Shell tip

Shell tip

In addition to piping frosting in the shape of shells, you can make interesting borders with this tip. To create a shell, hold the bag at a 45-degree angle with the tip slightly off the surface. Gently squeeze out the frosting while pulling the bag toward you. Stop squeezing to give the shell a pointed tip. To create a border, you can pipe out a line of shells that slightly overlap. You can also simply hold the bag at a 45-degree angle and squeeze the frosting from the bag in a straight or wavy line.

Leaf tip

Leaf tip

Making piped leaves for your decorative flowers (like the fondant rose on page 374) adds the perfect finishing touch— and they are quick and easy to make. Leaf tips come in a few sizes. To create the small leaves shown here, hold the bag at a 45-degree angle with the tip slightly off the surface. Gently squeeze the frosting from the tip and let it taper to a point. To create a border, pipe out a line of leaves, one after the other, but don't leave any space between them.

You are what you eat.

Made from sugar, fondant is soft and flexible and molds like clay. You can flatten it into a thin sheet with a rolling pin and then use it to cover a cake (instead of frosting). And because it's pliable, you can mold it into flowers or ribbons or bows or just about any shape you want. Along with tips on how to work with this edible product, I'll show you how easy it is to make fondant bumble bees, as well as beautiful roses to decorate your cakes and cupcakes!

Basic Steps for Working with Fondant

Helpful Tips

▶ Fondant dries out very quickly, so keep it in a sealed plastic bag. Take out only as much as you need and keep the rest covered.

▶ When working with fondant, the warmth of your hands will soften it. The more you work it, the softer it will get. If it gets too soft and becomes impossible to shape, wrap it in plastic and refrigerate for a few minutes.

1. Add color
To add color to white fondant, first knead it until soft and pliable. Shape it into a ball, flatten it a bit to form a disc, then press a well in the center. Add a drop or two of food coloring to the well. (For darker-colored fondant, add more drops, one at a time, after Step 2.)

2. Fold
To mix the coloring with the fondant, first fold the edges of the disc to seal the well, then continue folding the edges over and over to blend the color. I recommend doing this over the sink in case some of the coloring drips. And to prevent stained hands, wear food-safe plastic or latex gloves.

Basic Steps for Working with Fondant

3. Finish

Continue folding the fondant until it is uniform in color. The fondant may get a little sticky at this point. If it does, roll it into a ball, flatten it into a round disc, and wrap it in plastic. Refrigerate for a few minutes until it is workable.

4. Flatten

If you are going to roll out the fondant, first place a sheet of wax paper on a clean flat surface. Put the fondant on top and do the initial flattening by pressing it with the palm of your hand.

5. Roll out

With a rolling pin, roll out the fondant to the desired thickness. You can cut the flattened sheet into strips or different shapes with a knife or cookie cutter. Or use it to cover the cake for a super-smooth appearance.

How to Make a Fondant Bumble Bee

1. Shape the fondant into 7 pieces

Make one yellow rounded oblong piece (about $1\frac{1}{4}$ inches long and $\frac{3}{8}$ inch thick) for the body. Roll two white pieces into tube shapes (about $\frac{3}{4}$ inch long and $\frac{1}{8}$ inch wide) for wings; two tiny black balls for eyes; and a small black piece to make stripes (instructions for stripes are given in Step 3).

2. Make the wings

Taper one end of each of the white tubes. Place one of the tubes on a sheet of plastic wrap, then fold some of the plastic over the tube to cover. Starting from the tapered end, press the fondant with your thumb and flatten it to form a wing. Repeat with the other white piece. Set aside.

3. Make the stripes

To make the stripes, first flatten the black piece of fondant. Place it between two pieces of plastic (as you did with the wings) and flatten it to a piece about $1\frac{1}{2}$ inches long and $\frac{1}{16}$ inch thick. With a sharp knife, cut the flattened piece into two $\frac{1}{8}$-inch-wide strips for the stripes. Set aside.

4. Assemble the parts

Attach the eyes by gently pressing the two black balls on one end of the yellow body. Next add the stripes. Beginning at the underside of the body, wrap each stripe around until the ends meet. Pinch off any excess. Finally, press the wings on slightly behind the first black stripe (as shown).

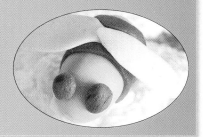

A rose by any other name would not taste as sweet.

Decorative fondant roses can add a touch of beauty and elegance to just about any cake. One of the best things about them is how deceptively easy they are to make. Just follow these simple directions and you'll be on your way. And even if your first attempt doesn't produce the results you want, no problem. You can take the rose apart and use the same fondant to try it again (and again if necessary). So take a deep breath, relax, and have some fun!

How to Make a Fondant Rose

1. Dye the fondant
Unless you've purchase colored fondant, you'll have to add the color yourself (Steps 1 through 3 beginning on page 372.) Of course, you can skip this step when making white roses. For red and yellow roses, add enough food coloring to produce deep colors.

2. Shape the 10 pieces
Roll one piece of fondant into a tube shape (about 2 inches long and $1/4$ inch thick) for the center of the rose. Make nine balls (about $1/4$ inch in diameter) for the petals.

3. Make the petals
Place one of the balls on a piece of plastic wrap, then fold some of the plastic over the ball to cover. With your thumb, flatten it to $1/16$-inch thickness. Repeat with the remaining balls. Set aside.

How to Make a Fondant Rose

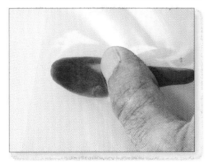

4. Flatten the tube
Place the tube-shaped piece on the plastic wrap, then fold some of the plastic over the tube to cover. With your thumb, flatten it to $^1/_{16}$-inch thickness.

5. Make the center piece
To create the center of the rose, roll up the flattened tube on a slight diagonal (as shown above). This will create a spiral-shaped center piece that becomes gradually thicker toward the bottom.

6. Add the first petals
Take one of the flattened petals and wrap it around the bottom of the center piece. Place a second petal on the opposite side and wrap it around the bottom (as shown above).

7. Add the remaining petals
Continue to add the remaining petals, starting each new petal at the middle of the previous one. This will cause the petals to overlap in a similar manner.

8. Flair the petals
Once all the petals are in place, gently flair them out for a more natural appearance.

Important Tips
Flattening fondant between two pieces of plastic is recommended for two reasons:

▶ It prevents any grease on your hands from touching the fondant.

▶ The fondant is easier to flatten.

METRIC CONVERSION TABLES

Common Liquid Conversions

Measurement	=	Milliliters
1/4 teaspoon	=	1.25 milliliters
1/2 teaspoon	=	2.50 milliliters
3/4 teaspoon	=	3.75 milliliters
1 teaspoon	=	5.00 milliliters
1 1/4 teaspoons	=	6.25 milliliters
1 1/2 teaspoons	=	7.50 milliliters
1 3/4 teaspoons	=	8.75 milliliters
2 teaspoons	=	10.0 milliliters
1 tablespoon	=	15.0 milliliters
2 tablespoons	=	30.0 milliliters

Measurement	=	Liters
1/4 cup	=	0.06 liters
1/2 cup	=	0.12 liters
3/4 cup	=	0.18 liters
1 cup	=	0.24 liters
1 1/4 cups	=	0.30 liters
1 1/2 cups	=	0.36 liters
2 cups	=	0.48 liters
2 1/2 cups	=	0.60 liters
3 cups	=	0.72 liters
3 1/2 cups	=	0.84 liters
4 cups	=	0.96 liters
4 1/2 cups	=	1.08 liters
5 cups	=	1.20 liters
5 1/2 cups	=	1.32 liters

Conversion Formulas

LIQUID		
When You Know	Multiply By	To Determine
teaspoons	5.0	milliliters
tablespoons	15.0	milliliters
fluid ounces	30.0	milliliters
cups	0.24	liters
pints	0.47	liters
quarts	0.95	liters

WEIGHT		
When You Know	Multiply By	To Determine
ounces	28.0	grams
pounds	0.45	kilograms

Converting Fahrenheit to Celsius

Fahrenheit	=	Celsius
200–205	=	95
220–225	=	105
245–250	=	120
275	=	135
300–305	=	150
325–330	=	165
345–350	=	175
370–375	=	190
400–405	=	205
425–430	=	220
445–450	=	230
470–475	=	245
500	=	260

INDEX

Abbreviations, common baking, 69

Accenting, as decorating technique, 359

All-purpose flour, 11

Allspice, 14

Almond-Berry Coffeecake, 274–275

Almond Biscotti, 125

Almond Crispies, 131

Almond paste, 20

Almond Poppyseed Muffins, 239

Almond Torte, Chocolate-, 306–307

Almond Triangle Puffs, 316–317

Aluminum cookware, 37

Angel food pan, 39

Angel wings. *See* Golden Palmiers.

Apple corer, 32

Apple Crispy, 192–193

Apple Crumbly, Cherry-, 194–195

Apple Filling, 89

Apple-Pecan Coffeecake, 270–271

Apple Pie, Mom's, 184–185

Apple Strudel, 312–313

Apple Turnovers, 314–315

Appliances, electric, 36

Arrowroot, 13

Artificial sweeteners, 12

Aspartame sweetener in baking, 12

Bakeware, basic, 38–39

Baking chocolate, 19

Baking powder, 11

Baking soda, 11

Banana Berry Bread, 250–251

Banana Cream Pie, Choco-, 180–181

Banana English Trifle, Mocha-, 348–349

Banana Nut Bread, 251

Banana-Nut Frosting, 78

Bar cookies. *See* Bars/squares, dessert.

Bars/squares, dessert
about, 146
preparing cookie crust for, 147
preparing pastry crust for, 146
recipes for, 148–157
storing, 147
tips when making, 147

Bars/squares, recipes for
Chocoberry Oaties, 157–158
Chocolate Pecan Bars, 150–151
Date-Nut Oaties, 157
E-Zay Lemon Squares, 148–149
5-Layer Choconut Bars, 154–155
Pumpkin Cheesecake Bars, 152–153
White Chocolate 'n Pecan Oaties, 157

Basket weave pie crust, 169

Beating ingredients, 42, 55

Beautiful Blondies, 144–145

Bee, making a fondant, 373

Berries, fresh, 22

Berry Bread, Banana, 250–251

Berry Coffeecake, Almond-, 274–275

Berry Pie, Triple, 187

Berry Whippy Cream, 99

Bicarbonate of soda. *See* Baking soda.

Biscotti, Almond, 125

Biscotti, Chocolate Almond, 122–123

Biscotti, White Chocolate Macadamia, 124–125

Biscotti cookies
about, 120, 121
recipes for, 122–125
steps for making, 120
storing, 121
tips when making, 121

Biscuit recipes
Blueberry Corn Biscuits, 230–231
Cranberry Butter Biscuits, 228–229
Mom's Buttermilk Biscuits, 232–233

Biscuits
about, 226
preparing dough for, 226
recipes for, 228–233
shaping methods for, 227
storing, 227
tips when making, 227

Bitchin' Brownies, 138

Blender, 36

Blending ingredients, 42, 54

Blondie recipes
Beautiful Blondies, 144–145
Coconut Blondies, 145
Maple Walnut Blondies, 145

Blondies
about, 136
add-ins for, 137
recipes for, 144–145
steps for making, 136
storing, 137
tips when making, 137

Blueberry Buckle, 276–277

Blueberry Buttermilk Muffins, 242–243

Blueberry Corn Biscuits, 230–231
Blueberry Crispy, Nutty, 193
Blueberry Filling, 90
Blueberry-Maple Corn Muffins, 247
Blueberry Puffs, 325
Blueberry Scones, 234–235
Boils, types of, 65
Bomb Cupcakes, Chocolate, 287
Bottle openers, 32
Bowls, mixing, 33
Bran Muffins, Raisin, 240–241
Bread flour, 11
Bread Pudding, 347
Bread recipes. *See* Quick bread recipes.
Brown sugar, 12
Brownie mixes, commercial, 8
Brownie recipes
    Bitchin' Brownies, 138
    Chocolate-Chocolate Brownies, 139
    Chocoroon Brownies, 140–141
    Marble Brownies, 139
    Soufflé Brownies, 142–143
Brownies
    about, 136
    add-ins for, 137
    recipes for, 138–143
    steps for making, 136
    storing, 137
    tips when making, 137
Buckle, Blueberry, 276–277
Bumble bee, making a fondant, 373
Bundt pan, 39
Butter, 18
    measurement equivalents for, 69
Butter Biscuits, Cranberry, 228–229
Butter-Butter Coffeecake, 266–267
Butter Crisps, Holiday, 335
Butter Pecan Coffeecake, 262–263
Butter Sauce, 87
Butter Tartlets, Canadian, 202–203
Buttercream, Chocolate, 76
Buttercream, Vanilla, 76
Buttermilk, 16
Buttermilk Biscuits, Mom's, 232–233
Buttermilk Muffins, Blueberry, 242–243
Buttermilk Muffins, Raspberry-
    Chocolate, 243
Buttermilk Pound Cake, 290
Butterscotch Cookies, Oat-, 111
Buttery Yellow Cupcakes, 282

"Cage free" eggs, 17
Cake
    about, 288
    assembling a two-layer, 289
    frosting a two-layer, 366
    recipes for, 290–307, 350–351,
        352–353, 354–355
    steps for making, 288
    storing, 289
    tips when making, 281
    See also Cupcakes.
Cake flour, 11
Cake frosting, commercial, 8
Cake mixes, commercial, 8
Cake pans, 38
Cake recipes
    Buttermilk Pound Cake, 290
    Chocolate-Almond Torte, 306–307
    Chocolate Heart Attack Cake,
        304–305
    Coconut-Coconut Cake, 291
    Debbie's White Cake, 294–295
    Devil's Food Cake, 302–303
    German Chocolate Cake, 300–301
    Greek Honeycake, 296–297
    Holiday Honey Cake, 354–355
    Pineapple-Carrot Cake, 298–299
    Rich 'n Delicious Chocolate Cake,
        292–293
    Southern Red Velvet Cake, 350–351
    Sponge Cake with Goodies,
        352–353
Cake server, 34
Cake turntable, 367
Can openers, 32
Canadian Butter Tartlets, 202–203
Candy Chocolate Chip Cookies, 107
Candy thermometer, 32
Canisters, storage, 27
Cannoli Cream, 94
Cannoli Puffs, 324
Caramel Sauce, 86
Caramel Sauce, Vanilla Cheesecake
    with, 210–211
Carrot Cake, Pineapple-, 298–299
Carrots in baked goods, 24
Cast iron cookware, 37
Cheese
    about, 17
    varieties of, 17

Cheesecake. *See* Cheesecake, baked;
    Cheesecake, no-bake; Cheesecake
recipes.
Cheesecake, baked
    about, 214
    preventing cracks in, 215
    recipes for, 216–223
    steps for making, 214
    storing, 207
    swirling method for, 214
    tips when making, 207
Cheesecake, no-bake
    about, 206
    recipes for, 208–214
    steps for making, 206–207
    storing, 207
    tips when making, 207
Cheesecake Bars, Pumpkin, 152–153
Cheesecake recipes
    Chocolate Swirl Cheesecake,
        220–221
    Italian Cheesecake, 216
    Lemon Chiffon Cheesecake, 212–213
    New York Strawberry Cheesecake,
        218–219
    Pumpkin Chiffon Cheesecake, 217
    Vanilla Cheesecake with Caramel
        Sauce, 210–211
    White Chocolate Cheesecake with
        Fruit Topping, 208–209
    White Chocolate-Raspberry Swirl
        Cheesecake, 222–223
Chef's knife, 33
Cherry-Apple Crumbly, 194–195
Chiffon Cheesecake, Pumpkin, 217
Choc-Choc Frosting, 77
Choc-Choc Muffins, 238
Choco-Banana Cream Pie, 180–181
Choco-Walnut Coffeecake, 268–269
Choco Whippy Cream, 99
Chocoberry Oaties, 157–158
Chocolat, Mousse au, 96
Chocolate, 19
    varieties of, 19
Chocolate Almond Biscotti, 122–123
Chocolate-Almond Torte, 306–307
Chocolate Bomb Cupcakes, 287
Chocolate Buttercream, 76
Chocolate Buttermilk Muffins,
    Raspberry-, 243

Chocolate Cake, German, 300–301

Chocolate Cake, Rich 'n Delicious, 292–293

Chocolate candy, 19

Chocolate Chip Cookies, 106–107

Chocolate Chip Cookies, Candy, 107

Chocolate Chip Hanukkah Rugelach, 333

Chocolate Chip Macaroons, 113

Chocolate chips. *See* Chocolate morsels.

Chocolate-Chocolate Chip Cookies, 107

Chocolate-Chocolate Brownies, 139

Chocolate Chunk Coffeecake, 260–261

Chocolate Cream Pie, 178

Chocolate Cream Puffs, 326

Chocolate Cupcakes, 283

Chocolate-Date Muffins, 253

Chocolate Frosting, German, 80

Chocolate Ganache, 92

Chocolate Ganache Tartlets, 201

Chocolate garnishes, making, 362

Chocolate Heart Attack Cake, 304–305

Chocolate Ice, 82

Chocolate Macaroons, 113

Chocolate morsels, 19

Chocolate Mousse, White, 95

Chocolate Nut Cookies, Flourless, 115

Chocolate Palmiers, 321

Chocolate Pecan Bars, 150–151

Chocolate Swirl Cheesecake, 220–221

Chocolate Tart, Strawberry, 197

Choconut Bars, 5-Layer, 154–155

Chocoroon Brownies, 140–141

Chopping ingredients, 52

Christmas Loaf, Fruity, 343

Cinnamon, 14

Cinnamon-Nut Coffeecake, 264–265

Cobbler, Peachy Blue, 191

Cobblers
    about, 161, 190
    recipe for, 191
    steps for making, 190

Cocoa powder, 19

Coconut Blondies, 145

Coconut-Coconut Cake, 291

Coconut Cupcakes, 284–285

Coconut Frosting, 79

Coconut Macaroons, Diabetic, 113

Coconut Macaroons I, 112

Coconut Macaroons II, 113

Coconut-Oatmeal Cookies, 111

Coffee Whippy Cream, 99

Coffeecake
    about, 258
    add-ins for, 259
    recipes for, 260–277
    steps for making, 258
    storing, 259
    tips when making, 259

Coffeecake recipes
    Almond-Berry Coffeecake, 274–275
    Apple-Pecan Coffeecake, 270–271
    Blueberry Buckle, 276–277
    Butter-Butter Coffeecake, 266–267
    Butter Pecan Coffeecake, 262–263
    Choco-Walnut Coffeecake, 268–269
    Chocolate Chunk Coffeecake, 260–261
    Cinnamon-Nut Coffeecake, 264–265
    Fresh Strawberry Coffeecake, 272–273

Condensed milk, 13

Confectioner's sugar, 12

Containers, plastic storage, 26

Convection ovens, 40

Conventional ovens, 40

Cookie crust. *See* Pie crusts, cookie.

Cookie Crust, Standard, 172

Cookie cutters, 32

Cookie dough, commercial, 6

Cookie recipes
    Almond Biscotti, 125
    Almond Crispies, 131
    Candy Chocolate Chip Cookies, 107
    Chocolate Almond Biscotti, 122–123
    Chocolate Chip Cookies, 106–107
    Chocolate Chip Hanukkah Rugelach, 333
    Chocolate Chip Macaroons, 113
    Chocolate-Chocolate Chip Cookies, 107
    Chocolate Macaroons, 113
    Chocolate Palmiers, 321
    Coconut Macaroons I, 112
    Coconut Macaroons II, 113
    Coconut-Oatmeal Cookies, 111
    Diabetic Coconut Macaroons, 113
    Flourless Chocolate Nut Cookies, 115
    Ginger Snappies, 130
    Gingerbread Dudes 'n Pals, 336–337
    Golden Palmiers, 320–321
    Hanukkah Rugelach, 332–333

Holiday Butter Crisps, 335

Holiday Rum Balls, 330–331

Mama's Shortbread, 132–133

Mexican Wedding Cakes, 117

Oat-Butterscotch Cookies, 111

Oat-Rageous Oatmeal Cookies, 110

Oatmeal-Raisin Cookies, 111

Peanut Butter Cookies, 108–109

Peanut Butter 'n Pieces Cookies, 109

Peanut-Peanut Butter Cookies, 109

Persian Walnut Cookies, 116

Spanish Polvornes, 334

Sugar Cookies, 128–129

Sugar Tots, 129

Walnut Puffs, 118–119

White Chocolate Macadamia Biscotti, 124–125

Cookie sheets, 38

Cookies. *See* Bars/squares, dessert; Biscotti cookies; Drop cookies; Golden Palmiers; Nut cookies; Refrigerator cookies.

Cooking spray, 18

Cookware, basic, 37

Cooling rack, 32

Copper cookware, 37

Corer, apple, 32

Coring ingredients, 53

Corn Biscuits, Blueberry, 230–231

Corn Muffins, Blueberry-Maple, 247

Corn syrup, 12

Cornberry Muffins, 246–247

Cornmeal, 11

Cornstarch, 13

Cranberry Bread, 342

Cranberry Butter Biscuits, 228–229

Cream, 16

Cream, Cannoli, 94

Cream, Mascarpone, 94

Cream, Pastry, 93

Cream cheese, 17, 207

Cream Cheese Frosting, 81

Cream of tartar, 14

Cream Pie, Choco-Banana, 180–181

Cream Pie, Chocolate, 178

Cream Puffs, Chocolate, 326

Cream Puffs, White Chocolate, 327

Creaming ingredients, 55

Crimping dough, 43, 63

Crispies, Almond, 131

Crisps
about, 161, 190
recipes for, 192–193
steps for making, 190
Crisps, Holiday Butter, 335
Crispy, Apple, 192–193
Crispy, Nutty Blueberry, 193
Crumbles
about, 161, 190
recipe for, 194
steps for making, 190
Crumbly, Cherry-Apple, 194–195
Crushing ingredients, 51
Crust. *See* Pie-crust recipies; Pie
 crusts, cookie; Pie crusts, pastry;
 Tart crusts; Tartlet crusts.
Crust, Flaky Pastry Pie, 173
Crust, Standard Cookie, 172
Crust, Sweet Tart, 174
Cupcake recipes
Buttery Yellow Cupcakes, 282
Chocolate Bomb Cupcakes, 287
Chocolate Cupcakes, 283
Coconut Cupcakes, 284–285
Pumpkin Cupcakes, 286
Cupcakes
about, 280
decorating techniques for, 364–365
garnishes for, 281
recipes for, 282–287
steps for making, 280
storing, 281
tips when making, 281
See also Cakes.
Custard, Lemon, 91
Cutting ingredients, 43, 55

Date Muffins, Chocolate-, 253
Date-Nut Bread, 252–253
Date-Nut Oaties, 157
Debbie's White Cake, 294–295
Decorating techniques, 358–359
for cakes, 366–367, 370–371
for cupcakes, 364–365, 370–371
Dessert bars. *See* Bars/squares,
 dessert.
Dessert squares. *See* Bars/squares,
 dessert.
Devil's Food Cake, 302–303
Diabetic Coconut Macaroons, 113

Doneness, testing for. *See* Testing-
 for-doneness techniques.
Double boiler, 37
Dough
commercial varieties of, 6–7
shaping techniques for, 60–63
steps for rolling out, 62
Dough scraper, 33
Drop cookies
about, 104
add-ins for, 105
recipes for, 106–113
steps for making, 104
storing, 75
tips when making, 75
Dudes 'n Pals, Gingerbread, 336–337
Dusting, as decorating technique,
 43, 359
Dutch oven, 37

Easter Pie, Fiadone, 340–341
Egg beater, 32
Egg sizes, 17
Egg wash, 44, 167
Eggs
about, 17
varieties of, 17
Eggs, cracking, 51
Eggs, separating, 51
Elephant ears. *See* Golden Palmiers.
English Trifle, Mocha-Banana, 348–349
Equal sweetener in baking, 12
Evaporated milk, 13
Extracts, 15
E-Zay Lemon Squares, 148–149

Fabulous Fruit Tart, 198–199
Fat varieties used in baking, 18
Fiadone Easter Pie, 340–341
Filling recipes
Apple Filling, 89
Blueberry Filling, 90
Cannoli Cream, 94
Chocolate Ganache, 92
Lemon Custard, 91
Mascarpone Cream, 94
Mousse au Chocolat, 96
Nut Filling, 90
Pastry Cream, 93
White Chocolate Mousse, 95

Fillings
about, 88
recipes for, 89–97
storing, 88
techniques for making, 88
5-Layer Choconut Bars, 154–155
Flaky Pastry Pie Crust, 173
Flour
as thickener, 13
sifted, 50
varieties of, 11
Flouring bakeware, 58
Flourless Chocolate Nut Cookies, 115
Foil, 27
Folding ingredients, 44, 55
three stages of, 56
Fondant
about, 44, 372
steps for working with, 372–373
tips when working with, 372, 375
Fondant bumble bee, 373
Fondant rose, 374–375
Food processor, 36
Frangipane Puff Pie, 318–319
Fresh Strawberry Coffeecake, 272–273
Frosting
about, 74
commercial, 8
recipes for, 76–81
steps for making, 74
storing, 75
tips when making, 75
See also Icing.
Frosting, as decorating technique,
 358. *See also* Piping.
Frosting a two-layer cake, 366–367
Frosting knives, 367
Frosting recipes
Banana-Nut Frosting, 78
Choc-Choc Frosting, 77
Chocolate Buttercream, 76
Coconut Frosting, 79
Cream Cheese Frosting, 81
German Chocolate Frosting, 80
Pineapple Frosting, 78
Vanilla Buttercream, 76
Whipped Cream Frosting, 80
Frosting spatula, 367
Frosting spreader, 367
Frosting tools, 367

Fruit
canned, 25
dried, 25
fresh, 23
frozen, 25
Fruit designs, creating, 363
Fruit Glaze, 101
Fruit spiral, creating, 363
Fruit Tart, Fabulous, 198–199
Fruity Christmas Loaf, 343
Fudge Sauce, 85

Gadgets, basic, 32–35. *See also*
Appliances, electric; Bakeware,
basic; Cookware, basic.
Ganache, Chocolate, 92
Ganache Tartlets, Chocolate, 201
Garnishing, as decorating
technique, 358
Gelatin, 13
Gele, Claudius, 311
Gentle boil. *See* Medium boil.
Georgia Peach Pie, 188–189
German Chocolate Cake, 300–301
German Chocolate Frosting, 80
Ginger, 14
Ginger Snappies, 130
Gingerbread Dudes 'n Pals, 336–337
Glaze, Fruit, 101
Gluten, 11
Golden Palmiers, 320–321
Goodies, Sponge Cake with, 352–353
Granulated white sugar, 12
Greasing bakeware, 58
Greek Honeycake, 296–297
Grinding ingredients, 51

Half-and-half, 16
Hanukkah Rugelach, 332–333
Hanukkah Rugelach, Chocolate
Chip, 333
Hard boil. *See* Rolling boil.
Heart Attack Cake, Chocolate, 304–305
High-altitude baking, 70–71
Holiday Butter Crisps, 335
Holiday Honey Cake, 354–355
Holiday Rum Balls, 330–331
Honey, 12
Honey Cake, Holiday, 354–355
Honeycake, Greek, 296–297

Ice, Chocolate, 82
Ice, Lemon, 83
Ice, Vanilla, 82
Icing
about, 74
basic formula for, 361
basic step for making, 74
recipes for, 82–83
storing, 75
tips when making, 75
See also Frosting.
Icing, as decorating technique, 358,
360–361
Icing dispenser, making, 361
Icing recipes
Chocolate Ice, 82
Lemon Ice, 83
Vanilla Ice, 82
Ingredient preparation techniques,
51–57
Ingredient substitutions, 28
Ingredient yields, 29
Ingredients, proper temperature of, 50
Irish Soda Bread, 344–345
Italian Cheesecake, 216

Juicer, citrus, 32
Juicing ingredients, 53

Key Lime Pie, 179
Knives, 33
Knives, frosting, 367

Lactose-free milk, 16
Ladle, 33
Lattice pie crust, 168
Lawrence, William, 207
Leavening agents, 11
Lemon Chiffon Cheesecake, 212–213
Lemon Custard, 91
Lemon extract, homemade, 15
Lemon Ice, 83
Lemon Meringue Pie, 186
Lemon Poppyseed Muffins, 244–245
Lemon Squares, E-Zay, 148–149
Lemon Tartlets, 201
Lime Pie, Key, 179
Loaf, Fruity Christmas, 343
Loaf pans, 38
Lowfat milk, 16

Macadamia Biscotti, White
Chocolate, 124
Macaroons, Chocolate, 113
Macaroons, Chocolate Chip, 113
Macaroons, Diabetic Coconut, 113
Macaroons I, Coconut, 112
Macaroons II, Coconut, 113
Mama's Shortbread, 132–133
Maple Corn Muffins, Blueberry-, 247
Maple Walnut Blondies, 145
Marble Brownies, 139
Margarine, 18
Marzipan, 20
Mascarpone cheese, 17
Mascarpone Cream, 94
Mascarpone Puffs, 323
Mashing ingredients, 52
Measurement conversions,
common, 69
Measuring cups, 34, 68
Measuring spoons, 34, 68
Medium boil, 65
Meringue Pie, Lemon, 186
Metric conversions
about, 69
chart for, 376
Mexican Wedding Cakes, 117
Microwave ovens, 40–41
Milk
about, 16
concentrated, 13
varieties of, 16
Mixers, electric
hand-held, 36
stand, 36
Mixing bowls, 33
Mixing ingredients, 54
Mocha-Banana English Trifle, 348–349
Mom's Apple Pie, 184–185
Mom's Buttermilk Biscuits, 232–233
Mousse, White Chocolate, 95
Mousse au Chocolat, 96
Muffin pans, 39
Muffin recipes
Almond Poppyseed Muffins, 239
Blueberry Buttermilk Muffins,
242–243
Blueberry-Maple Corn
Muffins, 247

Choc-Choc Muffins, 238
Chocolate-Date Muffins, 253
Cornberry Muffins, 246–247
Lemon Poppyseed Muffins, 244–245
Raisin Bran Muffins, 240–241
Raspberry-Chocolate Buttermilk
    Muffins, 243
Muffins
    about, 236
    add-ins for, 237
    recipes for, 238–247
    steps for making, 236
    storing, 237
    tips when making, 237

Neufchâtel cheese, 17, 207
New York Strawberry Cheesecake,
    218–219
Nut Bread, Banana, 251
Nut Bread, Date-, 252–253
Nut Coffeecake, Cinnamon-,
    264–265
Nut cookies
    about, 114
    recipes for, 115–119
    storing, 114
    tips when making, 114
Nut cracker, 33
Nut Filling, 90
Nut pastes, 20
Nutmeg, 14
NutraSweet sweetener in baking, 12
Nuts
    about, 20
    oven toasting, 20
    stovetop toasting, 65
    varieties of, 20
Nuts 4 Pecan Pie, 183
Nutty Blueberry Crispy, 193
Nutty Tartlets, Triple, 200–201

Oat-Butterscotch Cookies, 111
Oat-Rageous Oatmeal Cookies, 110
Oaties, Chocoberry, 157–158
Oaties, Date-Nut, 157
Oaties, White Chocolate 'n Pecan, 157
Oatmeal Cookies, Coconut-, 111
Oatmeal Cookies, Oat-Rageous, 110
Oatmeal-Raisin Cookies, 111
Oil can, 33

Oil varieties used in baking, 18
Orange extract, homemade, 15
Organic eggs, 17
Oven controls, 41
Oven gloves/mitts, 33, 40
Ovens, features of, 41
Ovens, preheating, 50
Ovens, types of, 40–41

Palmiers, Chocolate, 321
Palmiers, Golden, 320–321
Pans. See Cookware, basic; Bakeware,
    basic.
Parchment paper, 27
    lining bakeware with, 59
Paring knife, 33
Pasteurized eggs, 17
Pastry bags, 33
    assembling, 368
    decorative tips for, 370, 371
    filling, 369
    guidelines when using, 369
    See also Piping techniques.
Pastry brush, 34
Pastry Cream, 93
Pastry crust. See Pie crust, pastry.
Pastry dough blender, 34
Pastry Pie Crust, Flaky 173
Pastry wheel, 34
Patterning, as decorating
    technique, 359
Peach Pie, Georgia, 188–189
Peachy Blue Cobbler, 191
Peanut Butter Cookies, 108–109
Peanut Butter 'n Pieces Cookies, 109
Peanut Butter Pie, 177
Peanut-Peanut Butter Cookies, 109
Pecan Bars, Chocolate, 150–151
Pecan Coffeecake, Apple-, 270–271
Pecan Coffeecake, Butter, 262–263
Pecan Oaties, White Chocolate 'n,
    157
Pecan Pie, Nuts 4, 183
Pecan Topping, 101
Peeling ingredients, 53
Persian Walnut Cookies, 116
Phyllo dough, 7
Pie crusts, cookie
    basic recipe for, 172
    commercial varieties of, 9

cookie choices for, 163
    steps for forming, 162–163
Pie crusts, pastry
    basic recipe for, 173
    commercial varieties of, 9
    finishing touches for, 167
    steps for forming basket weave
        top, 169
    steps for forming bottom crust,
        164–165
    steps for forming/adding top
        crust, 166–167
    steps for forming lattice top, 168
    steps for forming starburst top, 169
Pie crust recipes
    Standard Cookie Crust, 172
    Flaky Pastry Pie Crust, 173
    Sweet Tart Crust, 174
Pie fillings, commercial, 9
Pie pans, 38
Pie recipes
    Choco-Banana Cream Pie, 180–181
    Chocolate Cream Pie, 178
    Fiadone Easter Pie, 340–341
    Frangipane Puff Pie, 318–319
    Georgia Peach Pie, 188–189
    Key Lime Pie, 179
    Lemon Meringue Pie, 186
    Mom's Apple Pie, 184–185
    Nuts 4 Pecan Pie, 183
    Peanut Butter Pie, 177
    Pumpkin Pie, 338
    Sweet Po-Tater Pie, 339
    Triple Berry Pie, 187
Pie server, 34
Pies
    about, 160
    storing, 161
    tips for making, 161
    See also Cobblers; Crisps;
        Crumbles; Pie crusts, cookie;
        Pie crusts, pastry; Pie fillings,
        commercial; Pie recipes; Pies,
        baked; Pies, no-bake/low-bake;
        Tarts; Tartlets.
Pies, baked
    about, 182
    recipes for, 183–189, 338, 339,
        340–341
    steps for making, 182

Pies, no-bake/low-bake
  about, 176
  recipes for, 177–181
  steps for making, 176
Pineapple-Carrot Cake, 298–299
Pineapple Frosting, 78
Piping
  about, 359
  basic techniques for, 370
Plastic wrap, 26
Polvornes, Spanish, 334
Poppyseed Muffins, Almond, 239
Poppyseed Muffins, Lemon, 244–245
Po-Tater Pie, Sweet, 339
Potato masher, 34
Pots. *See* Cookware, basic.
Pound Cake, Buttermilk, 290
Powdered sugar. *See* Confectioner's
  sugar.
Pudding, Bread, 347
Pudding, Yuletide, 346
Puff pastry dough
  about 7, 310
  inventor of, 311
  recipes for, 312–321, 323–327
  storing, 311
  tips when working with, 311
  using sheets of, 310
  using shells of, 322
Puff pastry recipes
  Apple Strudel, 312–313
  Almond Triangle Puffs, 316–317
  Apple Turnovers, 314–315
  Blueberry Puffs, 325
  Cannoli Puffs, 324
  Chocolate Cream Puffs, 326
  Chocolate Palmiers, 321
  Frangipane Puff Pie, 318–319
  Golden Palmiers, 320–321
  Mascarpone Puffs, 323
  White Chocolate Cream Puffs, 327
Puff Pie, Frangipane, 318–319
Puffs, Almond Triangle, 316–317
Puffs, Walnut, 118–119
Pumpkin Bread, 249
Pumpkin Cheesecake Bars, 152–153
Pumpkin Chiffon Cheesecake, 217
Pumpkin Cupcakes, 286
Pumpkin Pie, 338
Pumpkin purée, 24

Quick bread
  about, 248
  recipes for, 249–255, 342, 343,
    344–345
  steps for making, 248
  storing, 237
  tips when making, 237
Quick bread recipes
  Banana Berry Bread, 250–251
  Banana Nut Bread, 251
  Cranberry Bread, 342
  Date-Nut Bread, 252–253
  Fruity Christmas Loaf, 343
  Irish Soda Bread, 344–345
  Pumpkin Bread, 249
  Zucchini Bread, 254–255

Raisin Bran Muffins, 240–241
Raisin Cookies, Oatmeal-, 111
Raspberry-Chocolate Buttermilk
    Muffins, 243
Raspberry Sauce, 86
Raspberry Swirl Cheesecake, White
    Chocolate-, 222–223
Raw sugar, 12
Red Velvet Cake, Southern, 350–351
Reduced-fat milk, 16
Refrigerator cookies
  about, 126
  preparing dough for, 126
  recipes for, 128–133, 332–333, 334,
    335, 336–337
  shaping methods for, 127
  storing, 127
  tips when making, 127
Rice milk, 16
Rich 'n Delicious Chocolate Cake,
    292–293
Ricotta cheese, 17
Roll cookies. *See* Refrigerator cookies.
Rolling boil, 65
Rolling pin, 34
Rose, making a fondant, 374–375
Rugelach, Chocolate Chip
    Hanukkah, 333
Rugelach, Hanukkah, 332–333
Rum Balls, Holiday, 330–331

Sauce recipes, dessert
  Butter Sauce, 87

Caramel Sauce, 86
Fudge Sauce, 85
Raspberry Sauce, 86
Sauces, dessert
  about, 84
  recipes for, 85–87
  steps for making, 84
  storing, 84
Scones
  about, 226
  preparing dough for, 226
  recipe for, 234–235
  shaping methods for, 227
  storing, 227
  tips when making, 227
Scones, Blueberry, 234–235
Self-rising flour, 11
Serrated bread knife, 33
Serving spoon, 35
Shortbread, Mama's, 132–133
Shortening, 18
Shredder, 33
Shredding ingredients, 53
Sifter, 35
Simmer, 65
Skim milk, 16
Slicing ingredients, 52
Snappies, Ginger, 130
Soda Bread, Irish, 344–345
Softening ingredients, 51
Soufflé Brownies, 142–143
Southern Red Velvet Cake, 350–351
Soymilk, 16
Spanish Polvornes, 334
Spatula, 35
Spatula, frosting, 367
Spatula, rubber, 35
Spices, 14
Splenda sweetener in baking, 12, 67
Sponge Cake with Goodies, 352–353
Spoon, serving, 35
Spoon, wooden, 35
Spreaders, frosting, 367
Springform pans, 39, 215
Squares, dessert. *See* Bars/squares,
    dessert.
Squares, E-Zay Lemon, 148–149
Stainless steel cookware, 37
Standard Cookie Crust, 172
Starburst pie crust, 169

Steam ovens, 41
Stemming fruit, 53
Stirring ingredients, 54
Storage containers, bags, and wraps, 26–27
Stovetop controls, 41
Stovetop cooking
    basic techniques for, 64
    helpful tips for, 64
Stovetops, types of, 40
Strainer, 35
Strawberry Cheesecake, New York, 218–219
Strawberry Chocolate Tart, 197
Strawberry Coffeecake, Fresh, 272–273
Streusel Topping I, 100
Streusel Topping II, 100
Strudel, Apple, 312–313
Sucralose sweetener in baking, 12, 67
Sugar Cookies, 128–129
Sugar shaker, 35
Sugar Tots, 129
Sugar varieties, 12
Sweet Po-Tater Pie, 339
Sweet potatoes in baked goods, 24
Sweet Tart Crust, 174
Sweeteners, artificial. *See* Artificial sweeteners.
Sweeteners, liquid, 12
Swirly tops for cupcakes, 365

Tapioca flour, 13
Tart, Fabulous Fruit, 198–199
Tart, Strawberry Chocolate, 197
Tart crust
    basic recipe for, 174–175
    steps for forming, 170–171
Tart Crust, Sweet, 174
Tart pans, 39
Tartlet crust
    basic recipe for, 174–175
    steps for forming, 171
Tartlets
    about, 160
    recipes for, 200–203
    storing, 161
    tips when making, 161
    See also Tartlet crust.
Tartlets, Canadian Butter, 202–203
Tartlets, Chocolate Ganache, 201

Tartlets, Lemon, 201
Tartlets, Triple Nutty, 200–201
Tarts
    about, 160
    recipes for, 197–199
    steps for making, 196
    storing, 161
    tips when making, 161
    See also Tart crust.
Terms, baking, 42–47
Testing-for-doneness techniques, 66–67
Thermometer, candy, 32
Thickeners, 13
Thickening liquids, tips for, 13
Timer, kitchen, 35
Toaster ovens, 40
Tools, kitchen. *See* Gadgets, basic.
Topping recipes
    Berry Whippy Cream, 99
    Choco Whippy Cream, 99
    Coffee Whippy Cream, 99
    Fruit Glaze, 101
    Pecan Topping, 101
    Streusel Topping I, 100
    Streusel Topping II, 100
    Whippy Cream, 99
Topping, as decorating technique, 359
Toppings
    basic techniques for making, 98
    recipes for, 99–101
Tots, Sugar, 129
Triangle Puffs, Almond, 316–317
Trifle, Mocha-Banana English, 348–349
Trimming dough, 63
Triple Berry Pie, 187
Triple Nutty Tartlets, 200–201
Trivets, 35, 40
Tube pans, 39
Turnovers, Apple, 314–315
Turntable, cake, 367

"Upside-down" pies. *See* Cobblers; Crisps; Crumbles.
Utensils, useful. *See* Gadgets, basic.
Utility knife, 33

Vanilla Buttercream, 76
Vanilla Cheesecake with Caramel Sauce, 210–211

Vanilla extract, homemade, 15
Vanilla Ice, 82
Velvet Cake, Southern Red, 350–351
Venting dough, 47, 63

Walnut Coffeecake, Choco-, 268–269
Walnut Cookies, Persian, 116
Walnut Puffs, 118–119
Wax paper, 27
Wedding Cakes, Mexican, 117
Whipped cream, commercial, 9
Whipped Cream Frosting, 80
Whipped topping, commercial, 9
Whipping ingredients, 47, 55
    three levels of, 56
Whippy Cream, 99
Whippy Cream, Berry, 99
Whippy Cream, Choco, 99
Whippy Cream, Coffee, 99
Whisk, 35
Whisking ingredients, 55
White Cake, Debbie's, 294–295
White chocolate, 19
White Chocolate Cheesecake with Fruit Topping, 208–209
White Chocolate Cream Puffs, 327
White Chocolate Macadamia Biscotti, 124–125
White Chocolate Mousse, 95
White Chocolate 'n Pecan Oaties, 157
White Chocolate-Raspberry Swirl Cheesecake, 222–223
White sugar. *See* Granulated white sugar.
Whole milk, 16
Whole wheat flour, 11
Wooden spoons, 35
Wrap, plastic. *See* Plastic wrap.

Yeast, 11
Yellow Cupcakes, Buttery, 282
Yuletide Pudding, 346

Zester, 35
Zesting ingredients, 47, 53
Zucchini Bread, 254–255
Zucchini in baked goods, 24

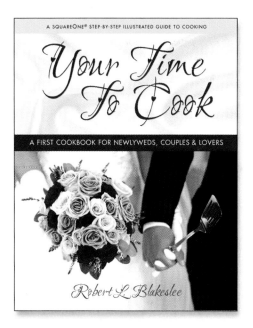

YOUR TIME TO COOK
A First Cookbook for Newlyweds, Couples & Lovers

Robert L. Blakeslee

For some people, cooking a meal is as easy and effortless as a walk in the park. But for others, even frying an egg may seem like a hike up Mount Everest. Designed for everyone who feels clueless in the kitchen, *Your Time to Cook* is a true "first" cookbook, packed with important kitchen essentials and cooking fundamentals—as well as a collection of basic, easy-to-prepare recipes.

Kicking off the book is an introduction to kitchen gadgets and gizmos, essential guidelines for stocking the pantry, and a review of common cooking terms and food-preparation techniques. Hundreds of magnificent full-color photos help make the information clear and accessible—whether it is a description of a how to chop an onion, scramble an egg, cook the perfect steak, or brew the best cup of coffee. Over 250 foolproof recipes include everything from breakfast favorites and party appetizers to hearty soups, salads, veggie side dishes, pastas, and seafood, as well as chicken, beef, pork, and lamb dishes. There is also a dessert chapter that's packed with your favorite sweet treats. To further ensure successful results, photos accompany each recipe's step-by-step directions, while practical tips and "tricks" make sure that each meal is not only picture perfect, but also perfectly delicious.

Whether you are a newlywed struggling in your first kitchen, a single out on your own, or just someone who would like to gain more confidence in the kitchen, *Your Time to Cook* is your key to cooking success.

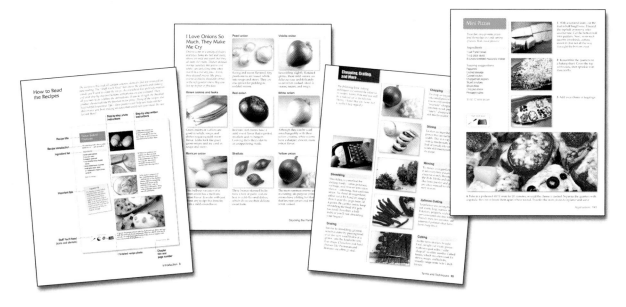

$29.95 • 416 pages • 8 x 10-inch hardback • ISBN 978-0-7570-0216-8

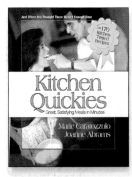

KITCHEN QUICKIES

Great, Satisfying Meals in Minutes

Marie Caratozzolo and Joanne Abrams

The authors of *Kitchen Quickies* know that you don't have time for hours of grocery shopping followed by hours of food preparation. Their solution? For starters, virtually all of their over 170 kitchen-tested recipes call for a maximum of only five main ingredients, minimizing time in the supermarket. Then most of the recipes take less than thirty minutes to prepare from start to finish! And these delicious dishes are actually good for you—low in fat and high in nutrients.

The book begins by guiding you through the basics of quick-and-easy cooking. Then ten chapters offer imaginative dishes, including sensational soups, sandwiches, salads, and pasta dishes; savory seafood, poultry, beef, and pork fare; meatless entrées; vegetable and grain side dishes; and luscious desserts. Next time you think there's no time to cook a great meal, let *Kitchen Quickies* prove you wrong. You may even have time for some "quickies" of your own.

$14.95 • 240 pages • 7.5 x 9-inch quality paperback • ISBN 978-0-7570-0085-0

GREAT NATURAL BREADS MADE EASY

Simple Ways to Make Healthful Bread

Bernice Hunt

This simple-to-follow, beautifully illustrated guide can show anyone how to make a spectacular loaf of artisan bread—even if they've never baked before. It explains how to mix, knead, shape, and decorate over 100 nutritious, mouth-watering loaves, including such classics as Honey Whole Wheat, Sourdough Rye, Italian Semolina, Jewish Challah, and French-Style Baguettes. There are also sweet rolls, muffins, flatbreads, bagels, biscuits, and much more. Also included is a chapter on luscious dips and spreads to accompany your freshly baked loaves.

If you love bread, but have avoided making your own because you thought the process was difficult, don't wait to discover the joys of *Great Natural Breads Made Easy*.

$16.95 • 160 pages • 7.5 x 9-inch quality paperback • ISBN 978-0-7570-0294-6

THE COMPLETE MUFFIN COOKBOOK

The Ultimate Guide to Making Great Muffins

Gloria Ambrosia

Expert baker Gloria Ambrosia shares an extraordinary collection of her favorite muffins that are not only sensational, but also quick and easy to prepare (you can whip up a batch in under thirty minutes). After revealing muffin-making basics, Gloria presents six chapters that are packed with over 130 muffin varieties, from sweet and fruity to rich and savory. Not just for breakfast, Gloria's muffins make delicious snacks, perfect accompaniments to soups and salads, and even welcome guests at the dinner table.

$14.95 • 216 pages • 7.5 x 7.5-inch quality paperback • ISBN 978-0-7570-0179-6

**For more information about our other cookbooks,
visit us at www.squareonepublishers.com**